D1415680

TANKS
And Other Fighting Vehicles

WRITTEN AND ILLUSTRATED
BY RAY HUTCHINS

GRAMERCY BOOKS
NEW YORK

ACKNOWLEDGEMENTS

Picture credits

Chapter 1: pages 5, 6(2), 8, 10, 11, 15, 16(2), 17, 20, 21, 22(2), 23(2), all The Tank Museum (TM).

Chapter 2: pages 24(2), 26(3), 27(2), 29, 30(3), 31, 32, 33, 34, 35, 36, 37(2), 43 (TM).

Chapter 3: pages 50,52, 53, 57, 60,65,66,67 (TM).

Chapter 4: pages 74, 83 (TM).

Chapter 5: pages 91, 92, 93 TM, 93 bottom, Ray Hutchins (RTH), 96 Israel Defence Forces (IDF), 97 TM, 98 top RTH, 98 bottom, 100,104 TM,

106 Chris Foss (CFF), 107 Krauss-Maffei-Wegmann (KMW), 108 TM, 110 CCF

Chapter 6: pages 119, 122 TM,

Chapter 7: pages 129 RH ALAN,130 top Perkins Engines Company, 130 bottom ZTS,133(3), 134 top NOVOSTI (London),134 bottom,135 top China North Industries Corporation (NORINCO) 135 Heavy Industries Taxila,

Chapter 8: pages 137 top Israeli Military Industries, 137 bottom TM, 138, 139, 140 CFF, 141 TMHyundai Precision & Industry Co Ltd,

Chapter 9: pages 145 no credit,146(2) RTH, 148 Vickers Defence Systems

Illustrations

Title, half-title and contents pages: Ray Hutchins (RTH).

Chapter 1: pages 6 TM, 7(2) RTH, 8(2), 9(2) 10 Midsummer Books Ltd (MBL), 12(2), 13(2), 14 map, 15,19 map RTH, 23 MBL

Chapter 2: pages 24, 25(2), 28(2) 29, 33, 34,36 RTH, 38 top MBL, 38 bottom, 39(2), 40/41 cutaway, 42 RTH

Chapter 3: pages 45(2), 46/47 cutaway, 48(2), 49(2),50, 51,53,54/55 cutaway RTH, 56 bottom MBL 56 top, 57 58/59 cutaway,60, 61(2), 62map, 64, 65, 66, 67(2) RTH

Chapter 4: pages 69(2), 70(2), 71, 72/73 cutaway,75(2), 76/77 cutaway,78(2), 79(2), 80(3), 81(3), 82map, 83(2), 84(3), 85(3), 86(3), 87(3) MBL

Chapter 5: pages 89(2),90(2), 91,94/95 cutaway,96, 97,99(3)100, 101map, 102(2), 103(30, 104, 105map,106,108, 109(2) RTH, 110 SPL, 111(3) RTH

Chapter 6: pages 113(2), 114(2), 115(2), 116(2), 117(2), 118(2), 119(2)RTH, 120 top, 2nd and fourth SPL, 3rd RTH, 121 top, 2nd and fourth SPL, 121 3rd RTH, 122, 123(3),124(2), 125(3), 126(2), 127(3), RTH

Chapter 7: pages 129,131(4), 132(2) MBL

Chapter 8: pages 138 MBL 140, 141,142 RTH

Chapter 9: pages 145, 147map, 148, 150, 151, 153, 155,157map RTH

Chapter 10: pages166/167 cutaway,168/169 cutaway,172/173 cutaway,176,178/179 cutaway RTH

Chapter 11:184 top RTH 2nd & 3rd, 185 top and bottom MBL, 185 centre RTH 185 top and bottom MBL,186(3) 187 top RTH, 187 middle and bottom MBL.(VDS), 149(2) RTH,150 VDS, 151 General Dynamics Land Systems (GDLS), 152 Sergeant Paul L. Anstine II (SPA), 153 GDLS, 154 top US Army, 154 bottom VDS, 155 US Army, 156(2), 158 Royal School of Artillery, 159 GDLS, 152, 153 SPA

Chapter 10: pages 160 KMW, 161 VDS, 162,163, 164(2) KMW, 165 GIAT Industries (GIAT), 170 GIAT, 171, 174, 175 VDS, 176 GDLS, 177(2) SPA180/181(2) GDLS

Chapter 11: pages 182 Steyr-Daimler-Puch, 183 top CFF, 183 bottom Alvis Hägglunds, 188 top Singapore Technologies Kinetics, 188 bottom ASCOD, 189GDLS 190, 191 KMW, 192 top MOWAG, 192 bottom Alvis Vickers, 193(2) GDLS

The publishers would like to thank the following for permission to use their photographs and illustrations:

Midsummer Books Limited, General Dynamics Land Systems, Giat Industries, Israeli Ordnance Corps, Israeli Military Industries, Krauss-Maffei Wegmann GmbH, Novosti (London), The Tank Museum,Bovington,Dorset,UK, Vickers Defence Systems.

This 2007 edition is published by Gramercy Books, an imprint of Random House Value Publishing, a division of Random House Inc., New York, by arrangement with Bounty Books, a division of Octopus Publishing Group Limited, 2-4 Heron Quays, London E14 4JP.

Gramercy is a registered trademark and the colophon is a trademark of Random House, Inc.

Random House
New York • Toronto • London • Sydney • Auckland
www.valuebooks.com

Printed and bound in China

A catalog record for this title is available from the Library of Congress.

ISBN: 978-0-517-22985-9

10 9 8 7 6 5 4 3 2 1

I dedicate this book to my wife, Yvonne, for her constant support and to my grandsons, William T. Hutchins, Tom Whitton, Conor Stockley and Bruce, Anthony and Martin Walker in the hope that it may interest them. The Author would like to thank: Soph Moeng for his advice and invaluable help; Chris Foss for general technical advice and Julian Mason for helping me with the artwork for the Russian tanks.

CONTENTS

FOREWORD

There are those prepared to claim that the tank was a phenomenon of the Twentieth Century; created to break the stalemate of one disastrous war, spearhead of the Lightning War in another and now become too big, destructive and expensive for present conditions. They can also point to a state of technological advance that almost fulfils the science-fiction writer's prophesy of weapons systems which change so rapidly that personnel are constantly training in new skills but are never ready to fight.

There is a certain amount of truth in this, if one restricts the topic to that of the Main Battle Tank, but that misses the critical point. Man the warrior has always sought to attack his enemies while protecting himself as far as possible and the armoured fighting vehicle is but another manifestation of this. That is a clumsy term, armoured fighting vehicle; tank is far more blunt and to the point but it is also too specific for a work such as this. Perhaps the generic term armour would be more appropriate. However as the author/illustrator shows, not only in words but with his vivid artwork, armour takes many forms, and it always has done.

The tank itself may have sprung from the mud-encrusted misery of the Great War but the concept pre-dates that period by a decade or more. Indeed if one considers warships or armoured trains the history of mechanised armour reaches back another fifty years or so. It was only awaiting a suitable source of power to be let loose on land. That came with the invention of the internal combustion engine and, somewhat later, the understanding that crawler tracks would enable heavier vehicles to move across country. From that time on it was a technical struggle between the conflicting ideals of maximum firepower, impregnable protection and unlimited mobility, a perfect balance that is yet to be struck.

Most of us are conditioned by our own culture and the media to think of the tank in terms of the Second World War. It was an important time and much that influenced military thinkers then is still with us. Right up to the present time the tank and its vast extended family has made the news and there is no reason to suppose that it will ever end. We still live in interesting times and, as the later chapters of this book show, the range of combat vehicles now available to the modern soldier is remarkable, both in terms of quantity and variety. Yet you will find, if you study these pages, that almost everything has existed before, in one form or another and there really is nothing entirely new under the sun. So what next?

Those industries that manufacture the huge main battle tanks are contracting and in many countries design work on new models is virtually at a standstill. At the same time there is a massive growth industry, and not just in the workshops of traditional industrial nations, in upgrading and improving existing types. Further down the scale, in the realms of infantry transporters and internal security vehicles, the range and variety of products is truly bewildering, so much so that even a comprehensive book such as this cannot hope to deal with everything.

For the future there is considerable interest at present in un-manned, remote control vehicles that might fight our wars for us and there are other new technologies particularly in the fields of armour protection and small but infinitely destructive weapons. The tank, as we know it, may slowly shuffle off the world stage but that will not mean the end of armour. Such vehicles will appear wherever there is conflict in the world and TV cameramen will inevitably focus on them where the action is. To study a work such as this is not just to indulge in a bit of armoured train-spotting, it is an informative briefing on what is happening in the world around us.

David Fletcher,
Bovington,
July 2004.

The Historian of The Tank Museum
Bovington
Dorset
England

CHAPTER ONE

The Birth of the Tank

From the earliest days, decisions reached in warfare were usually conditional upon the ability of one of the contestants to impose its will upon the other through the application of mobility. Mobility - the process, in its military sense, being the facility to move freely to, from and about the battle field - was, in its turn, controlled to some considerable extent by man's chances of survival. If fire-power became so intense that he could not move without being killed, mobility could be eliminated. On the other hand, if he could move so fast or was so heavily protected by armour that he became invulnerable, he could practise mobility and win battles and campaigns at will.

In fact, until the end of the 19th Century, neither firepower nor protection became so wholly dominant as to deny the practice of mobility one way or another without the use of many special devices. Although there had always been a place in armies for such expedients as chariots, armoured elephants and wagon-forts, the armed man on horseback or on foot possessed a high enough factor of survival to allow him to practise mobility without resort to specialised fighting vehicles.

The advent of quick firing artillery, which could engage targets indirectly from long range, and of rapidly firing machine-guns, which could annihilate men and horses far quicker than they could hope to close with and destroy the threat, engineered a revolution in warfare within less than two decades. When World War I broke out in 1914 the situation already existed whereby mobility was no longer economically possible for foot and horse armies. Either the soldiers were penned into trenches or slaughtered in their thousands when they attempted to cross open ground. Moreover, the massed artillery and machine guns, which produced these conditions of stalemate by enhancing the defence, were shown to be incapable of countering them in support of offensive action.

Some sort of new key was needed to unlock the powers of mobility again. The invention of the internal combustion engine in 1885 was to provide that key. Not only would it revolutionise society, it could provide the source of power which would drive an armoured and armed vehicle through the curtains of hostile fire and thereby carry the fight to the enemy. Even if wheeled armoured cars had not been mooted prior to 1914, their imminent invention would have been a certainty; and, even if caterpillar tracks to carry agricultural tractors across soft ground had not been suggested well before the turn of the century, something of that nature would soon have been on the drawing boards. As it was, French, Belgian and British armoured cars were in action within a few days of the outbreak of war in August 1914, and by October proposals were afoot to construct a cross-

Holts of Peoria, Illinois, had been building crawler tractors since 1906 and they made a trademark of the word Caterpillar. Conditions in the USA were far more conducive to the development of such tractors and this 75hp model was bought in large numbers by the British as an artillery tractor during the Great War. Holts played a key part in tank development, particularly in France and Germany, whereas the British pioneers tended to use rival designs such as the Killen–Strait or Bullock Creeping Grip.

country tracked vehicle capable of overrunning the thin, but impregnable, line of defended trenches which ran from the North Sea to the Swiss frontier. The simple motor cars, protected only by improvised armour plating and usually armed with one or two machine-guns, had demonstrated immense powers. So long as the roads remained open they dominated German cavalry and infantry.

First battle trials

When the first tracked armoured vehicles of rhomboid shape went into action on 15 September 1916, in the closing phase of the Battle of the Somme, they carried with them a faint British hope that, because they could traverse broken ground and wide trenches, they might help break the trench deadlock. More important, for the long term, they incorporated in one machine a universal

THE HORNSBY TRACTOR

Hornsbys of Grantham built a series of tracklaying tractors to the design of their Managing Director, David Roberts, starting in 1904. This huge machine, powered by an Ackroyd oil engine, took part in War Department trials and created sufficient interest to generate an order for a second tractor in 1909. Seen at the time as a means of hauling heavy artillery it played no direct part in the evolution of the tank beyond that of a source of inspiration. Indeed, Hornsbys found the potential market, both military and civil, to be so poor that they sold Roberts' patents to an American manufacturer.

Mark V (male) tanks of 9th (I) Battalion, Tank Corps, giving an obstacle crossing demonstration. Although virtually identical, outwardly, to earlier models the Mark V featured Harry Ricardo's 150hp engine linked to W.G. Wilson's epicyclic transmission to produce improved performance and one-man control.

weapon system that was both mobile, possessed inbuilt fire-power and enjoyed a measure of armoured protection. The facts that their tracks were likely to break down after 20 miles, that each hastily designed and constructed 'tank' (as they were called for security reasons) was very unreliable, that the armour was neither proof against the German armour piercing bullet nor, the most deadly threat, field artillery, and that the fire-power provided by 6-pounder guns and machine-guns was difficult for the crew members to apply, were merely transitory problems which time and redesign would eventually solve. The vital pointer to the future was exhibited by the handful of machines which not only managed to

THE FLYING ELEPHANT

A heavy tank developed in 1916 but cancelled the same year, this 100 ton monster was to carry a 6-pounder gun plus six machine-guns protected by 3-inch thick frontal armour. Powered by two 105 hp Daimler engines the tank carried an auxiliary set of tracks fitted under the bottom half of the vehicle which could be lowered and used on very soft ground. It was intended to be 26 ft long and carry a crew of eight.

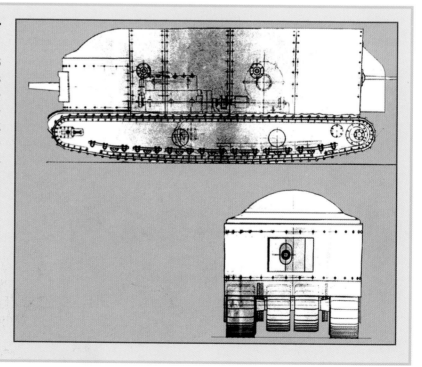

The short tracks and long body of Schneider's Char d'Assaut proved less than effective for obstacle-crossing when it was first introduced in the field; even fitted with extra 'nose and tail' ramps it still remained inadequate. Added to this the armour was thin and the vehicle burned easily.

cross the enemy frontline trenches but also advanced to the mouths of the enemy guns to knock them out. And, if the tanks were regarded only as a bonus to help the infantry forward (and in no way given special support by the infantry and artillery), that was something which could soon be rectified by study and by the dissemination of approved tactical drills prior to the next appearance of tanks in battle in April 1917.

Early developments

The fact remained that the tank's baptism of fire made plain that this new child of warfare had a promising future. Under the

direction of men such as Brigadier-General Hugh Elles and Lt.Col. J.F.C. Fuller, at HQ Tank Corps, the new weapon would rapidly be developed in technology and usage, moving towards the moment when it would no longer enter battle as an infantry ancillary but, instead, as a dominant weapon system with a role which supplemented and, on occasion, superseded the artillery in subjugating the enemy defences. In addition, it would soon begin to assume the role of cavalry as the principal means of exploiting mobility. Indeed, before the first rhomboid tanks had gone into action, the British tank designers were sketching

Continued on page 12

The M 280 sur Chenilles ('sur-chenilles' is French for 'on-tracks') was based on a large Schneider chassis developed at their Le Creusot works. It carried a 14/16 howitzer modified for this vehicle. It shared a common carriage with the 194 mle GPF and was driven by a petrol engine. There were only a few of these models produced.

ARMOURED CARS IN WORLD WAR I

Less than three months from the beginning of World War I the reported casualties, for both sides, were enormous and the hoped for, and expected, quick victory was unfulfilled. Stalemate evolved because both sides had the ability to secure entrenched positions behind barbed wire, protected with machine-guns and artillery, which withstood all but the most severe assaults.

At the end of October 1914 trench fortifications stretched in an endless belt from the North Sea to the Swiss Frontier occupied by troops living in squalor with little hope of release. It was supposed that the only method of breaking this deadlock was with artillery; however, this proved more than inadequate for the task. Indeed, in churning up the ground into a mud-filled morass it contributed to immobility and frustration. However, in the opening weeks of the war, as the German Army entered Belgium, destroying all the forts barring their way from

Liege through Brussels and Mons with heavy artillery, they were confronted by a weapon incorporating fire-power, survival and mobility.

Belgian innovation

The Belgians had adapted Minerva sports cars, fitting them with Hotchkiss machine-guns, searchlights and, a little later, with steel armour plates; these proved fast and efficient. They were joined later by a British Force equipped with fast, armed Lanchester and Wolseley cars. Within this Force was a brigade of Royal Marines carried in 50 or so motor buses, supported by a naval air squadron. This was an initiative of Winston Churchill who was then First Lord of the Admiralty and also responsible for the air defence of Britain. This Force was set up to protect the Belgian port of Antwerp but Churchill wanted also to prevent the Germans from setting up air bases that

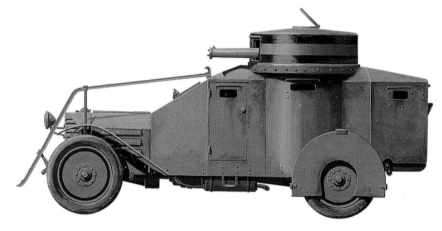

The Autoblinda Mitragliatrice Lancia Ansaldo IZ was one of the better armoured cars of World War I. It had a circular turret armed with twin machine guns. These cars proved to be very durable with some still in service with the Italian Army during the Spanish Civil War from 1936–1938.

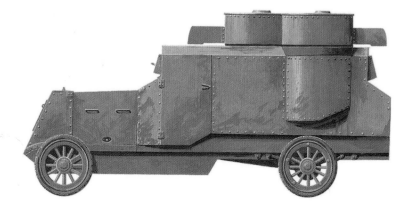

The Austin–Putilov was a variation of a UK Austin design with the bodywork produced by the Russian Putilov factory. It was more of an armoured truck than an armoured car. It was well suited to the rough conditions of the Eastern Front and went on to feature in the internal fighting that took place during the Revolution which started in October 1917 and led to the eventual overthrow of the Romanov dynasty.

The most sophisticated of the armoured cars was the 1914 Rolls-Royce Silver Ghost conversion which had the original Admiralty-Pattern turret, mounting a Vickers 7.7mm machine-gun. Some of these lasted well into World War II in India !

could be within bombing range of England, and, in particular, London.

At the suggestion of Commodore Murray Sueter, Churchill established an area of control of a radius of about one hundred miles from Dunkirk with the bases protected by the armoured cars of the Royal Navy under the dashing command of Commander C. R. Samson.

The influence and effect that these armoured cars had upon the German Military was greatly out of proportion to their numbers. They roamed freely ambushing enemy patrols with relative immunity because the only enemy weapon likely to do them harm was field artillery which had about a 30 to 1 chance of even hitting a stationary target at 300 yards and these armoured cars could easily move at 30 miles per hour or more! Each vehicle was said to be worth an infantry company when set against enemy cavalry. In fact the Germans ceased using cavalry in numbers on the Western Front and these cavalry units were sent to combat the Russians on the Eastern Front. Here the Russians had shown interest in armoured cars and had local improvisations and converted imports such as the Austin-Putilov. The Germans however had built only 15 armoured cars between 1904 and 1917 and these were used mostly in Romania and Russia. The Royal Navy had initiated these armoured vehicles but, at the end of 1915, these units were transferred to the Army in the newly created Machine Gun Corps.

In the West armoured cars were only serviceable until late 1914 because, by October, the trenches had reached the Yser Region where the Front Line stayed until 1918. However, during their brief spell of action in the early part of the war the Belgians demonstrated just what the armoured car could accomplish and their example was copied directly by the Germans and the British Royal Naval Air Service. After the Armistice, some of the old 1914 Minervas remained in operation with the Belgian Gendarmerie up until 1933!

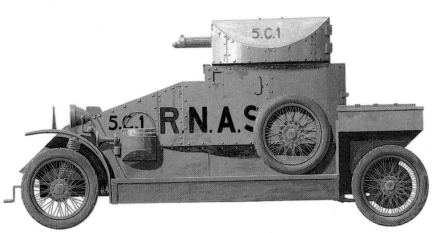

Lanchester armoured cars were used mostly on the Eastern Front and in Iraq, Romania, Persia (Iran) and Galicia. With Royal Navy crews they fought in support of the little recorded Russian campaign, during which they drove thousands of miles, in all weathers, over tortuous routes, often completely lacking in roads. They were proved reliable and fast, serving with the Russians until their participation in the war came to an end in 1917.

BRITISH TANK DEVELOPMENT IN WORLD WAR I

The last of the lozenge shaped tanks serving in any numbers was the Mark V (Male). This had a cupola for the commander and a provision for communication in the form of semaphore arms at the back of the hull. Earlier tanks could only communicate by homing pigeon!

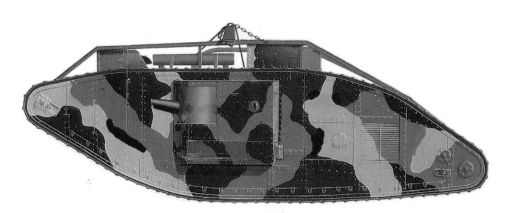

The idea of the armoured 'landship' was well established in fiction before the First World War, and proposals to construct such a machine had been made to all the European armies; but, because there was no requirement for this type of machine at the time the proposals were not taken up. However, after 1914, the situation changed and some far-sighted soldiers, such as Colonel E.D. Swinton, realising that the conditions existing on the Western Front could only be overcome by mobile armoured forces, used his position of influence to interest the British War Office in this new concept. A War Office committee was set up to investigate these proposals but its efforts came to nothing.

At this time the Royal Navy took a hand. Its Royal Naval Air Service had placed in service their armoured car squadrons and hence had at least some experience of armoured warfare. It was at this time that Winston Churchill became interested and set up the 'Landship Committee' to investigate the concept.

A 'big-wheel' machine was given the construction go-ahead and the committee's attention was drawn to a device known as the Pedrail which used a wide central track carrying loads and powerpacks above it. This was ordered for trials as were other caterpillar-like track forms which were ordered for experimental work. These included the Killen-Strait tractor, the Bullock Creep Grip tractor and the peculiar purpose-built machine which embodied the wheels of

a Daimler-Foster tractor and was known as the Tritton Trench-crossing machine; none of these were considered suitable and followed the fate of the Pedrail and were dropped.

Promising designs

Of these trial machines the Bullock tractor appeared to offer the most promise. Two of these vehicles were obtained from the United States for testing and although not intrinsically a war machine the tracks were found to be suitable for crossing mud and wire. William Tritton of Fosters of Lincoln was asked to redesign this tractor; he had been involved in the earlier design of the Tritton Trench-crossing machine and was later knighted for his efforts. He used the

Built in 1916 the Mark I tank, known in its prototype form as 'Mother', seen here, was the first tank to see action. The Mk Is created panic when they first appeared on the battlefield near Flers–Courcelette on 15 September 1916 during the Somme Offensive.

Bullock track and suspension to produce the 'No.1 Lincoln Machine' which was a more promising concept; however trials proved that the track was too narrow and gave constant trouble. Tritton designed a new track and other improvements which led to the construction of the vehicle known later as 'Little Willie'. The date was December 1915.

This was the first British tank and, although it appeared to meet the requirements of the Landship Committee, 'Little Willie' was still too unstable and considered unable to cross obstacles. Working with Tritton for the Landship Committee was Lieutenant Wilson who conceived the idea of enlarging the tracks into an 'all-round' form that resembled the 'lozenge' shape that characterised the tanks of World War I. The box of 'Little Willie' was modified to accommodate the new track outline which evolved into the machine named 'Mother'.

With this design the War Office became interested and after demonstrations held in Hatfield Park in January 1916 the design of 'Mother' was approved.

'Mother' was the prototype for the vehicles that appeared later as the Tank Mark I with an order for the latter of 100 placed by the British War Office in February 1916. The era of the tank as offensive weapon had arrived!

On 14 January 1916 'Mother' goes through her paces over obstacles in Poppleton's Field, Lincoln. Other similar obstacles, such as the trial trench, were also built at Hatfield Park, to demonstrate in front of VIPs and the Landship Committee. After these trials the vehicle went into production during February 1916.

One of the most successful tanks of World War I was the Renault FT 17. Production ran into thousands. They were used mainly in the infantry support role, but many other uses were found for them. In World War II the Germans took over many of them after the collapse of France in 1940. They were still in use up to 1944 when they were used by the Germans in the street fighting in Paris.

The Char d'Assaut of St. Chamond was even longer and clumsier than the Schneider. The very long hull restricted its use in action and it was therefore often relegated to the role of supply tank. However, it had a 75 mm gun and four machine-guns, giving it powerful weapon potential. It ran on a 90 hp (67 kW) Panhard advanced petrol engine which had electric drive.

Designs for a 100 ton shellproof tank, the 'Flying Elephant', due to cost and manufacturing difficulties, never got beyond the drawing board, and a faster, light 'Cavalry' tank, later known as Medium A or Whippet was designed.

The British were not alone in devising track-mounted armoured fighting vehicles. Without consultation with their Allies, the French were also building tanks. These were armoured assault guns: boxes on Holt tracks mounting a field artillery piece and machine-guns with the intention of moving into the front line to blast aside the German defences with direct, aimed fire.

Bogged down

The poor performance of the Holt track in mud contributed to the failure of these machines in April 1917. However, mud brought failure to the British tank too. Throughout the summer and autumn battles of Arras, Messines Ridge and Passchendaele, the British plunged their tanks into the quagmire stirred into porridge by intensive artillery fire. Since tanks in their infancy were only accorded low priority by the generals, it was expecting too much to hope that they would be given first choice of the most suitable ground upon which to operate. With artillery as the chosen means of assault to smash open a hole for infantry and cavalry, tanks were sentenced to operate in totally unsuitable conditions.

Nevertheless, the tank pioneers never ceased seeking better machines and preparing for the day when they would be given the opportunity to attack in the leading role across firm ground. While the Germans rejected tanks as a failure, both the British and the French stepped up production of improved vehicles. Armour that would stop the German armour-piercing bullet was fitted to the latest Mark IV tanks; while, as the Whippet tanks went into production for use in 1918, the French began manufacturing a small two-man tank which was to promote an entirely new concept of armoured warfare. The little two-man Renault FT 17

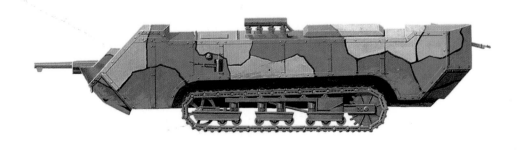

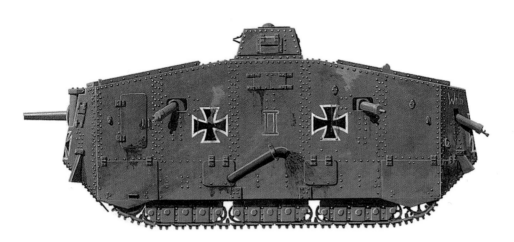

The A7V tank was Germany's only production tank. About 20 were made in time for battle in 1918. They served well in the first tank versus tank battle, when three A7Vs met two Male and one Female British MkIVs. This took place at Villers–Bretonneux (see page 18). This action was to strengthen the convictions of the Germans about the need for tanks.

with its single machine-gun in a one-man rotating turret was conceived by Colonel J.-B. Estienne as a mobile, armoured, machine-gun post; an 'infantryman on tracks' which could survive in large numbers in the forefront of battle.

New tactics

After the Battle of Cambrai plans for the campaign of 1918 could now be laid with due consideration of the part that tanks must play, while those for 1919 began to revolve around massed tanks in the central role. Too late, the Germans began to make tanks. For, while they could produce only 20 of their own machines for their March 1918 offensive, the Allies were on the eve of fielding thousands.

Initially, for the campaign of 1918, the Allies had to tackle the problems of defence against an impending German offensive of immense power, based on intelligence reports that a massed artillery barrage would open the way for strong infantry forces, which, in battle groups, were to penetrate the Allied lines by infiltration through the weaker spots. Because tanks were regarded as purely offensive weapons, their part in the defensive was expected to be insignificant. So, because they could only travel so short a distance on their own tracks, and there was a dire shortage of rail flats to move them from one threatened front

The 194 mle GPF gun, despite its bulk and weight, was able to cross terrain that other towed weapons of the time were unable to negotiate without difficulty. This weapon was still in use in the early days of World War II.

THE BATTLE OF CAMBRAI: 20-22 NOV 1917

For tanks to establish their place as a weapon in their own right, they had to win a resounding success upon which to base their claim. That opportunity came on 20 November 1917 across firm, rolling, ground unbroken by preliminary shelling, in the approaches to Cambrai. That day, at dawn, 378 British tanks, working with six infantry divisions, and the Cavalry Corps advanced simultaneously behind a delayed surprise artillery barrage from over 1,000 guns and assisted by aircraft of the Royal Flying Corps, which strafed the German guns, overran the dense German defences. Once through the front line the leading wave of tanks dominated the enemy by their presence and firepower as the infantry followed through the gaps.

From that moment onwards it was recognised that no advance would be likely if tanks were not present. After the successes at Cambrai the tank pioneers could draw up confident plans and propose new Armoured Fighting Vehicles which would be accepted and, in due course, dictate the terms of battle. They could now show beyond doubt that, without armour, there was no future for men or horses against modern weapons, especially the machine-gun, and that the mechanisation of warfare was inevitable.

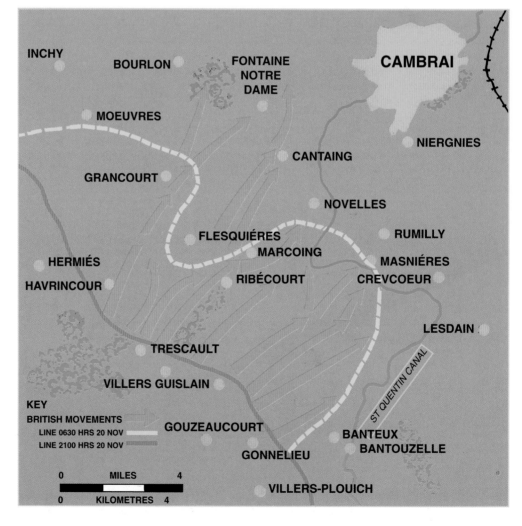

The Battle of Cambrai started at 6am on 20 November 1917. The tanks first had to cross three trenches. Working in teams and laying bundles of timber, known as fascines, each tank in turn dropped its bundle into a trench and the following tanks would then cross. Led by General Hugh Elles, the tanks advanced crossing the front trenches. The surprise effect of the appearance of the tanks through mist was too much for the Germans who turned and fled.

INCHY
BOURLON
FONTAINE NOTRE DAME
CAMBRAI
MOEUVRES
NIERGNIES
GRANCOURT
CANTAING
NOVELLES
HERMIÉS
FLESQUIÉRES
RUMILLY
HAVRINCOUR
MARCOING
MASNIÉRES
RIBÉCOURT
CREVCOEUR
LESDAIN
TRESCAULT
ST QUENTIN CANAL
VILLERS GUISLAIN
KEY
BRITISH MOVEMENTS
LINE 0630 HRS 20 NOV
LINE 2100 HRS 20 NOV
GOUZEAUCOURT
BANTEUX
BANTOUZELLE
GONNELIEU
0   MILES   4
0   KILOMETRES   4
VILLERS-PLOUICH

The Medium Tank Mark A, Whippet, was a British attempt to exploit the tactical opportunities that were created when heavy tanks had broken through enemy lines. It was less vulnerable than the Mark IV but restricted to the same 20-mile life. It was armed with two Hotchkiss machine-guns and had a rigid turret.

to another, they had to be spread thinly along the front in small groups. Yet when the offensive eventually came and carried all before it, even these tank packets frequently made significant defensive contributions when they counterattacked locally, and saved the day against major breakthroughs. While they did not play the major part in halting the Germans that summer, they were ready in July to strike the series of increasingly powerful blows which turned the tide and transformed the Allied defensive into a mighty counter offensive, which swept the demoralised Germans back upon their own frontier to bring a surprisingly rapid end to the war.

Several months before the end, the shape of the tank in future warfare could

The Tank Mark IV had two variants: the Tank Mark IV (Female) armed only with machine-guns for direct infantry support, and the Tank Mark IV (Male) which carried an additional 6-pdr gun. Some Mark IVs were known as Hermaphrodites because they were Male on one side and Female on the other.

clearly be foreseen by those who took the trouble to study it. The Germans recognised in tanks a decisive 'terror' weapon; the French saw them as an important adjunct to infantry, a means to restore the supremacy of the man on foot; the British tank enthusiasts and, to a less pronounced extent their American counterparts, envisaged them as a weapon of manoeuvre which would replace the cavalry and develop into an independent arm of decision in addition to a support for infantry.

In the immediate aftermath of Cambrai, Fuller had proposed using the new Mark V tanks to carry infantry machine-gun parties deep into the enemy lines as a new way of disrupting the enemy defensive system. Throughout the winter of 1917, he proposed tank raids in depth to disrupt the German offensive preparations. In April he drafted his famous so-called Plan 1919 which proposed a major offensive by massed Allied tank armies, using heavy tanks supporting the infantry to break through the front lines, and fast tanks and armoured cars of long-range capacity to drive deep into the enemy rear and strike a stunning strategic blow by wrecking command control and logistic systems.

Advances in design

Tank design and technology were advancing; already it had been shown that the speed of the Medium A Whippet might be increased from 8mph to something in the region of 20mph. The Medium C, with a speed of 7mph and a 140 mile radius of action, would be ready by 1919; and, as an unfulfilled long shot, also the revolutionary Medium D with a speed of 25mph and a range of 150 to 200 miles.

It had been shown that the day when tank would fight tank had arrived when,

MEDIUM B WHIPPET

Weighing 18 tons, the Medium B was longer and wider than the Medium A, but not so tall. Its shape was more like that of a heavy tank than its predecessor, but with a large fixed turret mounted on top at the front of the hull. The engine, a four-cylinder 100bhp Ricardo, was mounted in a separate compartment divided by a bulkhead from the crew of four. A total of 48 Medium Bs was built but none were used in action.

MEDIUM C

Although it was designed in late 1917, none of the 45 Medium Cs built actually left the factory until after the Armistice. They remained in service until 1925. At 20 tons its 150bhp Ricardo engine gave it a power-to-weight ratio of 7.5 while its fuel tanks held 150 gallons – over double that of the Medium A. Top speed was still only 8 mph, but its radius of action was 120 miles.

J.F.C. FULLER: TANK PIONEER

John Frederick Charles Fuller was born in 1878. Although a light infantryman he was appointed, in 1916, General Staff Officer I of the newly formed Tank Corps. During the Boer War he had seen service with mobile scouts. He was something of a military genius, well able to express his technical awareness and with considerable powers of persuasion. His was the dominant influence of the strategy and tactics which were first shown at the Battle of Cambrai.

He demonstrated that AFVs would be the key to future decision making and mobility. He also forcefully encouraged engineers to design faster, long-range vehicles to fulfil his ideas of tank-versus-tank actions and, as he enshrined in his Plan 1919, the deep penetration of enemy lines.

After the war he won approval for a permanent British Tank Brigade in order to experiment further with tank design, while, in 1927 he created the formation of an all-arms experimental force which was the forerunner of all armoured divisions to come. He fell from grace because of his alleged fascist associations; and, although he spied against his German 'friends', his loyalty was held suspect by his countrymen and he was denied any official appointment during World War II.

at Villers-Bretonneux on 24 April 1918, three British Mark IVs and seven Whippets ran into a scattered force of thirteen of the large, clumsy German A7V tanks. In the ensuing encounter honours were about even, with losses from tank gunfire inflicted on both sides, but as a result the Tank Corps came to the conclusion that, henceforward, all battle tanks should have an anti-tank capability.

The major tank battle of Amiens on 8th August 1918, which so completely shattered the German front, undermined the resistance of their troops and convinced their High Command of the need to end the war, provided sufficient, if not complete, evidence of the validity of Fuller's concepts.

Concept proven
Despite ventilation failures, which made it impossible for the machine-gun parties to breathe in the Mark V tanks, the feasibility of the armoured idea was demonstrated. Medium A tanks, along with armoured cars, did pass through the enemy lines and strike with telling effect many miles in the enemy rear. Unfortunately the horsed cavalry, which tried to work in conjunction with the Medium A tanks, were unable to do so but this, too, was a useful lesson. Tank losses had been high and breakdowns higher still, but it was plain that the total enemy anti-tank effort, based on field artillery, was insufficiently mobile to withstand a more mobile opponent.

Anti-tank weapons
The study of anti-tank measures now assumed a predominant place in the minds of commanders at all levels. While Fuller had contended, prior to Villers Bretonneux, that the tank would probably be the best anti-tank weapon; gunners, cavalrymen and infantrymen sought ways of securing their future by developing ways and means of their own to kill tanks. The advent of smaller, faster AFVs, allied to the likelihood that thicker armour would be used, made it desirable to introduce into the front line, specialised, higher velocity anti-tank guns with a far greater accuracy than the existing lower velocity

THE FIRST TANK-VERSUS-TANK BATTLE 24 APRIL 1918: VILLERS-BRETONNEUX

On 24 April 1918 the first encounter between German and British tanks took place at Villers-Bretonneux during the Somme Offensive.

Three groups of German A7V tanks were leading infantry through the smoke, gas and early morning mist towards the Bois d'Aquenne and the villages of Cachy and Villers-Bretonneux. Group 1, with three tanks, was making good progress towards the British infantry lines at Villers-Bretonneux and a nearby wood when it had to turn to protect its own infantry being attacked by the British who were still holding the village of Villers-Bretonneux.

Group 2, with seven A7Vs, also had problems, two had suffered damage, one had broken down and some were veering off course because of the fog. Yet this Group managed to reach its objectives without further casualties.

Mitchell attacks

Group 3 was moving towards the village of Cachy, well ahead of the infantry it was supporting. On its flank Lieutenant Mitchell's Mark IV 'Male' tank emerged from the Bois l'Abbé and engaged the advancing enemy with his 57mm gun. He was also giving gun support to two 'Female' Mark IVs which came under fire from two German A7V tanks, one of which was commanded by a Leutnant Biltz. Mitchell and his Section Commander, Captain Brown, saw the two A7Vs at a range of about 400m; and, while Brown departed on foot to contact and send back the two out-gunned 'Female' tanks, Biltz opened fire and damaged one of them. Mitchell manoeuvred to engage Biltz without at first scoring; but, later Mitchell halted to give his left sponson gunner a chance to hit Biltz's tank with three rounds of armour-piercing solid shot.

Meanwhile, Captain Price, in command of seven Whippets, was advancing upon Cachy intending to engage what he believed were only enemy infantry trying to enter the village. Price was unaware that the casualties that he was suffering were caused by a German tank and not by field artillery; he was alerted by airdropped information and retreated.

The main action ended with the Germans secure in Villers-Bretonneux but barred from Cachy by the well-timed British tank attack. Group 2 departed with Mitchell sending them on their way with a few optimistic rounds of 57mm shot at 1000m range before his tank broke a track.

Lessons learned

Before the mutual retirement of both sides Leutnants Bitter and Muller tried once more to seize Cachy; they failed to do so because their infantry were so cowed by frenzy of the battle going on around them. The battlefield was left to crippled and broken tanks, many of whose crews had dismounted and fought on as infantry.

Nevertheless it was Mitchell's conclusion that it was a great day for the German tanks. The lessons of Villers-Bretonneux were highly important, both sides drawing profound conclusions from it. The Germans were convinced that the need for tanks was strengthened, along with the validity of their shooting at the halt technique. HQ Tank Corps appreciated that this was but the first of many similar battles to come, one which showed a need to develop and practise accurate, on the move, shooting techniques and that, as soon as possible, all tanks should be armed with an anti-tank weapon. At once they began to replace the machine-gun sponsons on one side of the female tanks with 6-pounder gun sponsons, thus producing the 'hermaphrodite tank'.

Another lesson was that the tank gunners should have better training in the use of the much-improved armament that was to be installed in the later versions of these early, but very useful, tanks.

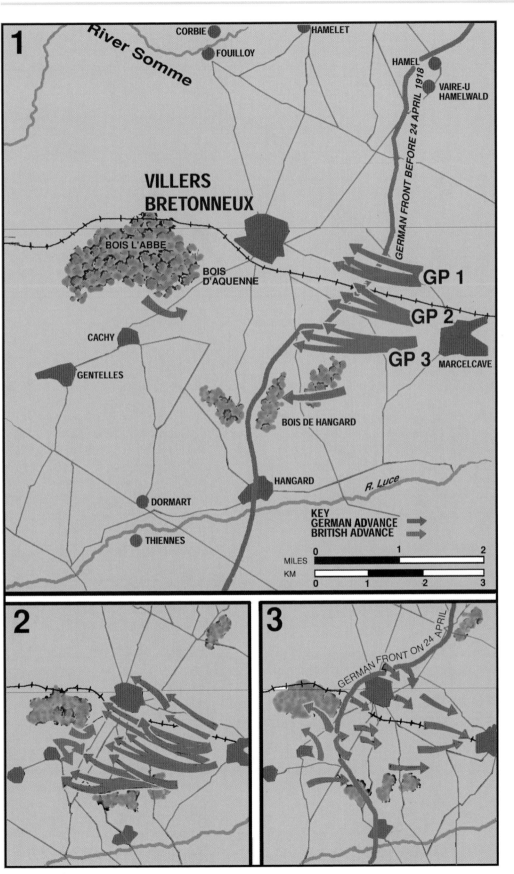

1

River Somme

CORBIE
HAMELET
FOUILLOY
HAMEL
VAIRE-U HAMELWALD

GERMAN FRONT BEFORE 24 APRIL 1918

VILLERS BRETONNEUX

BOIS L'ABBE

BOIS D'AQUENNE

GP 1

GP 2

GP 3

MARCELCAVE

CACHY

GENTELLES

BOIS DE HANGARD

HANGARD

R. Luce

DORMART

THIENNES

KEY
GERMAN ADVANCE
BRITISH ADVANCE

```
MILES   0              1              2
KM      0        1        2        3
```

2

3

GERMAN FRONT ON 24 APRIL

These three maps show the course of the Battle of Villers–Bretonneux, fought on 24 April 1918.

Map 1 conveys the opening moves on 24 April.

Map 2 shows the progress of Group 1 approaching to attack British infantry in Villers–Bretonneux and the wood beyond.

Map 3 shows Lt. Mitchell patrolling to the north where he was a spectator of the retreat of Capt. Price's Whippets.

field artillery pieces.

Before the end of the war, the Germans had a clumsy 13mm anti-tank rifle in service and had tried out flamethrowers, anti-tank mines, wide ditches and various kinds of barricade. But no single weapon or system on its own was effective, although a combination of several could hamper or even stop a small scale attack. Aircraft were also used – the German fighter planes making low-level attacks at Cambrai with a modicum of success. However, in the face of Allied air power and ground defences, these were very risky to press home.

Improved tactics

In the event, improved tank tactics, carefully worked out co-operation between artillery and infantry in close collaboration with tanks attacking by surprise in mass on relatively narrow frontages and the use of smoke screens, enabled attackers to attain the superiority of mobility over static defences. Aircraft helped, notably in reconnaissance to give warning of enemy defences and reserves and only sporadically in attacking gun emplacements. In this latter respect, clear reservations on the part of the airmen and tank men already existed. The question being asked was why was it not better for artillery, which delivered fire more safely, quickly and accurately, to do the job instead of aircraft, which were highly vulnerable to ground fire, were expensive, and also found difficulty in finding and hitting concealed, pinpoint targets?

Quite naturally, the challenge by anti-tank forces inspired tank forces to extend their repertoire. Not only would the speed, reliability, protection and mobility of the existing fighting machines be improved, but additional special types and devices would be introduced.

Further tank developments

Before 1919, among the many ideas actually in production were: gun carrier and personnel carrying tanks, tracked supply vehicles and bridging tanks, attachments to help tanks land from the sea and climb sea walls, pontoons to help AFVs swim and minesweeping devices and flamethrowing equipment; each being designed to improve the striking power, mobility and adaptability of fighting vehicles and to hasten the overall mechanisation of armies. For by now, in any case, the day of the horse on the battlefield was clearly nearly over. Vulnerable to fire, unable to cope with the heavy work demanded of them to shift modern equipment, their numbers were also in decline due to lack of demand. Civil agencies, on grounds of economy, were also disposing of horses in favour of machinery and thus inducing a rapid reduction in the horse.

FASCINES AND CRIBS

In order to improve the ability of heavy tanks to cross obstacles, bundles of brushwood, known as fascines, were made up (10 ft long and 4.5 ft in diameter) bound with chains. The fascine was then mounted on the nose of the tank ready to be dropped into a deep trench for the tank to move across. They weighed 1.5 tons and were later replaced by hexagonal timber cribs (seen here) which were lighter but equally as efficient.

PHILIP JOHNSON

Philip Johnson was born in 1987 and he became a trained engineer. As a civilian he helped to operate a railway system in South Africa during the Boer War. He joined the Fowler company in about 1906 where he worked on tractors and steamrollers for the Indian market. He enlisted himself in the mechanised transport company of the Army Service Corps in 1916 where he trained drivers on Mark I tanks before seeing action with them on the Somme. He was promoted to head a tank workshop in France in 1917 but quickly moved up to become the Chief Engineer of the newly formed Tank Corps.

Amongst his innovations were special tracks to enable Mark IV tanks to climb sea-walls which were proposed, but never used, to execute a landing to the rear of the enemy near Dunkirk; and a modified sprung suspension which enabled the Whippet tank to reach speeds of up to 20 mph, twice its design speed. This led on to the projected Medium D tank which was ordered from Johnson as the war ended in 1918.

He continued to work on this project at the Tank Design and Experimental Department and his ideas were to show the feasibility of all armoured fighting vehicles in the future.

The Medium D was the last British tank design of World War I proposed by Lieutenant Colonel Philip Johnson. The Mark D was intended to fill the new Tank Corps' requirements in 1919 for a purpose-built pursuit medium tank. It was designed during October 1918 but by the Armistice of the following month only this wooden mock-up had been constructed.

BRITISH TANKS: COMBAT AND SPECIALIST ROLES

Numerous versions of British tanks saw service during World War I. The Tank Mark I (Male) was intended to spearhead attacks; Tank Mark I (Female) was armed with four Vickers machine-guns, and was designed to deal with enemy infantry. Within months of the tank being introduced as a combat weapon, designs were being drawn up to introduce tanks in support and logistical roles. The Mark I tanks were subsequently converted to Tank Tenders (to carry supplies) and Wireless Tanks (to serve as communications centres). Tanks Mark II and III were unarmoured training machines built in small numbers pending delivery of the new Mark IV. Some Mark II tanks fought in the Battle of Arras in April 1917.

Right: A Tank Mark I (Female) showing the steering 'tail' which was later discarded because of its limited value.

Below: A Mark V Royal Engineer Tank fitted with a 20ft portable bridge. Connected to the forward placed jib the bridge could be lowered over trenches or other obstacles.

The Tank Mk IV (Female) was the most numerous tank of World War I. Early versions were armed with water-cooled Vickers machine-guns but these were replaced by air-cooled Hotchkiss machine-guns. Some of the later MkIVs were armed on one side with the Hotchkiss machine-guns and on the other with a 6-pdr gun. These were known as 'Hermaphrodites'.

Various types of anti-mine roller designs were tested on British tanks. The device fitted to the Mark V Royal Engineer Tank (bottom) has a hinged jib that carried a heavy roller forward of the hull. This could be lifted when not in use. A more permanent type of roller was carried on the experimental vehicle seen on the left. The weight of the timbers and rollers proved impractical.

CHAPTER TWO

Coming of Age

In the aftermath of World War I, which had witnessed a revolution in practically every aspect of the art of war, radical changes had to be made in the structure and the composition of armies. Quite apart from the introduction of AFVs, the development of air power, the sophisticated control and application of indirect massed artillery fire, the growth of modern transportation methods of a vast complexity of stores, and the ramifications of cable and radio communications during World War I had brought about a fundamental shift in manpower demands alongside a complete re-emphasis upon management systems and material and equipment procurement. The cavalry, artillery and infantry of all armies would hang on to their horses and traditional methods for the next couple of decades, but the progress of mechanisation and modernisation was sure to go ahead. In no branch of those armies was this more publicised than among the armoured units.

Among the world's principal armies there was almost a consensus about the future of tanks. Excluding the Russians and Germans (the former in political revolution, the latter denied tanks by the Treaty of Versailles) the opinion of the French, that tanks should remain an auxiliary to infantry and become an integral part of that arm generally prevailed. True, the French toyed with mobile mechanised forces, but their rejection of their use was copied by the USA, the Italians, the Japanese and, to a certain extent, the British. In the case of the British, however, there was a significant move towards independence for the tank arm, allied to quite a widespread desire to experiment with

Despite the drawback of the commander having to operate the main armament the SOMUA S−35, with its well−protected hull and manoeuvrability, was undoubtedly still the best Allied tank in 1940. Fitted with a radio and a 47mm gun, firing both armour−piercing shot and high explosive, it possessed refinements which had escaped British designers.

new techniques and vehicles. Due to the reluctance of the traditional arms, notably the cavalry and artillery, to adopt and man mechanical vehicles, it became necessary to perpetuate the wartime Tank Corps and it was given regular status in 1923. Its operational role would continue to be that of manning tanks and armoured cars, particularly the latter when engaged in the policing of India and the other extensive territories of the Empire. The experimental role covered examination of: a) the use of tanks in independent operations and b) the use of tanks in close support of infantry.

In fact the Colonial Powers, particularly Britain, France and Italy, had not only to take into account the need to police their territories but to do so as cheaply as possible. Therefore, although there was common ground within each army for the need of the three categories of tank which had evolved during the war, the 'heavies' of over 20 tons, the 'mediums' of between about 6 and 20 tons, and 'lights', a preference for 'lights' naturally took precedence in political and Treasury circles over the much more expensive heavier types. Hence, the attractions of the slow-paced little two-man Renault FT and its kind were considerable, particularly since a great many had survived the war and could easily be purchased. For this reason, French tank design, tied to the inflexible demands of infantry support, tended to concentrate mainly on improvements to the light tank by slight additions to armour, armament, power and pace without breaking away from the existing

The Char Leger R–35 (Renault Type ZM) was a light–infantry support tank designed to meet the 1933 programme. Its turret was hand–traversed and carried a 37mm short–barrelled gun. The R–35 was the most numerous French tank in 1940, about 2,000 being built. Sales were made to Poland, Turkey, Romania and Yugoslavia. Even the Germans used captured vehicles and converted many to artillery tractors.

Coming of Age

Sir John Carden and Vivian Loyd built one and two-man machine-gun carriers (or Tankettes) in the late 1920s. This, the first two-man machine, was christened 'The Honeymoon Tank' by the press, during trials at Farnborough.

Carden-Loyd Tractors Ltd was subsequently taken over by Vickers-Armstrongs who developed the Mark VI machine-gun carrier used extensively by the British and many foreign armies. All early examples were powered by the Model T Ford engine.

Vickers Medium Mark IA tanks were first developed in 1922 and the first production models were delivered as Light Tank Mk I. It was later classified as a Medium tank because lighter tanks were being introduced into service at this time.
It had a crew of 5 and was armed with a 3pdr QF gun, 4 Hotchkiss and 2 Vickers 0.303 machine-guns. It weighed 11.7 tons and was powered by a 90 hp air-cooled Armstrong-Siddeley V-8 engine.

and inefficient concept of a one-man, rotating turret in which the commander was also compelled to grapple with the work of loading, aiming and firing the main armament. Even the heavy Char B, with which the French experimented in the 1920s retained the one man turret, as did the medium tanks and light tanks to come. Only the 70 ton superheavy Char 2C forsook this arrangement, but only ten of these were made.

Changing shapes

In Britain, by contrast, strikingly original and imaginative designs were produced and put into service. Abandoning the rhomboidal heavies and concentrating on the fast, long range Medium D for experiments with an independent role, Elles and Fuller kept an open mind over what sort of infantry support tank was needed. It would, they thought in 1920, be a light machine, but it might easily have to be a heavily armoured one. In the event,

Known as the 'Sixteen Tonners', although in fact they weighed more than that, the three A6 series tanks were prototypes for a new model Medium Tank. New features were twin turret cupolas for the commander and observer and additional machine-gun turrets at the front. Following trials three more tanks, designated Medium Mark III were built but the programme was then cancelled due to cost.

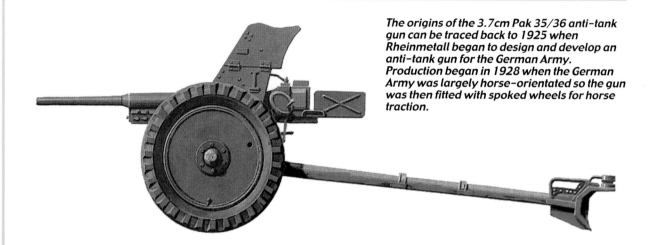

The origins of the 3.7cm Pak 35/36 anti-tank gun can be traced back to 1925 when Rheinmetall began to design and develop an anti-tank gun for the German Army. Production began in 1928 when the German Army was largely horse-orientated so the gun was then fitted with spoked wheels for horse traction.

The Vickers Light Tanks had their origins in the Carden-Loyd tankettes designed and produced in the 1920s. The Mark I had a two-man crew and a small turret carrying a 7.7mm (0.303 inch) machine-gun. The Mark IA had better armour and the Light Tank MkII had an improved turret and modified suspension. The Marques improvements in design continued up to the Mark VIc which had a 15mm (0.59 inch) heavy machine-gun. These designs went on to improve suspension, armour and cross-country performance.

the abandonment of the overambitious and overcomplex Medium D, allied to the failure to produce a derivative Infantry Light Tank, led to the British War Office striking out on a new tack in their efforts to procure a single machine which might fill both the light infantry support role and the experimental function. A request for help from the private firm of Vickers Limited in 1922 coincided with a desire on the part of the War Office to produce a tank which, as a machine-gun carrier, could fill the main operational role in India, especially if war with Afghanistan broke out again, and also form the basis of a family of tracked AFVs which could carry artillery, infantry, or act as ambulances and in other operational roles. Quickly produced in prototype, the 11ton Vickers so-called Light Infantry Tank was almost at once adopted as the British Army's Medium Tank with an order that eventually ran to 160. In the event, the Indian Army declined to take the Vickers medium (machine-gun version) on the grounds of expense and complexity. Yet this tank's design was to prove an enormous step forward, particularly in its three-man turret, where the gunner had only to aim and fire the gun and the second man load the gun and operate the radio, leaving the commander to perform his duties without undue distraction by crew tasks.

The 5cm Pak 38 saw action first in 1941 during the invasion of the Soviet Union when it was supplied with the, then, new type of tungsten-cored ammunition known as AP40. This offered a considerable increase in armour penetration. This proved to be the only gun/projectile combination to penetrate the armour of the new T34/76 Russian tank.

Arms versus armour

The armour and armament of the Vickers Medium also gave an indication of the direction in which tank design was heading. Ostensibly a light tank, its armour thickness of 6.5mm (later raised to 8mm) provided virtually no protection against shell splinters or bullets. Its 47mm (3-pdr) gun, however, representing as it did the first attempt to fit tanks with a higher velocity anti-tank weapon, deprived the tank of a high explosive shell such as was fired from the 57mm (6-pdr) gun fitted to the very first tanks. Yet the Medium, while it possessed good mobility, improved reliability and an acceptable armament, was from inception an inadequate combat vehicle due to its poor armour. Even so it was vastly superior to a very small 2ton light tank being proposed whose backers contended that sixteen of these machines costing £500 each had equal combat value to one vastly superior medium tank costing £8,000. This series of one or two man tankettes, which came on offer in 1926, were little more than lightly armoured boxes on tracks: open topped, devoid of a turret and armed with a single machine-gun. Attractive as these tankettes were to the parsimonious, most tank soldiers, who recognised a death trap

Design work by Vickers during 1936 made the A9 a superior tank to the cancelled A6 series. They were first designed to perform the duties of reconnaissance and pursuit normally carried out by the cavalry. They were in service from 1938 to 1941. The British 1st Armoured Division, which had A9 and A10, operated west of Dunkirk and was in action subsequent to that evacuation.

J. WALTER CHRISTIE: INFLUENTIAL DESIGNER

Few were made of the 1931 Christie T3 tank which combined his sloped armour, a round, rotating turret, big-wheel suspension, and was powered by an ex-aircraft 338hp Liberty engine. It had a profound influence on Russian, and to a lesser extent on British, tank design. It had a crew of three, but Christie gave little attention to fighting compartment design because his attention was focused mostly almost exclusively on automotive aspects of tank design.

J. Walter Christie was born in 1865, the last year of the American Civil War. He was an experienced engineer, learning from the shop floor. He came late to AFV design, in 1915; but, soon caught up, designing a self-propelled howitzer with a big-wheeled suspension. He was a man who was far more interested in ideas than production, he even made models before converting the ideas to blueprints.

On the entry of the USA into World War I in 1917 he was prompted to design a light tank. This was the M1919 which was fitted with sloped armour and the option to move either on wheels or tracks. After the war, in 1921, he improved the M1919 with sprung suspension, and in 1922, he designed the first of four amphibious vehicles which were later developed into the Landing Vehicles Tracked, which spearheaded many of the Allied invasions from 1942 in World War II.

His 1928 fast tank, with a road speed of 70mph on wheels and 42 mph on tracks became a trendsetter which brought orders from the US Army to develop a smaller medium tank to have sloping armour (Christie's idea) and a rotating turret. This was the T3 tank, powered by a Liberty aero engine of 338bhp. Christie delayed in delivering production models of this tank because his mind was on further fresh proposals for even faster airborne tanks, so he was dropped by the US Army.

Russian interest

However, by then the Russians, and later the British, took up his ideas and intended production. Once again his sponsors found Christie a difficult person to work with, but they pursued his ideas nevertheless. The Russian BT-2 looked very similar to the Christie T3 but it was completely redesigned by Russian and US engineers. Similarly, the British firm of Nuffield redesigned because it discovered that only the big wheel suspension had value. Yet Christie's ideas remained with many of the future tanks, amongst them the Russian BT tanks and later, the T-34, T-54, T-55, and T-62 models, and the British Cruiser tanks Mark III to Mark VII, and many other front-line service tanks into the 1980s.

This Christie prototype was supplied to Great Britain in 1936: forerunner of all British Christie Cruisers.

Russian BT-7 fast cruiser tanks on manœuvres during the 1920s. The BT-7 was based on the American Christie design.

when they saw one, called the idea 'positively wicked'. For the next eight or nine years the debate would be kept alive by the tankette's protagonists, but was finally dropped in favour of light, turreted tanks, many of which incorporated minor features thrown up by the tankette designers. Nevertheless, in the guise of infantry weapon carriers they were to enter service in large numbers and, in the wars of the 1930s and 1940s, their vulnerability would be exposed. The British Bren gun carrier, the French Renault UE and the Italian Fiat Carro Veloce 33 were amongst this number.

Interest increases

The British exercises in the latter half of the 1920s and the start of the 1930s attracted world wide notice and extensive emulation. Coinciding, as they did, with the initial stages in the period of political tension which led up to World War II, it was natural that armies which had held back from modernisation and mechanisation should try to catch up through short cuts by studying others. Some went much faster and farther than the rest.

The Christie revolution

Among the tardiest were the Americans. Although they at once set in motion experiments intended to copy the British, they were denied a convincing trial since almost all their equipment remained of World War I vintage and therefore lacked the ability to carry out high speed, long distance manoeuvres. They were not only deficient in a modern communication system but also firmly held in check by the Infantry Branch who, invoking the Act of Congress, which gave the Infantry exclusive rights to tanks, refused to allow the Cavalry Branch to have tanks or to use these vehicles in the traditional cavalry role of reconnaissance and exploitation.

Nevertheless, within the USA, one man, J. Walter Christie, designed and built fast, lightly armoured tanks, worked on a revolutionary big-wheeled suspension, and caught the eye and imaginations of both soldiers and politicians, not only in Washington but in several other nations too. Christie's 'tank' of 1928, with its 337hp aero engine, a speed of 26mph on tracks or 50mph on wheels with the tracks removed, its 13mm armour, and its two token machine-guns, may not have met the minimum standards demanded of

The Russian BT2 was developed from the BT1 which, in turn, was copied from the American Christie M-1931 (T3) tank. The BT2 was very similar to the BT1 but differed by being fitted with a modified turret with a 37mm gun and ball-mounted 7.62mm machine-guns. They were still in service in 1940.

a combat vehicle, yet it certainly indicated a new way ahead in the search for high-speed vehicles of good cross-country performance and long range capability. Developed as the so-called M1931 (or T3) with a fully rotating turret, it would attract purchasers from Poland, Russia and, much later, Britain. It could easily have been adopted by the USA, too, if Christie had not been such a difficult man to deal with, but eventually official interest in the patents was allowed to lapse. Partly because of this business impasse, but largely as a result of the state of the national economy at a time of financial crisis and squabbles between the infantry and cavalry, the creation of a genuine independent tank arm in the USA,

Arguably one of the finest tanks of the inter-war period the Vickers-Armstrong Mark E was an impressive export success for the Newcastle company. Even so it was rejected by the British Army as being unsuitable.

Believing that tank warfare had altered little since World War I, the Renault R 35, originally the Renault ZM, carried on the two-man infantry support role. Trials began in 1935 and in the same year came into production. This is the R 35 prototype showing the original twin machine-gun armament and lack of cupola on the turret.

employing largely British methods, was delayed until the eve of the outbreak of World War II.

Further experiments

Between 1925 and 1926, the studies and experiments of the British Army provided a clear definition of the shape of mechanised armies of the future. Using a single heavy tank, the Independent of 32 tons, the Vickers Medium tank, a few tankettes, armoured cars and cross-country load and personnel carriers as test beds for a whole variety of technical trials, they formed the component parts of a so-called Experimental Mechanised Force, which developed new types of AFVs and a fresh concept of warfare far beyond the point which notions had reached in 1919. Pursuing the concept of independent operations by tank forces, they devised the outline of an organisation which would come to be known as the Armoured Division, a

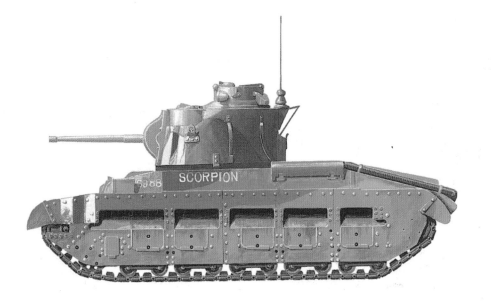

The Matilda II was the best British infantry-type tank and the only one to withstand the anti-tank guns of the German Army; despite its unreliability and mere 60 mile radius, it performed well in combat at Arras and in the Western Desert and went on to gain a good reputation with the 8th Army in the desert campaign.

Coming of Age

formation of all arms carried in fully cross-country fighting vehicles with the capacity to engage in almost every type of operation, from reconnaissance, full-blooded assault of an entrenched position, close combat as well as long range strategic exploitation. As the principal armoured weapons needed for this kind of formation, they envisaged a medium tank of about 16 tons, which was evolved from the Vickers Medium and the Independent; light tanks of about 6 tons for close reconnaissance and protection duties; armoured cars for long range reconnaissance; self-propelled artillery, supplemented by close support tanks to

provide high explosive and smoke and machine-gun carriers to move the modern infantryman, in relative security, to the pivot points on the battlefield upon which the AFVs would base their manoeuvres.

Armour improves

Exploration of the future support role of tanks for assault infantry was simply an extension of what had been formulated during World War I with the exception, in the face of rapidly improving and enlarging anti-tank weapons, it was reluctantly conceded that the light infantry tank must fail. Fuller's suspicion

The T37 series of the USSR was based on the British Carden–Loyd amphibious tank. T37A, as designated in 1935, shown here, had the original balsa wood side floats replaced by a combined welded/rivetted metal construction. Production ended in 1936 but many were still in service in 1942.

A key feature of the new era of armoured warfare pioneered by the Royal Tank Corps was centralised command. It was the cornerstone of all work done by Charles Broad, Percy Hobart and others. General Broad is seen here in the specially adapted Medium Command Tank 'Boxcar' during one of the epic exercises on Salisbury Plain.

of 1920, that only a heavily armoured tank had a chance of survival when compelled to advance at walking pace, was admitted in the face of the threat posed by high velocity anti-tank weapons. A gun such as the Oerlikon 20mm gun, with a muzzle velocity of 2,000 feet per second, or the German 3.7cm Pak 35/36 of 1928, would easily penetrate armour of 14mm, such as that which protected the latest 18-ton British Medium tank A6 (known as the 16-tonner). Therefore the sort of well-armoured vehicle which came to be called the Infantry (I) Tank, in 1930 was stated to need 25mm of armour – a thickness which increased steadily in the course of the next few years, as anti-tank guns with a calibre of anything from 25mm to 76mm were announced by their manufacturers. By the mid 1930s, for example, 60mm of armour was regarded as necessary to defeat the existing 37mm and 47mm guns with their muzzle velocities of about 2,600fps. Thus a race between gun and armour was started which, in the years to come, would impel an irresistible increase in the size, weight, power plant and cost of AFVs – the bigger the gun, the larger the turret, needed to mount it, and the larger the turret the

larger the tank and its engine had to be if mobility was to be assured.

Advanced communications

Another vital addition to AFV ancillary devices, occupying a foremost place in the consideration of tank leaders during the 1920s, was communication equipment, above all radio receivers and transmitters. From the outset in 1916, they had envisaged the need for the internal and external communications for AFVs, and a few of the very bulky radio sets of the day had been employed at the Battle of Cambrai to relay reports from the front. But not until the mid 1920s, as miniaturized sets working in the high frequency ranges, designed, originally for aircraft, became available was it possible to fit them easily into tanks. From 1930 onwards crystal controlled sets were being used by the British Tank Corps, which, in 1931 during a famous large scale exercise, demonstrated how one man, speaking over the radio, could control a mass of AFVs on the move.

Russia joins the race

Russia, under the urging of Chief of Staff Marshal Tuchachevsky, during a

The T26 was a Russian licence-built version of the Vickers 6-ton light tank Models A & B, examples of which were purchased in 1930 together with other lighter types.

massive reorganization and rearmament programme early in the 1930s, went much faster. Taking Vickers and Christie designs as the foundations of the many thousand tanks they would build in new factories, they opted, also, to create both armoured divisions and special infantry support units. By the mid-1930s, they would have in service the T26 series of tanks, copied from the privately made Vickers 6-ton light tank, the BT2 fast medium tank, based on the Christie T3, and a few heavy tanks similar to the

Vickers 16-ton tank and the Independent. Yet all along, under the tutelage of British and American engineers, they were training their own engineers, men such as M. Koshkin and Z. Zotin who developed the BT2 into the 'medium' 28ton, the T34, and the early heavies into the 46ton KV1. These revolutionary tanks, coming into service in 1941, would establish a long line of fighting vehicles still in service in the 1980s. In common, they mounted the 76mm dual purpose gun (which could fire all kinds of ammunition), and was so

The Soviet T-28s were clumsy and unsuccessful. They were inadequately armoured and under-gunned. The main armament was a short 76.2mm gun with machine-guns mounted in two forward turrets.

A Russian heavy tank KV-1 shown at the armoured training camp at Lulworth in England, having been presented to Britain by the Soviets during World War II.

well armoured that none of the anti-tank guns in service in 1940 could penetrate them except at point-blank range. The introduction of these tanks did, indeed, call for a revision in tank weight designations. Henceforward the heavy tank stood at 40 tons and above, and that for mediums between 25 and about 40 tons, ratings that would not last for long as the gun/armour race moved faster and faster.

German rearmament

Coming late to the tank race due to the total ban applied by the Treaty of Versailles, the Germans suffered badly at first from lack of tank designers and suitably equipped and experienced factories. A secret mutual aid agreement with the Russians in the 1920s had partially helped fill the gap, but it was 1933 before tank building on a large scale was started on the eve of Adolf Hitler's rejection of the Treaty of Versailles and the

A Russian SMK (Sergius Mironovitch Kirov) Heavy Tank used during the Russo-Finnish War where it proved unwieldy and was abandoned as a project. Externally it was almost identical to the T-100 Heavy Tank.

Coming of Age

The Kleiner Panzerbefehls wagen (small armoured command vehicle) was a command version of the PzKpfw I Light Tank. Although widely used they proved too small for the task and were later replaced by modified versions of later tanks.

commencement of German rearmament. However, in terms of philosophy and policy, the Germans by then had, to some extent cleared their minds. While many of their senior commanders tended to cling to the notion that AFVs must remain subsidiary to infantry, but to assume the reconnaissance role from cavalry, the thoughts and demonstrations thrust on them by Colonel Heinz Guderian produced gradual acceptance of a radical system initially based on British practice. Rejecting, for economic reasons, the construction of heavy or special infantry support tanks, Guderian postulated Panzer (armoured) divisions, composed of all arms which would work in collaboration through battlegroups. The tank, concentrated at the decisive, weaker

points of the enemy defences, would be the dominant weapon. To achieve his aim within a tight defence budget (in which the air force received a higher priority than either the army or navy), Guderian had to make do with relatively cheap AFVs. He opted to sacrifice armour protection in favour of quite high speeds and maximum reliability: 39mm was the thickest armour fitted. Having rejected heavy tanks, he selected three operational types: a light tank, the PzKpfw II of 10 tons and a speed of 30 mph, for reconnaissance; a medium tank, the PzKpfw III of about 20 tons with a high velocity 37mm gun and a speed of 25mph, for anti-tank combat; and another medium, the PzKpfw IV of about 20 tons with a low velocity, short 75mm gun and

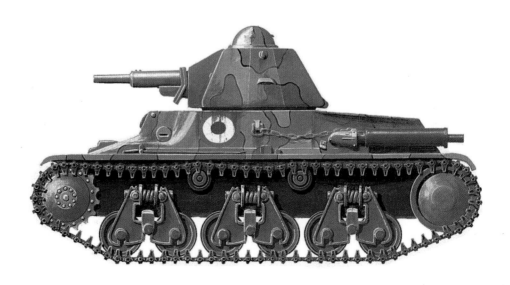

Installation of the SA 38 37mm L33 gun gave the Hotchkiss H-35 a respectable performance, with the only major disadvantage being that the commander had to work the gun!

Even though it was intended as a training vehicle the PzKpfw II became the major strength of the German Panzer divisions for the assaults of Poland and Czechoslovakia, and, later, France.

speed of 25mph, for close support purposes. It was Guderian's greatest contribution, perhaps, to the startling power of Germany's armoured forces that he insisted, against the resistance of doubters, upon relatively high expenditure on equipping each tank with a good HF radio set. By so doing he ensured maximum tactical control down to the lowest level in his panzer divisions and a vast increase in their direction and flexibility of operation.

French concepts

Compared with Germany's AFVs, those of France, its most powerful likely opponent looked, on paper, far stronger. Even the light R35s and H35s, weighing between 10 and 12 tons, had about 40mm armour and a 37mm gun as main armament, while the latest medium, the SOMUA S 35 with its 55mm armour and 47mm gun and the heavy Char B of 32 tons with 60mm armour and a 47mm and short 75mm gun, looked decidedly superior. Yet all suffered from the French addiction to the one man turret, and a tank doctrine and organisation which were positively detrimental to effective combat employment. For the French, while conceding in the early 1930s that horsed cavalry must give way to armoured vehicles, merely tried to substitute tanks and armoured cars for the horse. Their three Light Mechanised Divisions (DLM), which contained the elements and assumed the approximate shape of an all-arms panzer division, were destined to be

The TNH P–S Light Tank was a Czechoslovakian tank which, after the German occupation, remained in production for the German Army from 1939 to 1942. More than 1,400 were produced under the designation Panzerkampf- wagen 38(t) Ausf S to Ausf G.

Panzerkampfwagen III (SdKfz 141) Ausf J heavy tank

Cutaway drawing key

1 Commander's cupola
2 Turret ventilator
3 Co-axial machine-gun
4 5 cm KwK L/42 gun
5 Spare road wheels
6 Maybach HL 120 V 12 engine
7 5 cm ammunition stowage
8 Idler wheel
9 Shock absorber
10 Suspension bump stop
11 Propeller shaft
12 Turret base rotary junction
13 Battery
14 Torsion bar
15 Road wheel
16 Track drive sprocket
17 Final drive
18 Steering clutch
19 Driver's seat
20 Steering levers
21 Gear shift lever
22 Steering brake
23 Instrument panel
24 Maybach-Variorex transmission
25 Hull gunner/radio operator's seat
26 Hull machine-gun
27 Machine-gunner's head pad
28 Turret ball race
29 Turret side hatch
30 Turret stowage box

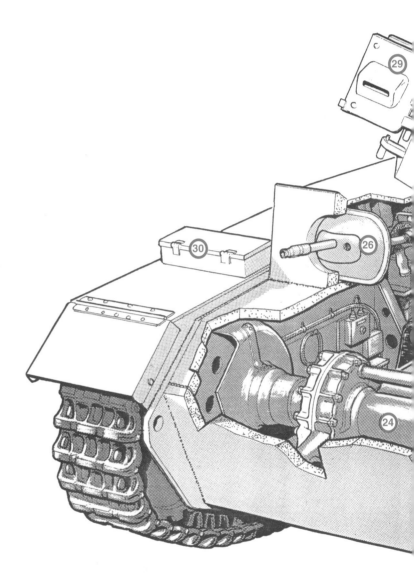

©Ray Hutchins '88

The PzKpfw III Ausf G was used by the Afrika Korps and proved most effective against the more lightly armoured British infantry tanks whose heavier weight made them less mobile than the Panzer III which also had the advantage of having a 50mm L/42 gun. This gun proved inadequate against the Soviet T 34 and so the Ausf J was upgraded with the longer-barrelled KwK 39 L/60 gun.

employed spread out across a wide front in reconnaissance and only to be concentrated if a breakout ever looked likely. Likewise, the heavy and light tanks committed to infantry support were to enter battle in diluted form. Therefore neither the command, control and logistic systems, nor the techniques of their employment had been developed before battle was joined in earnest in May 1940. For this state of affairs France had her generals far more than anybody else to blame.

British developments

British AFV development also fell short of the German standard, and differed from the French, but for different reasons. Political priorities and ineptitude mitigated against the acquisition of main battle tanks. Financial precedence was given to the navy and air force over the army, and the emphasis within the army was placed upon cheap light tanks and armoured cars exclusively for imperial policing, since British foreign policy withheld a commitment of the Army to a Continental war. Not until 1938 was there any likelihood of Britain committing herself to fighting Germany at the side of France, and by then starvation of funds, vacillation within the Army Council and a far too small tank manufacturing industry precluded the production of sound medium and heavy tanks in time for a war in 1939.

The British lead in tank matters of the 1920s had been dissipated. By 1938 only armoured cars and the 5-ton Vickers Mk VI were in large scale production. Failure to put the A6 16-tonner into production had broken the line of development for medium tanks by Vickers. That led to the construction of cheap 'stop gap' tanks with inferior combat capabilities, incipient unreliability and a shape and size which, unlike their German counterparts, impeded later adaption to thicker armour and to bigger guns when the need arose. The 15-ton A9 and A10 mediums were a match for the German Pz III, but underpowered and prone to break down. The A13, based on the Christie and full of promise began life as the first product of the newly built Morris factory; but it proved a haven for mechanical defects of all kinds despite extensive redevelopment from its forebear, the faulty Christie M1932 tank. False economy also bedevilled the I Tank types. In fact, the A 10 cruiser was originally intended as a so-called 'Woolworth's Tank' but its defects and, above all, thinness of armour, brought about the change of status. In its place came A17, the Matilda Mk I, whose inefficiency as a fighting machine was wholly the product of financial skimping; weighing only 12 tons, with a speed of just 8 mph and only one machine-gun, there was little its crew of two men could do in cramped quarters to make it battleworthy. Its one saving grace was 65mm of armour that made it proof against German 37mm guns. Better was the later Matilda Mk II which had a 40mm gun in a three-man turret with 80mm armour and a speed of 15 mph. This tank would become 'Queen of the Battlefield' for a short time but was soon passed over for further development. Even so the British Army went to France in 1940 ill-equipped to fight a modern tank war and not ready for the German attack.

Japanese developments

Japan's first step towards tank design began in 1918 with the arrival of some Mk V tanks from England, Renault FT tanks from France and, later, deliveries of British Mk A tanks. Little more was accomplished until 1925 when a domestic design programme was launched. During the period up to the early thirties a number of developments were carried out to keep themselves abreast of the most advanced foreign designs, when the first studies concentrated on wheeled armoured cars, but terrain conditions in the Far East favoured tracked vehicles.

A line of small tracked vehicles, classified as tankettes, started in 1932 and the first Japanese tankette, known as the Type 94, was shown in 1934. Further adaptions of the Type 94 were developed but abandoned when the Japanese Imperial Staff considered the entire tankette concept outdated.

After Japan became involved in full-scale war with China in 1937 several more powerful and specialised vehicles were designed and produced, but in the meantime development continued by Mitsubishi Heavy Industries on a light tank, powered by the same diesel engine as the Type-89-B Medium Tank. Prototype construction included a model fitted with a 37mm gun and weighed 7 tons. This was the HA-GO which was standardised as the Type 95 (Kyugo) Light Tank.

The most remarkable achievement of the Japanese tank designers was the policy of 'dieselisation' initiated in 1933 for the Type 89 Medium Tank. This policy gave the advantage of reduced fire hazard, lowered fuel consumption and eliminated the difficulties of acquiring petrol. In 1945 Japan was considered the most advanced nation in the field of diesel development and was way ahead of the Allies and Germany.

The most outstanding Japanese tank of World War II was the Type 95 (HA-GO) Light Tank. It was developed in 1933 and gave mobility and speed to Japan's newly formed mechanised brigades. It was built by Mitsubishi Heavy Industries and weighed 7.4 tons. Armament consisted of a 37mm gun plus two 7.7mm machine-guns. It had a crew of three. The 6-cylinder air-cooled diesel engine provided 110hp and gave the Type 95 a speed of 25mph.

CHAPTER THREE

The Tank Proves Itself

The German armoured forces were not fully prepared for the campaign against Poland which began on 1st September 1939 to form the beginning of the Second World War. Of the 3,000 tanks available, only 98 were Pz IIIs and 211 Pz IVs, the remainder being light tanks of which the Pz Is were little more than weapon carriers, based on the early tankettes, which had been acquired for training purposes. The fact that the Germans overcame the Poles within three weeks was the result of concentrated German offensive action by land and air forces. The Poles had only a small, outclassed, air force and 225 tanks, of which but a handful were modern versions of the outmoded Vickers 6-tonner. Nevertheless, the action of panzer divisions was undeniably a prime cause of the Polish collapse; at no stage could the Poles, hanging on behind linear defences of the old kind, match the mobility of the fast, mobile formations. The Germans, spearheaded by armour, struck at the heart and brain of a nation virtually unhindered and won the war with the loss of only 217 tanks and 8,000 dead. Yet it might have turned out easier still had the German infantry performed better, for, denied close armoured support as they were, due to the concentration of all tanks in elite formations, they tended to hang back in attack. The remedy would soon be forthcoming.

Prior to the next campaign in the West, many of the unbattleworthy Pz I tanks were converted to armoured assault guns, along with over 50 Pz IIIs, to work specifically in the van of the infantry divisions assault. These updated versions of the 1917 French chars d'assaut, cheaper and easier to build than the more sophisticated turreted tanks, would play an increasingly big role in the years to come in all armies. In the German Army, however, they would exclusively take the place of heavy or I Tanks as that role was envisaged by the French, British, Russian and US armies.

The death knell of the light tank, in any role other than that of reconnaissance, was sounded during the campaign in the West of May/June 1940. The losses on both sides were very high. Still with less than 3,000 tanks to tackle some 3,600 belonging to the Allies, the Germans had significantly increased the number of gun-armed machines at the expense of those armed only with machine-guns. At the same time they had raised the number of full panzer divisions from six to ten and, at Luftwaffe insistence, were embarked on a scheme whereby the heavy 88mm anti-aircraft gun should be deployed as often as possible in the forefront of battle to take on the dual role of anti-tank gun. This

One of the first self–propelled gun conversions of the PzKpfw I tank was the Geschützwagen mounting a 15 cm sIG 33 infantry howitzer. It was high and very awkward giving the crew only limited protection, but it pointed the way to requirements for the future.

tactic, first tried out during the Spanish Civil War in 1937, was to have a significant impact in a campaign in which the number of tank versus tank battles was far exceeded by those in which tank fought field-mounted anti-tank guns; and, in which the inadequacy of the 37mm guns to penetrate the thick British Matildas' armour was only compensated for by the intervention of 88s and 105mm field artillery firing over open sights.

The gun versus armour lesson was not lost on either the Germans or the British. In the immediate aftermath of the campaign, the Germans would set in train a rapid re-equipment of their tank and anti-tank forces. The Pz III's 37mm gun, which was already in course of

replacement by a short barrelled 50mm gun (to the disgust of Guderian who would have preferred to go the whole hog and fit the more powerful, longer barrelled version) would be phased out, while the long barrelled 50mm would gradually replace the 37mm field piece with the rest of the army. Simultaneously, the construction of assault guns would be increased towards the point at which enough would be available to support all the infantry formations, a condition which battle losses and insufficient production would for ever frustrate.

For their part, the British, virtually disarmed and expecting invasion after the collapse of France (a collapse attributed more to bad generalship than inferior

When the United States entered the war in late 1941 the Light Tank M3A1 was the main combat version of the M2/M3 light tank series. It had provision for mounting three machine-guns with a 37mm (1.46in) main gun.

Light Tank M3A3 – Stuart V

Cutaway drawing key

1 .30in Browning anti-aircraft machine-gun
2 Turret periscopes
3 Turret traverse control
4 Elevating handwheel
5 Commander's seat
6 37mm gun recoil guard
7 Wireless aerial
8 Gunner's seat
9 Turret ball race
10 Exhaust silencer
11 Continental 7-cylinder radial engine
12 Hull stowage box
13 Spare track links
14 Engine cooling fan
15 Clutch
16 Idler wheel
17 Propeller shaft
18 Main suspension unit
19 37mm ammunition stowage
20 Road wheel
21 Driver's seat
22 Gear shift lever
23 Steering brake levers
24 Clutch pedal
25 Transmission
26 Track drive sprocket
27 Hull gunner's seat
28 Driver's periscope
29 .30in Browning machine-gun
30 Pistol ports
31 Driver's hood locators
32 37mm gun
33 0.30in Browning co-axial machine-gun
34 Gyro-stabiliser
35 Spotlight

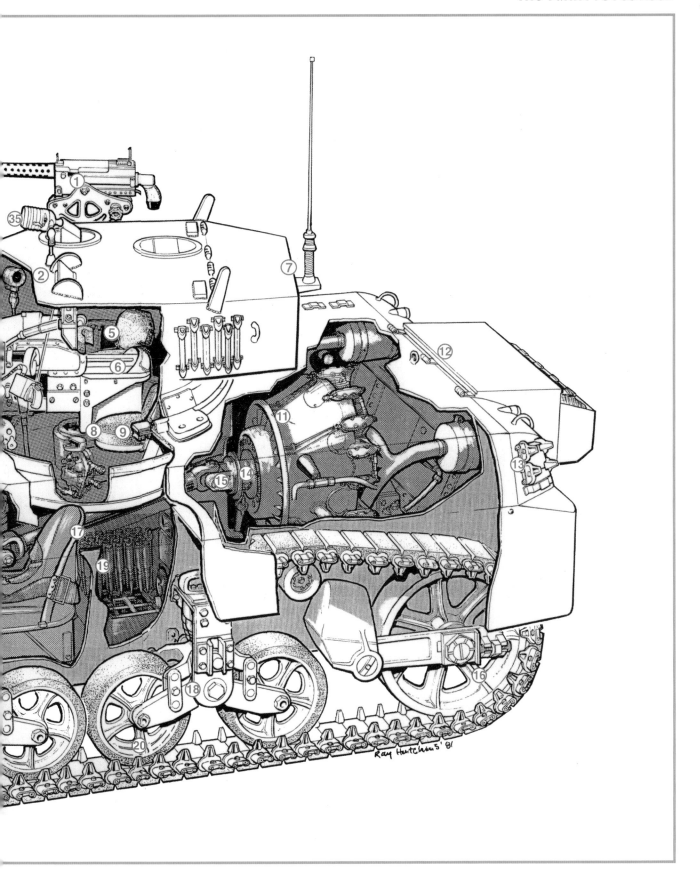

The Tank Proves Itself

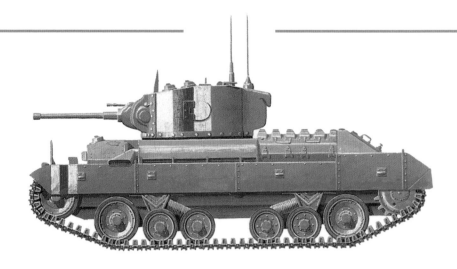

Although slow like the Matilda, the Valentine III/IV was one of the more successful pre-war designs. It was mass-produced from 1941 and fought throughout the North African desert campaigns. This was a sturdy vehicle and able to be rearmed with better guns as the war progressed.

equipment) had to make do with whatever could be built in haste. Convinced as they were that tanks were now a dominant weapon, that armour must be increased on all tanks to 80mm at least, and, that the 40mm gun must be replaced by a 57mm (6-Pdr) gun, they were compelled by the dire circumstances to take whatever they could get. In addition to the light, medium and heavy tanks then in production, plus the next generation to come, the armed forces therefore had foisted upon them a large collection of lightly armoured wheeled vehicles whose combat worthiness was suspect to say the least. Meanwhile, despite the desire of the tank experts to increase the proportion of medium to I Tanks, the factories continued to turn out more I Tanks because of the priority given to these machines in the days when infantry support seemed the more likely role. Not until the beginning of 1941 was

the next generation medium tank, with thicker armour and a 57mm gun, approved (the tank which eventually came into service one year too late in 1943 under the name of Cromwell) along with a hastily designed 38 ton I Tank to be called the Churchill. Yet still, production of the 57mm gun was delayed because there were not enough 40mm guns to equip the army as it was; and, it was reasoned, anything was better than nothing.

Gunnery lessons

The years to come would reveal that a mass of inferior equipment might easily be defeated by small batches of superior weapons properly handled, as already had proved the case in the West to the German advantage. Yet, even if the lesson was digested that: dispersed tank forces (on the French model) would fall victim to concentrated tank attacks (in the

The Cromwell was built to a 1941 General Staff requirement for a 'heavy' cruiser. It was nearly 50% heavier than the Crusaders it replaced because experience had shown that lack of armour and inadequate firepower were greater deficiencies than lack of speed.

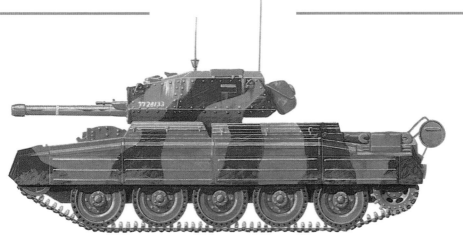

The Crusader III was the first tank to be fitted with a really effective gun, the 6 pdr replaced the 2 pdr of earlier Crusader models. Its suspension was its great strongpoint which was so tough that it could exceed its theoretical top speed.

German manner); and that a gun/armour race of considerable impetus was in progress, scant attention was paid to bad shooting by tank and anti-tank gunners of both sides. The technique of hitting pin-point targets at variable ranges out to about 1,000 metres had not advanced much beyond the point to which British tank gunnery experts had carried it in the early 1920s. The difficulty that commanders and gunners found in judging the range beyond 400 yards because of unreliable ammunition, primitive firing gear and poor optical instruments, quite apart from the unsteadiness of composure of many crewmen when under fire, all contributed to some wildly inaccurate shooting even at very close range. Considerable quantities of ammunition were expended for poor results, and it would be almost two years before this matter came to be taken seriously in hand by any of the contestants.

Mechanical upsets

However, a larger proportion of tank losses was due to mechanical failure rather than enemy action. Breakdowns, even minor ones, could cause wide fluctuations in tank strength; and, for the next two years, no tank force suffered more seriously from this than the British. Each tank, with the exception of the Valentine, had one or more chronic ailments, such as few tanks of other nations had, in such profusion. The A9 and A10 medium tanks (usually called cruisers) suffered, among other things, from frangible tracks; the A15, Covenanter cruiser had a bad engine-cooling system for which no remedy sufficient to make it battle worthy could be found without complete redesign; the A16 Crusader cruiser was bedevilled by water pump and engine lubrication problems which caused many breakdowns; and the 38 ton Churchill, rushed through design into production, was a nest of troubles. It was

Introduced in 1943 the Churchill was essentially designed for a return to trench warfare; as such it was a classic infantry tank, slow although heavily armoured. Its chassis was subsequently used for a host of specialist vehicles.

The Tank Proves Itself

Cromwell tanks move up to their start line for one of the many breakout battles which took place in Normandy in 1944. Despite the much improved quality of British armour, the price of attacking German positions was often very heavy.

The Josef Stalin IS-2 heavy tank was introduced in early 1945 and was the most advanced heavy tank of the period and a major influence for subsequent British and American designs. Good as it was the Russians thought that it could be improved, the result being the IS-3 which mounted the larger 122mm (4.8 inch) gun.

bad enough that, for the first two years of war, the makers could not be persuaded to make nearly enough spare parts to replace failures. It was disastrous also that when, as the result of breakdowns in battles during which the British were more often in retreat than on the advance, they frequently left behind, in enemy hands, brand new and, quite often, almost undamaged machines from already depleted holdings.

German restrictions

Not that the Germans for all the triumphs made possible by armoured forces, were without their troubles. The sharp campaigns of 1939, 1940 and early 1941 all benefited from being of short duration, providing intervening periods to refurbish worn machinery and make replacements. But the German war economy ran on a shoestring. At the start of the greatest campaign of all against Russia in June 1941 it could provide only 3,200 tanks (with production at only 125 tanks a

month) and could mount only a small proportion of the artillery and infantry units in tracked or half-tracked vehicles that were able to keep up with the tanks. The rest travelled either in wheeled vehicles with a poor cross country performance, marched on their feet, or were drawn by horses. It was indeed one of the most remarkable military achievements of history that this relatively small but expert force was able to rout a huge Russian army which included some 17,000 to 20,000 tanks of the mainly Christie and Vickers type, none of which were grossly inferior to the German models.

But it was the factor of overstretch on German mechanical reserves and an inadequate logistic system, and their inability to keep up the pace of advance into the depths of the Russian heartland, which led them to fall short of totally annihilating the enemy. Though the German motorised formations out-manoeuvred and outfought the Russian armies, they never possessed that last

reserve of strength and mobility to carry them to the ultimately decisive points in the enemy rear. Always there were just enough Russians, with a few tanks and guns, standing in the way; and as winter mud, cold and snow blanketed the front, it was the appearance in ever increasing numbers of the KV-1 and T-34 tanks which brought a deadly chill to German hearts when they found themselves confronted by fighting vehicles which were markedly superior to their own.

Russian surprises
Both of these new Russian machines made an enormous impression when the first few put in an appearance in June and July 1941. Just at a glance their combination of protection, firepower and mobility could be recognised. Even the long 50mm anti-tank gun had difficulty penetrating the KV-1's 106mm sloped frontal armour, while the T-34's sloped 60mm glacis plates presented problems at all but the shorter ranges. The sloped armour at 50° to the angle of attack doubled the protective factor of armour plate. But it was the 76mm gun with its dual capability of firing a good HE round and a devastating solid shot which raised these tanks to a new plain of excellence.

The poor quality of Russian crew training and lack of leadership (escalated by political purges and heavy initial battlefield losses), plus the disadvantage that the crew found in controlling the tank and gun in the T-34 two man turret,

militated against full effectiveness. Even so, it was clear to the Germans that tank warfare and tank design had achieved a new plane. Perhaps to an even greater extent than before, the tank battle which would confer battlefield superiority to one side or the other would be won by the side whose tanks could not only penetrate the enemy armour, while at the same time providing a reasonable, if not absolute, level of protection against enemy shot, but, could also expedite the enemy's destruction by a vast improvement in the standard of shooting at longer ranges and against pin point, hard targets.

Enter the Tiger
So, the Germans, with the energy of desperation, improved armament of the Pz IV with a long, high velocity 75mm gun, in place of the original short close support version; and designed and produced the heavy tank, Tiger I, with an 88mm gun, which could deal easily with the KV-1. Also, they produced a 43ton medium tank, the Panther, with an even longer 75mm gun than the one for the Pz IV. They also introduced far more sophisticated optical instruments and gunnery techniques to assist crews to hit targets with a minimum of wasted, ranging shots.

It was to the credit of the tank officers of the United States Army that, in the summer of 1940, when they laid down the armament for their future main battle tanks, they specified the mounting of a

Continued on page 56

THE LEGENDARY T-34 MEDIUM TANK

The T-34 was one of the main war-winning weapons of World War II. It was produced in such large numbers and in so many variations that entire books have been written about it without exhausting its qualities and exploits.

The updating, in 1938, of the BT-7, first known as the A-20 and A-30, and, later, the BT-IS, was then further developed with a heavier gun and increased armour becoming known as the T-32. Many features of this marque can be seen in the T-34.

The T-34 went into production in 1940, and, as the T-34/76A, mass production, with yet more armour, soon followed. By 1941 the marque was well established and it gave the Germans a nasty shock when they confronted it during their invasion of the Soviet Union.

Massive production
Production lines were disrupted during 1941 but improvised factories carried on producing in ever increasing numbers. Even though the finish on most was poor they were proven to be excellent fighting machines. Apart from their main role of battle tank, they also served as reconnaissance vehicles; engineering tanks; recovery vehicles and even as a personnel carrier simply by carrying infantry, called 'tank descent' personnel, on the hull over long distances. These troops became the scourge of the Germans as they advanced through the liberated Soviet Union and Eastern Europe.

The T-34/76C was an improved model fitted with a larger turret containing two hatches instead of the previous design having one. The T-34/76D was fitted with a hexagonal turret and wider mantlet and jettisonable exterior fuel tanks. The T-34/76E had all-welded construction and a cupola fitted to the turret, while the T-34/76F was identical to the T-34/76E except that its turret was cast and not welded.

First models mounted a 7.62cm (3in) gun but these were replaced later by an 85mm (3.34in) gun using a turret taken from the KV-85 heavy tank. These models were designated T-34/85 and some remain in service to this day. Special assault gun versions mounting the 85mm gun were introduced; and, later, 100mm (3.94in) and 122mm (4.8in) artillery pieces were developed as were engineer, tractor, mine-clearing and flame-throwing versions.

However, it is as a main battle tank that the T-34 makes its claim to fame. The availability of thousands of these tanks gaining mastery of the battlefield gave the Soviet Forces the tactical and strategic initiative to put the Germans on the defensive and to win the 'Great Patriotic War'.

If the measure of a tank's quality is the ability to accept improvement, then the Russian T-34 has to be classed as one of the best. In 1943 the hull was adapted to take a new turret, mounting an effective 85mm gun and, what is more, the new turret was capable of taking an extra crewman, freeing the commander from his duty as loader. This example was captured by the Allies during the Korean War.

Crude, tough and available in large numbers the T-34/76 was an impressive machine by any standards. The combination of Christie suspension, a rugged V-12 diesel and sloped armour with an effective 76mm gun was a tribute to its designers. If it had a failing then the two-man turret, with the commander having to take on the task of loader was one. Infantry tank riders were a common feature of warfare on the Eastern Front.

INFLUENCE OF T-34 ON GERMAN TANK DESIGN

Designed, basically, by M. I. Koshkin from the original BT, A-20 and A-30 tanks, the T-34 was produced on a massive scale. It was a complete surprise to the German Army when making its combat debut at Grodno (Belorussia) on 22 June 1941. There was even a question of whether to build some for the German Army, but this proved impracticable. The general design of the T-34 prompted the Germans, greatly influenced by the T-34's capabilities, to design the Panther tank. The overall design of the tank facilitated mass production and gave easy maintenance and repair in the field. The T-34 of Koshkin can rightly claim to be Russia's equivalent of Mitchell's Spitfire; an analogy that proved even too true when both designers died giving their efforts to provide their countries with warwinning weapons.

Sherman Firefly VC Medium Tank

Cutaway drawing key

1 17-pdr Gun MIV or VII in mount No 2
2 .30in co-axial M1919A4 machine-gun
3 .50in HB M2 flexible AA machine-gun
4 Commander's cupola
5 Commander's periscope Mk6
6 Loader's hatch
7 British wireless set No. 19
8 Signal pistol
9 17-pdr ammunition stowage
10 Commander's seat
11 Loader's seat
12 Escape/driver's hatch
13 Driver's periscope (shown on opposite side for clarity)
14 Portable fire extinguisher
15 Driver's seat
16 Chrysler A-57, multibank, 30-cylinder, liquid-cooled, 425hp petrol engine
17 Range finder
18 2x12 volt batteries in series
19 Power train (transmission)
20 Gearshift lever
21 Parking brake lever
22 Steering levers
23 5 gallon fresh water containers
24 Equipment chest
25 Ventilator
26 Radio antenna
27 First-aid box
28 3.5in thick gun-shield
29 1.5in thick mantlet
30 Binoculars
31 Periscope M.4 with Telescope M.38

32 Air cleaner manifold
33 Clutch assembly
34 Fan assembly
35 Radiator
36 Final drive housing
37 Track return rollers
38 Suspension bogie
39 Track drive sprocket
40 Track idler
41 Volute spring

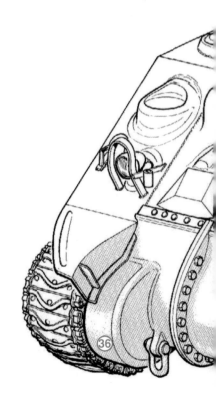

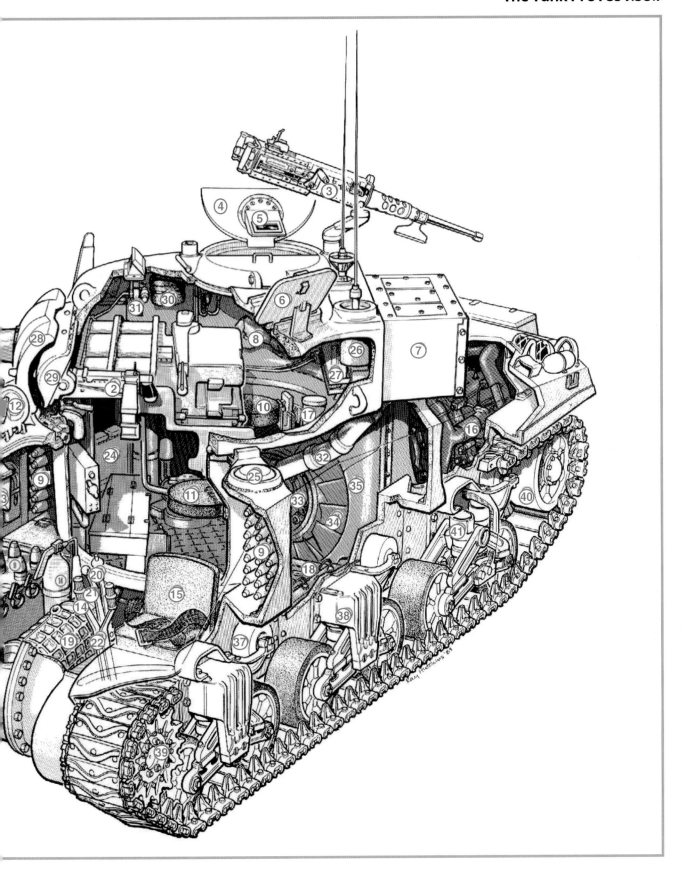

Another of the war winning tanks was the M4 Sherman. It first saw action at the Battle of El Alamein when the impact on the Afrika Korps was considerable. The Sherman came along with a turret allowing a 360° traverse enabling its 75mm (2.95in) gun to deal with any of the German tanks then in service.

75mm dual purpose gun. The selection was based entirely upon studies of tank warfare and vehicle performance in Europe, since not until the autumn of 1939 had the Americans a sufficient number, even of light tanks armed only with machine-guns, to conduct experiments with what came to be known as the Armoured Force. Hindered by shortage of funds and the opposition of the traditional arms, the American tank enthusiasts were compelled to break away from the Cavalry and Infantry in order to make what they considered sufficient progress at a time in history when it began to look as if an involvement in war was imminent. They adopted many ideas from the Germans, notably that of battle groups; but, it was with the British with whom they collaborated closest in vehicle design, and the British who were eager customers for any tanks the Americans could supply as a result of their design efforts.

American tank limitations

But for use in 1941, the only tank of possible battleworthiness that could come from the US factories was the light 12 ton M3, General Stuart, with only a 37mm gun and 38mm armour. It was not until early in 1942 that a tank mounting the 75mm gun would appear in numbers, and even this machine suffered from severe combat limitations due to the circumstances of its creation. For although the Americans knew that a fully rotating three man turret was essential, in the summer of 1940 they had neither the design, nor the manufacturing capability, to deliver such a machine until mid-1942. They could,

The Sherman M4A3 (Sherman IV) was one of the most developed of all the Sherman variants used until 1945. Apart from its Ford 373 kW (500 hp) petrol engine it was fitted with horizontal (HVSS), rather than vertical, volute suspension.

Built in vast numbers and available to all Allied armies the M4 Sherman tank was arguably one of the most important weapons of the war. Variations are almost endless, here is an M4A1, which had a cast hull and was powered by a nine-cylinder, radial air-cooled engine.

however, adapt an existing experimental Medium tank M2 to mount a 37mm gun in its upper turret and the 75mm with restricted traverse in a side sponson, low in the hull. The 30 ton M3 Medium which evolved would have armour of 88 mm and incorporate that high level of reliability which was a by-word for nearly all American built tanks. In its original form known as the Lee, the version that was improved as a result of British suggestions, would enter battle in May 1942 as the General Grant and, at a stroke, project into the desert war against the Germans and Italians the same gunnery and tactical upgrading as was occurring in Russia.

The Allies outgunned

Not only did the introduction into battle of the Grant, at the Battle of Gazala, coincide with the introduction of the Pz III tank, with its long 50mm gun - soon to be joined by Pz IV with its long 75mm gun - it also coincided with a series of heavy defeats in which numerically inferior German forces shattered British units whose Crusader, Matilda and Valentine tanks, armed only with 40mm guns, were so badly out-gunned that their very survival became problematical. Only the Grant could stand up to the improved armament of the German tanks; but, the Grants were also at some disadvantage

The M3 Grant was the 'British' version of the M3 Lee. It differed from the Lee in that the turret had an overhang to accomodate a radio set. The turret was fitted with a 37mm weapon which was found to be powerless to penetrate enemy armour so, as a stopgap, the Americans fitted a sponson mounted 75mm gun which proved relatively efficient.

Medium Tank M3A4 General Lee V

Cutaway drawing key

1 Commander's cupola
2 Pistol port
3 37mm ammunition stowage
4 Turret traverse gear
5 37mm gunner's seat
6 Air cleaner
7 Engine clutch
8 Engine cooling fan
9 Chrysler Multibank engine
10 Exhaust pipe
11 Idler wheel
12 Return roller
13 Road wheel
14 Volute spring suspension
15 Rear propeller shaft
16 37mm turret basket
17 Radio operator's seat
18 .30in Browning hull
     machine-gun
19 Handbrake lever
20 Clutch pedal
21 Track drive sprocket
22 Transmission
23 Driver's seat
24 Gear shift lever
25 Steering levers
26 75mm gun
27 75mm Gunner's seat
28 Gun traverse handwheel
29 Gun elevating handwheel
30 Gunner's periscope
31 Recoil Guard
32 75mm ammunition stowage
33 37mm gun
34 .30in Browning machine-gun

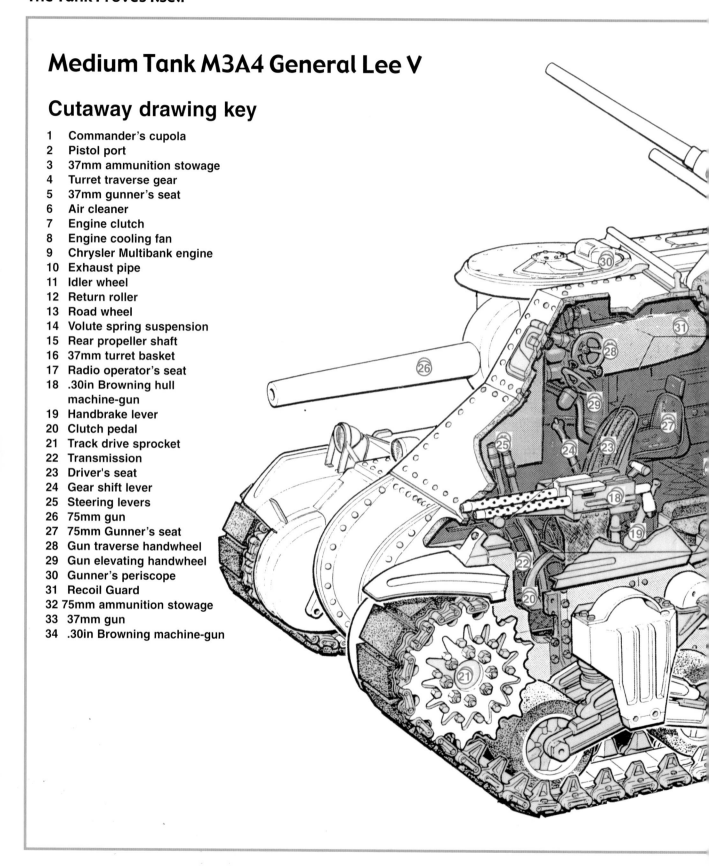

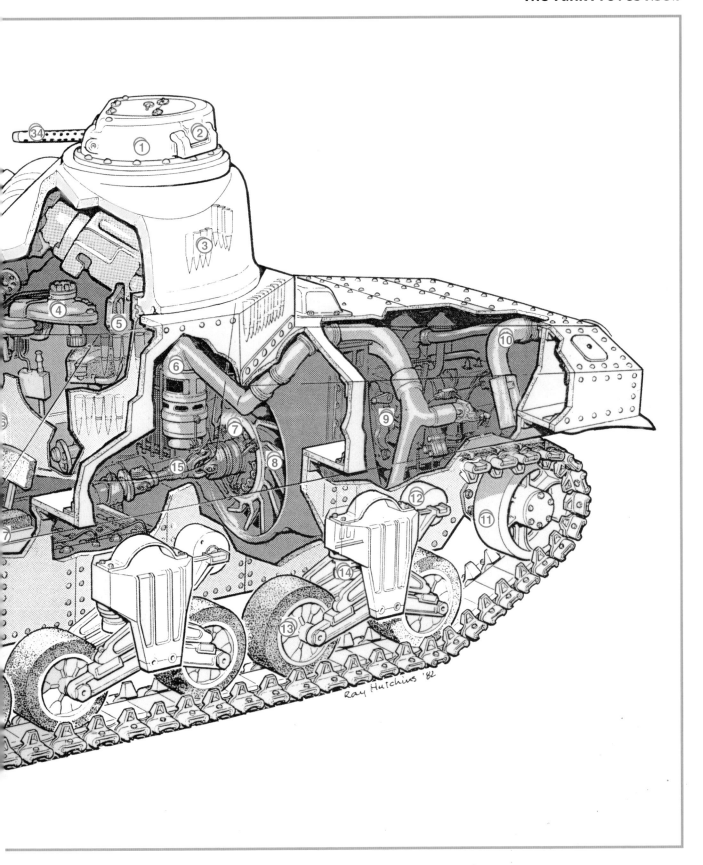

Ray Hutchins '82

The American Medium M3, Lee, tank, was accepted by the British with but one modification. In order to conform to British practice a new turret was designed that permitted the radio set to be accommodated at the back, not in the hull as on the American version. In this form it was known, in Britain, as the General Grant although in North Africa they nicknamed it 'Egypt's Last Hope'.

due to the inescapable problem of having to expose their tall hulls in order to fire the 75mm gun over open sights at the enemy.

Added to the British reticence in settling agreed tactical doctrine to make their tank units co-operate effectively with those of artillery and infantry, and their unwillingness to use their 3.7inch anti-aircraft gun in the anti-tank role, in the manner of the equivalent German 88mm gun, was the British habit of charging, in the Balaclava style, that was so often their undoing. In most cases it would have been admissible to stand back and shoot from behind cover at the enemy guns. However the tendency to charge was largely the product of the

need to close the range to give the obsolete 40mm guns a chance of hitting and penetrating small targets. The advent of the 75mm with its HE shell and AP round, which could be fired effectively from behind a crest, not only offered a safer way of engaging the enemy, but led to a swing of opinion from one tactical extreme to another.

At the nadir of British fortunes in the desert, when they were forced back to El Alamein in July 1942, the tacticians abetted by gunnery experts, were ordering that all anti-tank shooting must take place indirectly from a turret-down position, thus abandoning the far superior method of direct shooting from hull-down positions. That this was a viable

Jagdpanzer IVs (SdKpfw IV) were in great demand. They had a 7.5cm gun, as fitted to the Panther V and well-sloped superstructure of very thick armour. This tank-buster proved equal to any of the Allied tanks in the field.

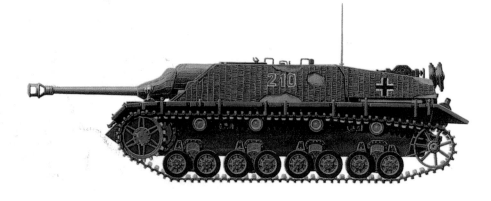

Used to tow heavy artillery and equipment the SdKfz 9 schwerer Zugkraftwagen 18t was the largest of all World War II halftracks. It was used mainly as a recovery vehicle and later versions were powered by the Maybach engines similar to those fitted to PzKpfw IV tanks.

arrangement for the Grant was arguable. However, its application to the Crusader tank, armed with the 57mm gun and above all, to the American Sherman, which arrived in Egypt in September 1942, had to be firmly rejected.

Weight decisions

The arrival of the 33 ton Sherman marked the same sharp turning point as did the almost coincidental production of the German Pz IVF. Both with dual-purpose 75mm guns mounted in three-man turrets behind armour of, respectively, 81mm and 80mm, they could fire a good high explosive round, smoke and armour piercing shot. In effect the moment had arrived at which it was no longer necessary to separately specify infantry tanks and the medium cruiser or cavalry tanks. From now onwards it would be possible for a single medium tank to perform a multiplicity of roles. Although there would be a continued need for light tanks, such as Stuart, in the reconnaissance role, there was a persistent demand for heavy tanks above 40 tons: such as the 56-ton German Tiger I, the 40-ton British Churchill Mark VII, the 55-ton American M6A2 and the 45-ton Russian Josef Stalin 1. But, the day of the heavy tank would pass the moment that the medium tank reached about 50 tons; since, above that weight, the transportation of tanks by ship, or railway or across obstacles, approached the point of insuperability. Indeed, the Germans much preferred the Panther to the Tiger and the Americans abandoned their M6A2 because of shipping restrictions.

The Tiger II, called by the Western Allies 'The King Tiger', in German Königstiger, utilised the latest sloped armour and carried a long-barrelled 88mm high-velocity gun. The first 50 vehicles were fitted with the Porsche turret, as shown, but these were cancelled because it was found that the electric transmission used too much copper; subsequent tanks had Henschel turrets. The Tiger II was safe from almost all Allied tanks at most ranges.

STALINGRAD TO KHARKOV AND KURSK
NOVEMBER 1942 - AUGUST 1943

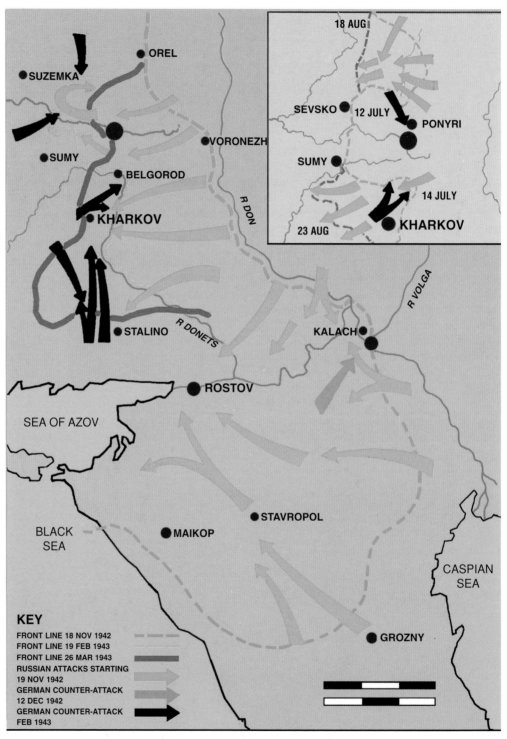

OREL

SUZEMKA

SUMY

VORONEZH

R DON

BELGOROD

KHARKOV

R VOLGA

STALINO

R DONETS

KALACH

ROSTOV

SEA OF AZOV

STAVROPOL

BLACK
SEA

MAIKOP

CASPIAN
SEA

GROZNY

18 AUG

SEVSKO   12 JULY   PONYRI

SUMY

14 JULY

23 AUG   **KHARKOV**

KEY

FRONT LINE 18 NOV 1942
FRONT LINE 19 FEB 1943
FRONT LINE 26 MAR 1943
RUSSIAN ATTACKS STARTING
19 NOV 1942
GERMAN COUNTER-ATTACK
12 DEC 1942
GERMAN COUNTER-ATTACK
FEB 1943

The Russian counter-offensive of mid-November 1942. It isolated the Wehrmacht besieging Stalingrad leading to the destruction of von Manstein's Sixth Army and began to roll back the Germans towards Kursk and Kharkov in the Ukraine.

RUSSIA TURNS THE TIDE

The German drive to the Caucasus and Stalingrad lasted from June to November 1942. General von Paulus's Sixth Army reached the outskirts of Stalingrad on 23 August 1942 where he confronted the insurmountable obstacle of the makeshift, but determined, defences of the city. Paulus called for reinforcements, leaving the protection of his flanks to the troops of the German satellite countries of Hungary, Italy and Romania. Despite ferocious resistance from the defenders, Paulus hoped to deliver Stalingrad to Hitler as a Christmas present but, unknown to him, the Russians were preparing a counter-attack.

While Stalingrad's forces tenaciously clung to their positions, General Georgi Zhukov was secretly massing a huge force north of the city along the shores of the River Don. On 19th November the Russians struck, catching von Paulus completely by surprise and surrounded the Wehrmacht's Sixth Army. He cabled Hitler for permission to withdraw from the city but Hitler refused and rejected requests for a retreat, commanding von Paulus to take Stalingrad or die in the attempt.

On advice, Hitler recognised that von Paulus would have small chance of salvaging the situation if German forces did not lift Zhukov's siege of the German garrison; in consideration of this he commissioned General von Manstein to prepare a relief force, called Army Group Don, to break through to the city and restore the German front.

The loyal Paulus made no attempt to break out of the Russian encirclement and kept the German 6th Army in place until the new year. Hitler was adamant that von Paulus should stay put, but on 31 January von Paulus was captured and the 6th Army surrendered with the collapse of the German offensive.

Army Group A, under the command of General List, was pulled out of the Caucasus and the remnants of von Bock's Group B and von Manstein's Army Group Don were regrouped to prevent a rout. In the north a Russian offensive had re-opened part of the rail line between Moscow and Leningrad enabling the siege of Leningrad to be lifted. It was only in the Crimea that the Germans held their positions.

The Stalingrad victory inspired the Red Army which lost no time pursuing the Wehrmacht to the west. By 7 February Kursk fell to the Russians, but von Manstein rallied his forces and retook Kursk albeit with a much diminished position. There was a lull in the battle from April until July 1943 during which time both sides reinforced their armies. The Red Army was defending a front stretching from Orel to Stalingrad with a bulge in the area of Kursk, while the Germans occupied a smaller area adjacent to the River Donetz. The Russian positions were more exposed than the Germans which invited an attack by the Wehrmacht when the conflict was renewed.

The Battle of Kursk

Equipped with the newest tanks and supported by the Luftwaffe a large German force attacked on 4 July 1943 with an assault on the Kursk bulge. The German Tiger and Panther tanks and Elefant SP guns were far superior to the Russian KV 1s and T-34s but the Russian tank reserves outnumbered those of von Manstein's forces and, although the Wehrmacht inflicted losses twice those of the Soviets, the Red Army could still afford to sustain these greater losses. As many as 3,000 tanks were involved in the week long battle and on 13 July von Manstein was forced to retreat to save the German Army being completely destroyed by Zhukov's Red Army forces. After their defeat at Kursk the Wehrmacht were pushed back to the Russian border and Hitler's ambitious hopes for Operation Barbarossa were well on the way to being finally closed. Kursk is considered to be the greatest tank battle ever.

CANADIAN AND AUSTRALIAN TANKS OF THE PERIOD

Canada had no tank units at the beginning of World War II, but training and familiarisation started on old World War I tanks. Because of the submarine activity in the Atlantic there was little hope of obtaining tanks from the United Kingdom and, at that time, the United States was not involved in the war; so, the only thing the Canadians could do was to build their own, starting from scratch.

The Canadians adopted many of the main mechanical, hull and transmission components of the M3 but added a rotating turret. Building this tank from scratch was a major achievement for Canadian industry. The prototype rolled off from the Montreal Locomotive Works late in June 1941 and was called Cruiser Tank Ram Mk I. This prototype carried the 40mm gun. The Ram Mk II mounted the 6-pdr 57mm (2.244in) gun and turned out to be a remarkably effective design. Production proper began at the end of 1941. The Ram never saw action. They were sent to the United Kingdom with Canadian armoured regiments but, as the M4 Shermans were pouring off American production lines, Canadian units were issued with Shermans and the Rams were used only for training.

Thus, the Rams were withdrawn but many had their turrets removed and were called Ram Kangaroo; these provided a simple and efficient troop carrier. These were widely used in the campaigns after D-Day. Others were converted to artillery observation posts and were termed Ram Command/OP tanks.

Australian efforts

1939 Australia's armed forces had virtually no tanks and no heavy engineering background to produce them. With knowledge gained from the USA and the UK they produced their first design, the AC1 (Australian Cruiser), again based on the M3. The first prototypes were ready in January 1942 and were given the name 'Sentinel'. This was a remarkable achievement since the Australians had to develop the means of production, even as the tanks were being built.

Another marque of the Sentinel was the Sentinel AC3 which mounted a 25-pdr (87.6mm 3.45in) gun which eventually proved inefficient against armour. A further model, the AC4 was to mount a 17-pdr gun, a prototype of which was built but never went into production.

Canada had no armoured forces in 1939 but their expanding army needed to equip itself with tanks because of the world situation. The Ram tank utilised the chassis of the M3 Grant but mounted its main armament in the turret rather than in a sponson.

The Japanese Type 95 KE-GO light tank proved to be very useful against infantry during the early part of World War II but it soon became outclassed when it was confronted by American Marine tanks in 1943.

JAPANESE AND ITALIAN TANKS OF THE PERIOD

Mitsubishi Heavy Industries were responsible for the production of most of Japan's tank manufacture. The Type 95 light tank was developed to meet the needs of the Japanese Army in the early 1930s, with the first two prototypes being completed in 1934. These were tested in China and Japan and the type was then standardised, Mitsubishi calling it the HA-GO and the Japanese Army the KE-GO. Over 1,100 Type 95s were built before the end of production in 1943, although it has been claimed that production continued until 1945. The Type 97 CHI-HA medium tank was a replacement for the obsolete Type 89B. Almost 3,000 were built up to the middle of World War II. It was considered the best Japanese tank to see any great amount of active service. Although it was considered a fairly advanced design, it was handicapped by an inadequate gun.

World War II brought no dramatic innovations by the Italians as far as armoured vehicle design was concerned. In one aspect they were abreast of tactical thinking by becoming interested in the tank-destroyer concept. When Italy entered the war they found that their existing tanks were out-gunned by British armour in North Africa so Fiat-SPA and Ansaldo combined to use the chassis of the old L.6/40 and mount a powerful 47mm version of the Austrian Böhler dual-purpose anti-tank/infantry support gun, one of the hardest hitting anti-tank guns of its day. This venture produced the Semovente L.40 da 47/32 which went straight into service from 1942 onwards. When the Italians surrendered in 1943 the Germans quickly took over as much Italian equipment as possible, the Semovente L.40 da 47/32 was part of this booty.

The Type 97 CHI-HA medium tank was a replacement for the obsolete Type 89B. Almost 3,000 were built up to the middle of World War II. It was thought to be the best Japanese tank to see any great amount of active service. Although it was considered a fairly advanced design, it was handicapped by an inadequate gun.

ANTI-TANK GUNS OF WORLD WAR II

Prototypes of the Ordnance, Q.F., 17-pdr were introduced into the British Army in 1942. It went on to be one of the most powerful Allied anti-tank guns. It could penetrate any enemy tank at long ranges and firing rates of 10 rounds per minute were not uncommon. Some of these guns served in the British Army into the 1950s and they are still in service in armies around the world.

Regarded by many as the finest anti-tank gun in the world when the Second World War began the British 2-pdr (40mm) was capable of penetrating 42mm of armour at 1,000m range. The gun came complete with a two-wheeled carriage that unfolded to create a cruciform platform and the gunner was provided with a two-speed, geared traverse system to enable him to track .

The Semovente L.40 da 47/32 was used by the Italian army in North Africa and during the early part of the Italian campaign and by the Germans thereafter until the end of the war.

Replacing the earlier 3.7cm and 5cm weapons the 7.5cm Pak 40 became the standard anti-tank gun of the specialist battalions of the German Army. It was an excellent weapon, first used in 1941, it continued in service until the end of the war. A tank gun version was also used in great numbers.

The threat posed by anti-tank rifles had been a scourge of the inter-war years. The German 28mm heavy anti-tank gun Schwere Panzerbuchse 41 was an improved weapon on the same lines. It used a tapered bore, 28mm breech, 20mm at the muzzle, firing a tungsten core anti-tank round (the Gerlich principle) and it could penetrate 52mm of armour at 500m.

This self-propelled anti-tank carriage was an early attempt to mount the famous '88', the 8.8cm Flak 18, on to a 12-ton tractor half-track. There were only a small number produced to see action in France in 1940.

CHAPTER FOUR

The Essential Weapon

Something of even greater importance than a readjustment of tank philosophy and design was taking place in the latter half of 1942. The British victory at El Alamein and the isolation of the Germans at Stalingrad by a Russian counter-offensive, marked the high tide of German expansion. For the Allies it was a reversal from the defensive to nearly three years of almost ceaseless advances, leading to the overwhelming of the Axis nations. In the East, Japan would be capable of further advances to continue her startling conquests of 1942, but this was largely a war on sea, and in the air, in which land warfare took place on terrain that automatically denied fighting vehicles a prominent role.

Only in Europe and North Africa did armies clash on the grand scale, employing fighting machines of ever increasing power, size and number. Now, indeed, the German numerical inferiority was so acute, and their technical superiority so eroded, that they could no longer withstand the attrition of ceaseless battle in which they lost irreplaceable quantities of equipment. Although Germany raised her production to a far higher level it could not replace losses which reduced average panzer division strengths from about 200 tanks, in the summer of 1942, to 27 in February 1943. Moreover, their opponents' production had now reached such quantity that it became a matter of expressed policy among British, American and Russian commanders that tanks could be sacrificed in very large numbers if a tactical advantage could be obtained. In any case, even when scores of tanks were knocked out, the casualties among their crews were rarely as proportionately high as amongst the infantry. Such was the life saving quality of armour compared with battle dress.

In the winter of 1942/43 the Germans faced up to the need to restructure their armoured forces. Although General Heinz Guderian's arguments would sustain tank production at a reasonably high level, he was faced by a strong caucus who disclaimed tanks as being too costly and difficult to build by comparison with other, cheaper, weapons, some unproven and a few quite useless, but weapons which could be manufactured in large quantities. A strong desire to give infantry greater anti-tank protection stimulated a swing of fighting vehicle production towards self-propelled guns of limited traverse with calibres up to 128mm, and armour as thick as 250mm as on the enormous 70-ton Jagd Panzer VI. At the same time the infantry were stiffened by more field anti-tank guns of 75mm and over and helped in the fortification of their positions by the employment of vast

Most powerful of the Italian armoured vehicle destroyers, Semovente M.41M da 90/53s, were armed with the 90mm (3.54in) anti-aircraft gun mounted on an M.15/42 tank chassis. They were used in the North Africa campaign and were much respected.

quantities of hand laid mines. Concurrently, the Artillery arm, eager to play a far greater part in the anti-tank battle, began to make chemical energy, hollow charge shells which, when fired at relatively low velocities, had the capability, through exploiting the Monro effect, of blasting a hole in armour with a jet of molten debris. Also, similar low velocity, short-range rocket propelled weapons, called panzerschreck by the Germans and bazooka by the Americans, were given to the infantry in large quantities.

Each new device, particularly those produced in quantity, was bound to contribute something to the defence and make the job of fighting vehicle crews more exacting. But, as is the nature of such things, each weapon's limitations could be found and subverted. SP guns could be outflanked and, inherently, were at a disadvantage to tanks with fully rotating turrets. Relatively immobile anti-tank guns and field artillery could also be outflanked

or destroyed by indirect artillery or tank gun fire. Hollow charge weapons, whose effectiveness was degraded when the round was spun or fired at higher velocities, suffered from significant ballistic inaccuracies. Infantry held anti-tank weapons were vulnerable to shell fire and enemy infantry who specialised as tank escorts. Anyway the hollow charge warhead could be defeated by spaced armour.

Tactical decisions
Fundamental to the effective employment of the various kinds of fighting vehicle in their endeavours to overcome opposition lay the need for co-operation between all arms. Towards the end of 1943, the Russians improved the armament of the T-34 with an 85mm gun, making it the 3-man-turret T-34/85; the Americans gave the Sherman a slightly better 76mm gun; and the British took delivery of the fast and reliable Cromwell; but, each of these new AFVs was vulnerable to the current

British Archer AFVs were an adaptation of the Valentine infantry tank mounting a 17-pdr (3in/ 76.2mm). They were used by the Royal Artillery and proved to be very useful weapons. The rear facing gun could have been a liability, but the gunners put it to advantage by using them from ambush positions and then driving away from the action with the barrel still pointing to the rear!

Designed as the main weapon of Tank Destroyer Command's mobile units, the American M10 mounted a 3in (76.2mm) gun in an open topped turret. The armour was relatively thin-skinned, the weight of better armour being sacrificed for all-round speed in action.

anti-tank weapons, and liable to very heavy losses if thrown into battle without the close support of artillery, accompanying infantry and engineers, let alone air power. The ways in which the other arms worked tactically with tanks were the products of careful study, training and execution in the tactical field, and are here not discussed, but the tools of that co-operation were often special fighting vehicles, most of them armoured, all of them designed to keep pace with the tanks wherever tanks could go.

Increased mechanisation

Tank manoeuvres usually depended upon momentum to sustain mobility. Momentum could soon be lost if the artillery and infantry did not travel in vehicles with cross country performance. So, as the war progressed and industrial output expanded, an increasingly high proportion of guns and infantry were carried in specially built tracked or half-tracked vehicles, or in obsolete tanks with their turrets and main armament removed.

Air/land communications

To link these disparate elements of combat teams together, a plethora of radio sets were fitted to fighting vehicles so that they could speak to each other, passing information, giving and receiving orders from commanders who tended to control from the front instead of from a remote headquarters behind the gun smoke. Communications, as the British tank pioneers and Guderian had long ago foreseen, were the key to making fighting vehicles work efficiently, and in linking the air arm to land warfare, which was equally important, specialised as the air arm was in its functions.

In a war in which air power played a central part, it was natural that aircraft, which frequently co-operated with

The M18 Hellcat was the fastest of all AFVs during World War II. It was an ideal tank-hunter, armed with a long 3in (76mm) gun. The M18 had good power-to-weight ratio with excellent acceleration and agility. It was in production from July 1943 to October 1944 when 2,507 of them were built.

armies, should also be employed as special tank hunters. Ineffectual attempts to do so were made by the Russians on a small scale in 1941, but it was not until 1942 that the British and the Germans attempted it seriously. To begin with, aircraft were armed with forward firing cannons of between 20 and 30mm calibre, and at once enthusiastic and exaggerated claims for success were filed, particularly by the Germans in Russia. Such claims have never been adequately substantiated; indeed, if full credence were granted to them it is unlikely that enough Russian tanks would have remained to advance to the German frontier and beyond between 1943 and 1945!

Similarly, the claims by British pilots to have destroyed large quantities of tanks in North West Europe in 1944 and 1945, by the use of rocket projectiles, are wide open to challenge, particularly since certain precise investigations on the spot suggest many claims were overstated. What of fuel, ammunition and vital stores reaching the front line troops? A costing of the effectiveness of aircraft versus fighting vehicles would probably show that the difficulties of finding concealed, small hard targets in the forward area, were well protected by anti-aircraft fire which could destroy a disproportionate number of expensive aeroplanes. Indeed, special anti-aircraft tanks were built.

Balancing the books

Costing, both in its monetary as well as its material and time consuming aspects, raised many problems for the makers of fighting vehicles and for those who aspired to defeat them. A balance had to be struck between the price of an article and its combat effectiveness. It was as useless to create a very few highly expensive pieces of machinery, which were bound to be destroyed without significant results, as it was to make vast quantities of cheap and totally vulnerable weapons. It could be argued that the enormously expensive concrete defences which the French and Germans had erected along their common frontiers, prior to 1939, were a complete waste of outlay when costed against the relatively cheap and ubiquitous mechanised armies which had outmoded and broken them. Similarly, the German coastal fortifications stretching from Norway to Spain, had only a limited role in contributing to a defence against the coming Allied invasion of 1944.

It had to be admitted, however, that the so-called Atlantic Wall, while strengthening the defences against fire and making possible savings in manpower, also had the effect of compelling the Allies to indulge in very complex and expensive countermeasures to overcome them. Among those countermeasures were to be found not only the special

The Elefant was unreliable, and despite it having a main armament of the 8.8cm gun, it proved too cumbersome. More importantly it carried no kind of self-defence, enabling Soviet tank-killer squads to swarm over them to place lethal charges that either blew off their tracks or otherwise disabled them.

Panzerkampfwagen VI Tiger Ausf E heavy tank

Cutaway drawing key

1 8.8cm Kw K36 L/56 gun
2 7.92mm MG34 machine-gun
3 7.92mm MG34 machine-gun
4 7.92mm machine-gun ammunition
5 Smoke generator discharger
6 Escape hatch
7 Commander's seat
8 Commander's traverse wheel
9 Revolver port
10 Traverse gearbox
11 Commander's shield
12 Gunner's traverse handwheel
13 Gunner's elevating handwheel
14 Gunner's seat

24 Steering unit
25 Steering wheel
26 Gearbox: 8 forward, 4 reverse gears
27 Driver's seat
28 Handbrake
29 Accelerator
30 Foot brake
31 Clutch
32 Shock absorber
33 Torsion bar suspension
34 Overlapping bogie wheels

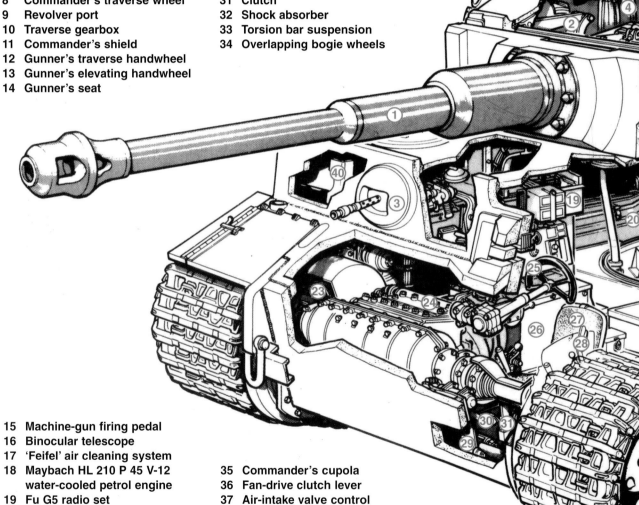

15 Machine-gun firing pedal
16 Binocular telescope
17 'Feifel' air cleaning system
18 Maybach HL 210 P 45 V-12 water-cooled petrol engine
19 Fu G5 radio set
20 8.8cm ammunition bins
21 Hydraulic traverse foot control
22 Hydraulic traverse unit
23 Disc-brake drum

35 Commander's cupola
36 Fan-drive clutch lever
37 Air-intake valve control
38 Petrol primer
39 Petrol tap
40 Machine-gun ammunition storage

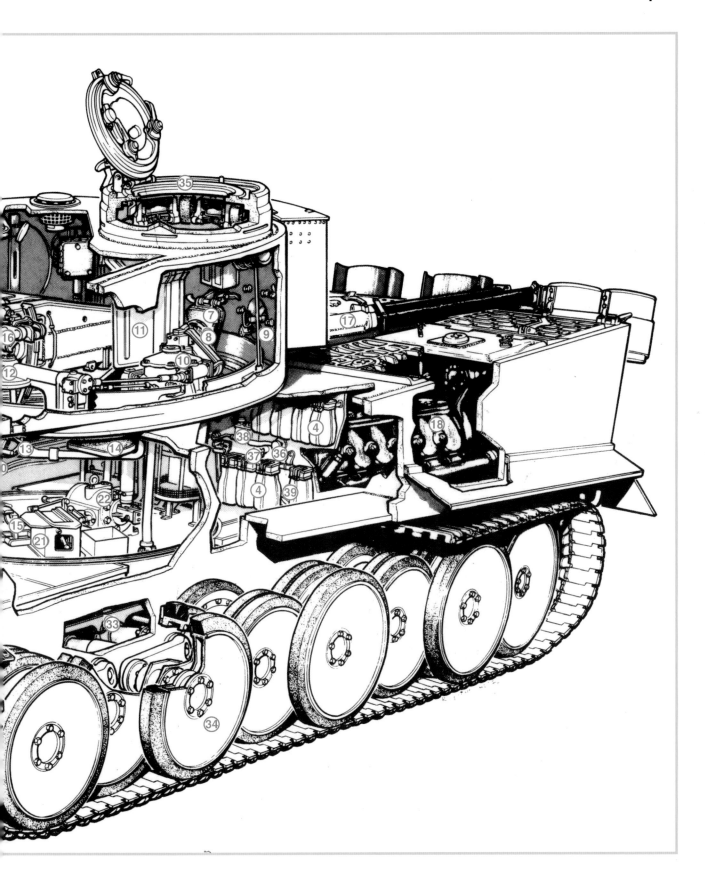

GENERAL HEINZ GUDERIAN: FATHER OF THE *PANZERTRUPPE*

Using the tank as the dominant weapon, he formed the *Panzertruppe*, working in close conjunction with other arms as an offensive formation. He was enthused by the ideas of Fuller and the British tank experiments in the 1920s and early 30s. By pressing hard for Panzer divisions, influencing Hitler with his ideas, he was able to form the Panzer Division in 1935, commanding it himself. He was promoted to command an Army Corps in 1938, and took part in the occupation of the Sudetenland and Austria, before further advancement to become Chief of Mobile Troops at the end of 1938.

Commanding the Mechanized Corps in 1939 he made his name with tank actions in Poland, and, in early 1940 he won public acclaim and his troops' devotion, at the head of the dramatic thrusts to the Swiss Frontier and the English Channel.

During the invasion of the Soviet Union his verve and dare to make calculated risks won him striking victories. His hot-headedness, however led to him being dismissed for disobeying orders when at the gates of Moscow.

He was recalled to Germany to become Inspector-General of Armoured Troops in early 1943 and spent the next two years struggling to repair damage to the *Panzertruppe* inflicted during battlefield neglect by retraining and re-equipping his tank units.

All the successes of his men during the struggles from 1943 to 1945 were to his credit. Appointed Army Chief of Staff in July 1944 his responsibilities for the hopeless situation on the Eastern Front were beyond even his capacity as leader.

Generaloberst Heinz Wilhelm Guderian was born in 1888. He started his military career as a light infantryman and became a specialist in radio. He had great insight into technology and was a charismatic leader. He served within the Great German General Staff, for Motorised Troops, in 1922 where he showed his organisational talent. He was amongst the elite who formulated the philosophy and shape of German forces of 1939.

Although he preferred heavy tanks Guderian opted for lighter tanks because of expense, they were the 10 ton light tank and two medium machines of about 20 tons: the Mark IV, for close support, armed with a 75mm gun and the Mark III tank-killer, armed with a 37mm gun.

Similarly he was unable to control the actions of his *Panzertruppe* after D-Day, 6th June 1944, because of the direct interference from Hitler, otherwise the Allies might have faced an even more aggressive foe than the one they fought on the beaches of Normandy.

The PzKpfw VI Tiger had thick armour and mounted a version of the dreaded 88 mm anti-aircraft/anti-tank gun, making it an outstandingly powerful design. Although not particularly agile it could command the battlefield. It was first encountered by the British army in Tunisia and then confronted the Allies on all fronts.

landing craft, required to carry fighting vehicles to the hostile shore, with the tanks, self-propelled guns and armoured personnel carriers comprising what was by now a typical European style mechanised army, but, also, a large number of different kinds of specialised vehicles equipped to deal with beach defences and inland fortifications in as rapid and economic a manner as possible.

Preparations for invasion

The siege train which the Allies assembled for the invasion of June 1944 had its roots deep in the history of fighting vehicles. Nearly all the functions which had to be catered for had been defined and tackled before. The main difference now lay in the far more sophisticated and ingenious methods adopted to meet the demands of those planning the invasion and that 'armour should be used in the forefront of the attack in order to dominate the enemy defences before the infantry came ashore'.

First ashore, therefore had to be ordinary gun tanks, Duplex Drive (DD) Shermans, which were made to float by surrounding them with a collapsible canvas screen and driven through the water by screws powered by the main engine. With these Sherman DDs established at the water's edge and advancing up the beach, teams of other obstacle clearing tanks would be landed to a drill procedure.

Other Sherman variants

There were minesweeping Sherman Crab tanks, using a normal Sherman tank fitted with a rotating drum of flailing chains mounted on a boom ahead of the tank and beating the ground ahead to clear mines and Armoured Vehicles Royal Engineer (AVREs). These were Churchill tanks. Some had mortar firing, heavy, high explosive charges to demolish concrete and other emplacements, to which also could be attached a number of different devices and attachments to enable

Probably the finest German tank of the war the PzKpfw V Panther. The first prototypes were completed in September 1942 with production following, without proper trials, shortly afterwards. The many mechanical problems that occurred in the early days were overcome and confidence in the vehicle grew. It first saw action on the Eastern Front in the battles for Kursk.

Panzerkampfwagen V Panther (SdKfz 171) Ausf G heavy tank

Cutaway drawing key

1   75mm L/70 gun
2   7.92mm MG34 machine-gun
3   7.92mm MG34 machine-gun
4   Ventilator
5   Commander's cupola
6   Gun cradle
7   Sighting telescope TZF 12a
8   Loading/escape hatch

36   Oil pressure pump
37   Batteries
38   Final drive
39   Sprocket
40   Return roller
41   Limited suspension stop
42   Shock absorber
43   Swing-arm bearing bracket

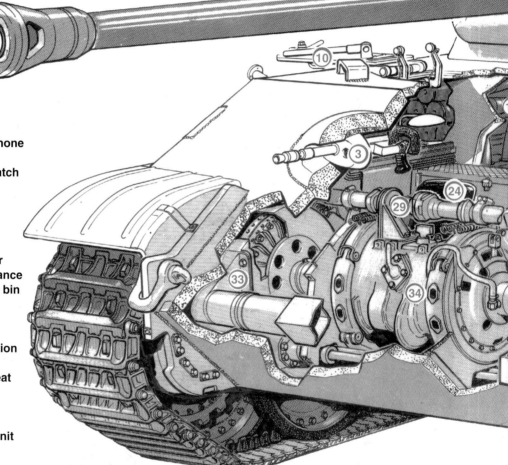

9   Commander's microphone
     and handset
10   Wireless operator's hatch
11   Turret traversing gear
12   Elevation handwheel
13   Engine ventilator
14   Cooling air inlet
15   75mm ammunition
16   Balance/elevating gear
17   Gun compensator/balance
18   Spent 75mm cartridge bin
19   Maybach engine
20   Gun cleaning kit
21   Spare track links
22   Machine-gun ammunition
23   Gunner's seat
24   Wireless operator's seat
25   Instrument panel
26   Spent machine-gun
     ammunition container
27   Hydraulic traversing unit
28   Compressor
29   Brake link
30   Steering lever
31   Driver's seat
32   Machine-gun firing pedal
33   Track brake cooling duct
34   Gearbox
35   Track brake

44   Suspension crank arm
45   Interleaved road wheels
46   Idler wheel
47   Torsion bar suspension

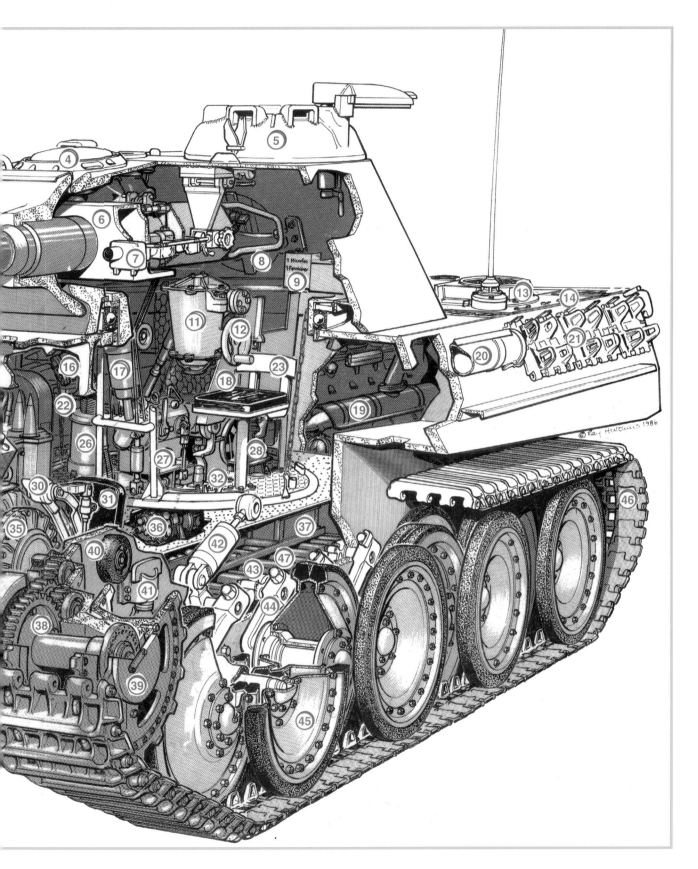

The Sherman DD or Duplex Drive Sherman provided the fire support necessary for the safer landing of the D-Day troops in their amphibious assault on the Normandy beaches. It was an M4 medium Sherman tank fitted with a floatation collar and twin propellers.

engineers to clear or cross obstacles with minimum exposure to fire special hand or rocket laid charges. Other AVREs were fitted with carpets which unrolled ahead of the AVRE on soft ground to help other vehicles get over while yet more carried long bridges to mount sea walls and cross streams and/or fascines to fill ditches.

Flamethrower tanks
Systematically the siege train would grind its way through the extensive minefields and obstacles that were to be found both along the Atlantic Wall and, to a lesser, but no less deadly extent, shielding inland defence systems. Joining in against pill-boxes, fortified houses and trenches would be Crocodile flame-throwing tanks. These were Churchill VII tanks fitted with a bow mounted flame gun (with a range of 120 yards), towing a trailer which contained 400 gallons of flame fuel (napalm) under pressure.

Adept as these specialised AFVs were in performing their duties, and capable as the DDs, Crabs and Crocodiles were functioning as gun tanks, the last two usually required support by other tanks on their special task. This was all the more necessary in 1944 when Allied armour, overwhelming though it was in numbers, was seriously out-classed in combat by the German Tiger and Panther tanks. Unreliable though these new German vehicles continued to be since their hasty introduction to service (respectively, in September 1942 and July 1943), they could out-gun all their opponents (with the exception of the Russian JS heavy tanks) and were proof frontally at all but the shortest ranges against the mass of 75mm and 76mm tank guns opposed to them.

It was commonplace for a few, or just a single, Panther or Tiger to hold up and knock out ten or more Shermans, Churchills or the newly introduced Cromwell.

Churchill AVRE, also fitted with deep wading gear, mounting a Bullshorn anti-tank mine plough at the front and a Porpoise skid trailer at the rear. These trailers could be used to carry ammunition, fuel and a wide range of other supplies.

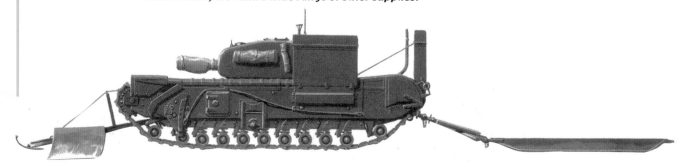

The Sherman Crab had 43 chains mounted on a drum powered by a takeoff from the main engine. It had side-mounted wirecutting discs to cut through barbed wire, screens to shield the front of the tank and a device to follow contours. It was the most widely used mine flail tank of World War II. The odd-looking device at the hull rear is a station-keeping marker to guide other flail tanks.

Only one Allied anti-tank gun, the long British 76mm (17-pdr), could penetrate the Tiger in front, and even this powerful piece could be defeated by the well sloped 120mm glacis plate of the Panther.

Sherman Firefly

Indeed, had it not been for the determined reversal of British tank policy which compelled the authorities (against their fixed resolution) to fit the 17-pdr into the Sherman (producing the Sherman Firefly), the British would have invaded Europe in the summer of 1944 lacking a tank that could hold its own, and leaving the rest as hostages to enemy depredations. The British, having fallen behind in development of the Cromwell, had also faltered in the development and production of its successor, the 33-ton Comet, with a good, modified 17-pdr gun called the 77mm. The Americans, deciding that quantity was better than quality, in 1943 had abandoned the Sherman's 76mm armed successor – the T 20, in favour of up-gunning and up-armouring the Sherman. Useful though the so-called Easy Eight Sherman with its 76mm gun would be, it could not hope to cope with the German tanks and heavily armed SP guns. Not until an improved T 20 with a 90mm gun and 110mm frontal armour – the 42-ton Pershing – came into service towards the end of 1944, would parity be partly restored. By then the war was in its closing stages and Germany's fighting vehicles were so seriously in decline, as her frontiers contracted and her industry was destroyed, that they ceased to be a factor in battle.

The Churchill Crocodile, unlike Sherman versions, was one of the most widely used flamethrower tanks of WWII. It towed a special trailer that carried the flame fuel and the nitrogen gas cylinders. The flame gun was mounted in the hull front thus retaining the 75mm gun.

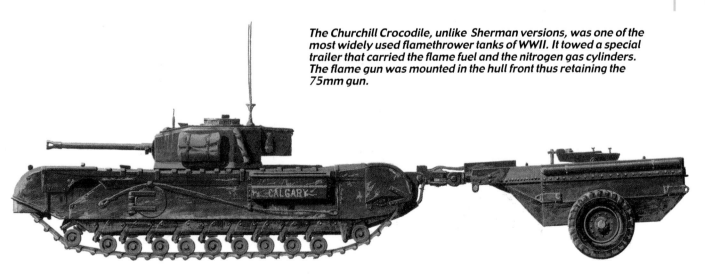

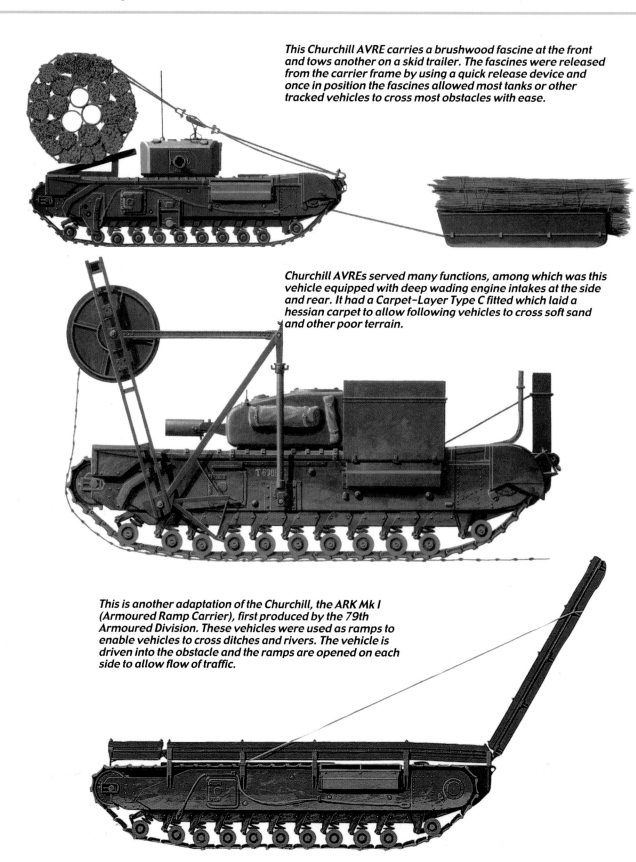

This Churchill AVRE carries a brushwood fascine at the front and tows another on a skid trailer. The fascines were released from the carrier frame by using a quick release device and once in position the fascines allowed most tanks or other tracked vehicles to cross most obstacles with ease.

Churchill AVREs served many functions, among which was this vehicle equipped with deep wading engine intakes at the side and rear. It had a Carpet–Layer Type C fitted which laid a hessian carpet to allow following vehicles to cross soft sand and other poor terrain.

This is another adaptation of the Churchill, the ARK Mk I (Armoured Ramp Carrier), first produced by the 79th Armoured Division. These vehicles were used as ramps to enable vehicles to cross ditches and rivers. The vehicle is driven into the obstacle and the ramps are opened on each side to allow flow of traffic.

The Canal Defence Light was actually never used for its original purpose. The Grant CDL was intended to replace a normal gun turret with one housing an intense light to illuminate battlefields at night. Although not used for their original purpose to light up the landing beaches they did good service providing 'artificial moonlight' to illuminate the crossings of the Rhine and Elbe in early 1945.

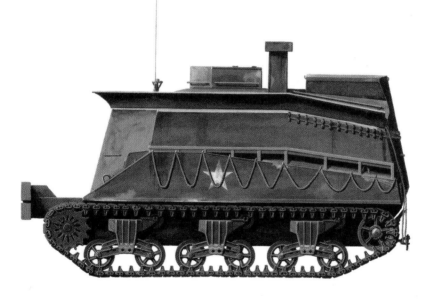

The Sherman BARV (Sherman Beach Armoured Recovery Vehicle) could operate in 3.03 m (10 ft) of water. It featured a high box-type superstructure and mounted a nudging nose to push vehicles out of the water. The crew usually included a trained diver.

The Sherman Crocodile was a British development that failed to impress the US Army in its flamethrower mode. Only four were built. The flame-gun itself was mounted on the right of the hull gunner's escape hatch.

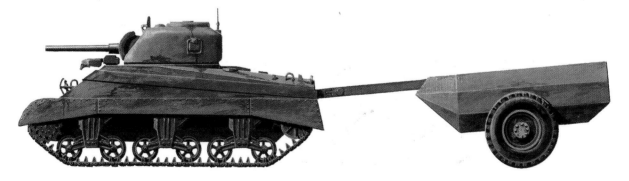

THE FINAL BATTLES FOR GERMANY: SEPTEMBER 1944 – MAY 1945

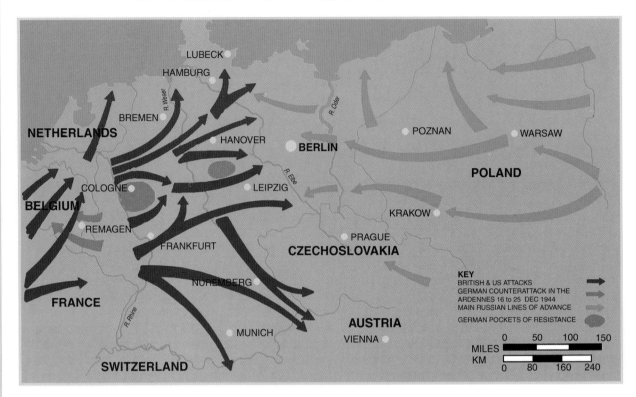

When the Ardennes offensive was called off on New Year's Day 1945 the Germans began transferring divisions to the Eastern Front. The Russians stormed the whole front on 12th January 1945.

Germany's arms production had fallen drastically and its transport system was under constant air attack. Troop movements became desperate and deadly slow. Guderian's SS Panzer Corps were diverted to Hungary instead of protecting Berlin as Guderian had planned. Armoured troops went from one crisis to another, always outnumbered and deprived of supplies and spares with their tanks falling to pieces. Many tanks had to be abandoned. However, they kept their pride and combat skills as they had done over six years of fighting. Although many were technically inferior to their opponents, the Allies poured thousands of tanks against the German defences. Among these the American M26 Pershing and the Russian JS2s could hold their own

and the crews of the latest M4A3 Easy-eight Shermans and the British upgraded Comets gained confidence with the improved protection of the reduction in fire hazards.

Overwhelming odds

Just 700 German tanks faced up to 4,000 Russian AFVs on 12 January 1945 and were in retreat until the Russians ran out of supplies, then the disparity in numbers was compensated by this logistical breakdown. Local tank-versus-tank battles were usually fought in the German favour with chaotic supply routes finally causing a break in the Russian advance. The Russian supply system would have been further impaired had it not been for the Americans providing them with 400,000 wheeled load carriers to fill the gap caused by the Russians' lack of manufacturing capacity. Russian Forces reached the River Oder in mid-January 1945.

On 22 March the last considerable German tank force, composed of 27 Panthers

The T34-85 was the standard medium tank of the Soviet Army at the end of World War II. After a successful war career the T34-85 continued in production initially in the Soviet Union, and then with its two Warsaw Pact allies Czechoslovakia and Poland. It saw combat in Korea, Israel, in the 1982 Lebanon War, and the various conflicts in Yugoslavia and against South Africa when that country entered Angola.

and 28 Tiger tanks, barred the way to Berlin against massed Russian infantry and tank assaults, shooting with excellent results from prepared positions. The Russian tank attack withered leaving their infantry to go to ground.

Soviet advances

Tank attacks resumed when a Russian flanking column, supported by artillery, seized a village sheltering the German Command Post and reserve Tiger unit. The Germans retreated in confusion under a smoke screen to reassemble in time to face the Russians, silhouetted by the smoke screen, emerging from the village. A mere handful of German AFVs were lost but the 'field was strewn with up to 60 burning and disabled T-34s when the Russians were massacred. However, despite local reversals like these, the Russian T-34s and IS-2s,

with excellent infantry support, went on to conquer Berlin and on to the River Elbe and towards northern Germany.

Last ditch battles

In the West even fewer German tanks stood guard and, as the Allies rebounded from the setback of the Ardennes 'Battle of the Bulge', they began remorselessly grinding down German resistance, crossing the Rhine at Remagen on 7 March 1945, by way of a captured bridge. On a broader front, started on 22 March 1945 the Allies began their final advance eastwards. In Italy a single under strength panzer corps, numbering a fifth of their enemy, had held back the Allies for almost two years, but was finally overwhelmed by superior Allied forces who swept on into Austria until the day of the German surrender in April 1945.

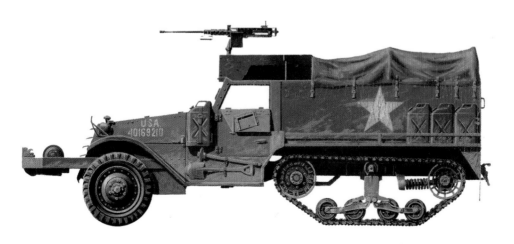

A virtual trademark of the US Army, the Half-Track Personnel Carrier M3, was also used throughout World War II by other Allied forces, including the Red Army. It could carry up to 13 crew.

Armed with the same calibre gun as the Jagdpanzer IV, the Marder II was used in large numbers on all fighting fronts, but because of its height, lacked the low-profile protection of the former tank.

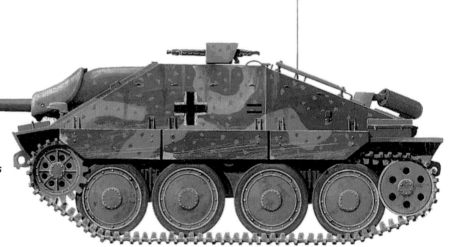

Using the chassis of the PzKpfw 38(t) the Germans produced a light Panzerjäger along Sturmgeschütz lines.

This resulted in the Jagdpanzer 38(t) für 7.5cm Pak 39, or Hetzer (baiter, as in bull-baiting), becoming one of the best of all German Panzerjäger tank-busters of World War II.

The Type 4 HO-RO combined the Type 97 medium tank with the Type 38 150mm (5.9in) howitzer which was mounted where the turret of this Japanese tank would normally have been.

The official name of the SdKfz 164 was Nashorn
(rhinoceros), but the name most usually used was
Hornisse (hornet). It was the first Panzerjäger to
mount the 8.8cm Pak 43/1. It used the same
chassis as the Hummel.

The Hummel
('Bumblebee') was a
purpose-built
German vehicle that
used components
from the PzKpfw III
and IV. It was a very
successful weapon
and was used on all
fronts. This self-
propelled howitzer
remained in
production until the
end of the war.

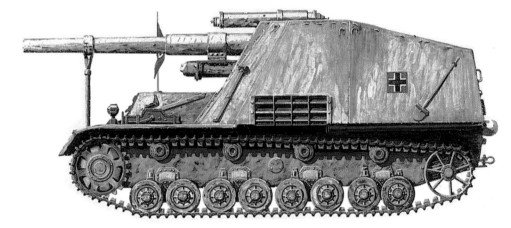

The German StuG III was armed with a long 75mm gun and was a close fire-support
version of the PzKpfw III tank. It was produced in considerable numbers, sometimes
taking the place of battle tanks in Panzer formations.

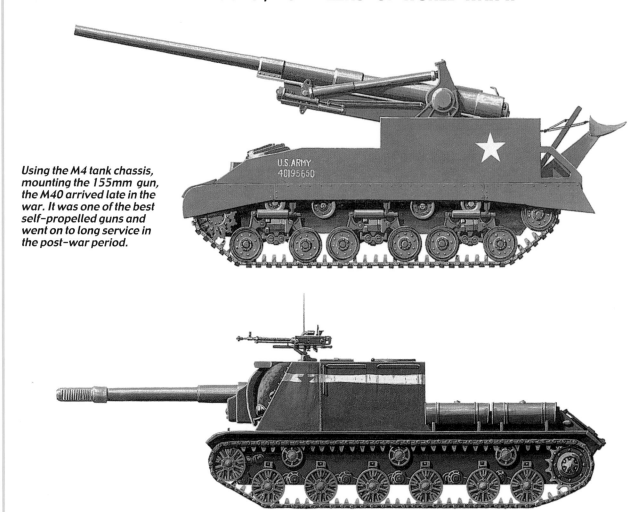

Using the M4 tank chassis, mounting the 155mm gun, the M40 arrived late in the war. It was one of the best self-propelled guns and went on to long service in the post-war period.

A conversion of the IS-2 tank the Soviet ISU-152 carried a powerful 152mm howitzer, designated M1937, which was housed in a large, heavy, mantlet on the front of the thick superstructure. It proved to be of great value to the Red Army in direct support of their tank and motorised infantry divisions.

After seeing the 'pulpit' that housed the 12.7mm machine-gun, British soldiers called the US M7 the 'Priest'. The ammunition for the 105mm howitzer was not a standard British Army type which caused severe problems with logistics.

Mounting a 25-pdr gun on a Valentine tank chassis, the Bishop was an early attempt by the British to produce a self-propelled gun. It was not a success and was rapidly replaced by the Priest.

The Sexton was based on the Ram tank, this vehicle was produced by the Canadians and carried the British 25-pdr gun. It was reliable and well-liked. It served for many years after the war.

A conversion of the T-70 light tank, the Soviet self-propelled SU-76 carried the 76.2mm gun. It was not popular with its crews who called it the 'Bitch' on account of its poor tarpaulin cover.

CHAPTER FIVE

Global Influences

The aftermath of the Second World War left behind great fleets of tanks, many of which were hopelessly outclassed by the new generation of heavily armoured and armed machines which had appeared towards the end.

As at the conclusion of the First World War, a wholesale programme of scrapping began when armies reverted to peacetime economy. Unlike 1919, however, strenuous research and development into new fighting vehicles was continued by the victors with a view to preventing a lapse into inferiority such as the British and Americans had suffered in the 1930s, and, unlike the aftermath of the First World War, the period of disarmament was of very short duration due to the mutual mistrust between the Western and Eastern blocs which later converted into the Cold War and the first of the series of the limited wars which have continued since.

The Soviet strength, viewed from the West, in terms of fighting vehicles, presented the threat of immense numbers of the proven T-34/85, IS-1 and IS-2 heavy tanks; and, the just revealed menace of the new 46ton JS-3 which had a 122mm gun and 200mm sloped armour.

Weakened though Russia was by an horrendous war it was clear, by 1948, that her recovery might soon be sufficient to enable her to undertake a strong and rapid advance into Western Europe if she chose.

The West had little to meet this challenge, having abruptly disarmed and faced economic crisis; also, Britain and France were distracted by troubles within the boundaries of their Empires. Forced 'to live on the hump' of wartime equipment production, each nation had scrapped the bulk of their obsolete fighting vehicles and now had in the front line the best of the obsolescent ones, with some that were almost obsolete in reserve.

As for the next generation of machines, their production was delayed or minimised until the need arose. Thus the USA made do with M26 General Pershing, with plans laid for an improved version, the 44ton M47 General Patton and the smaller M24 Chaffee.

The British had the Comet, plus a slowly increasing number of the new 42ton Centurion fitted with a 17-pdr gun and 121mm sloped glacis plate, and plans for a new breed of medium AFVs called the FV200 series. In terms of battlefield performance, the West had to face up to the problem of withstanding an enemy with something like a 5:1 adverse ratio, whose mobility, armament and armour were at least comparable to their own.

The M26 Pershing Heavy Tank, later reclassified as medium, entered service with the United States Army in 1945. Its 90mm gun proved good in combat and was the direct precursor of the M47/M48 Patton and the later M60 main battle tanks. They did good work during the Korean War.

Experiments by the Americans in the 1950s to design the 32-ton T95 tank, with a variable suspension, came to nought. Further research and development was focused on improving protection and fire-power. Yet in the existing state of the art protection could be only marginally improved by better sloping, increased thickness and, to help to combat Chemical Energy ammunition, the spacing of armour plates. The penalty, however, was inevitably an increase in weight at a time when a rising trend of thought regarded a reduction in weight to about 32tons rather than an increase to over the 50ton mark. Nevertheless protection went on being increased, raising the weight of the Centurion, for example, to 52tons and the American M48 to 48tons, leading further to the heavy British Conqueror with 200mm armour at 65tons and the US M103 at 55tons with 178mm armour! It was decided, therefore, that only greatly improved fire-power would give the chance of obtaining significant advantage over the enemy, and it was in this field that

least progress had been made with the notable exception of the advances made by the Germans during the war years.

To add to this the well-made traversing and elevation mechanisms, sensible ammunition stowage and accurate guns gave the German crews an edge over their opponents, made keener by well thought out fire control procedures, they were well in advance of Allied gunnery systems.

Not even the Germans had solved the problem of range finding, which became increasingly critical as ranges of engagement extended beyond the previous norm of about 1,200 yards. While the technique of shooting against tanks had, from the first, been based on judging distance to target, then firing a ranging shot and making correction on observation of its fall, this was now becoming impractical. Obviously there were compelling reasons to hit the enemy with your first shot before he could hit you.

The increased size of ammunition calibres severely reduced the amount of

The M41 Walker Bulldog was named in honour of General Walton T. Walker, Ground Forces Commander in Korea, who died in a jeep accident in 1950.
The M41 was of particular interest in that it was not, as was usually the case, designed around the gun with a suitable engine fitted later; but with its starting point the 500hp flat six engine. The designers decided first to specify the amount of traction power they could achieve first before deciding on a suitable gun.

The Light Tank M24 Chaffee came into service in late 1944 and served well until the end of World War II, but its real impact came afterwards during the Korean War and other conflicts. Post-war it formed the basis for a new family of armoured vehicles.

The M103 was designed to provide long-range support for the 90mm armed M48 tanks and to counter the Soviet IS-3 tanks which were armed with 122mm guns. The M103, like the British Conqueror heavy tank, was difficult to manoeuvre, both being phased out of service in the 1960s.

ammunition carried and observation was often impossible, because the far higher velocity of shot caused it to land at the target whilst still obscured by flash, smoke and the dust of discharge. Improvements to ammunition had been among the subjects seriously tackled during the war. The use of low velocity projectiles with Chemical Energy (CE) warheads was one line of approach, but naturally this made range-finding all the more critical. Most work was done in high velocity shot because its flight path almost coincided at the shorter ranges with line of sight through a gunner's telescope, thus minimising the range finding difficulty, while solid shot was less easily defeated by spaced armour than CE warheads. By the

time the war was over the shot itself had been improved in material, density and shape which reduced the chances of it breaking up against armour, while its velocity had been increased from the 2,600fps of 1939 to something in the region of 4,000fps. The British Armour Piercing Discarding Sabot (APDS) round, which enabled a relatively greater charge to be applied to the base of a smaller and lighter shot, thus giving it higher speed, was very successful and remains in service. Simply, the shot was cased in a jacket (or sabot) of some light material, which fell off after the projectile had left the barrel.

The Americans, for their part, tried to develop a smooth-barrelled gun firing fin-

The M47 was one of the earlier members of the armoured vehicle family that stretched from the M26 Pershing tank through to the M60 series. It saw action in Korea before being replaced by the much improved M48 Patton.

stabilised ammunition, but this attempt, along with their variable suspension, failed for the time being and left them dependent, for some time, on other nations for the supply of high velocity main armament.

Larger guns

Main armament, as would be expected, did not often decrease below 75mm calibre because, to obtain sufficient kinetic energy to penetrate existing armour thickness, larger calibres with higher velocities were needed, while lower velocity CE rounds were also in need of larger diameters in order to burst through thicker armour.

The Russians and Warsaw Pact powers adopted guns either of 100mm, 115mm or 122mm, and the Americans and British (and thus the NATO powers) settled initially for 76mm, 90mm and 120mm. The British, in the meantime, had designed a very good new 83.4mm gun (20-pdr) and then developed it into the gun which, in the 1980s, was to be found on nearly every NATO tank and those of other nations too. This 105mm gun can fire almost any kind of ammunition invented – be it shot, CE, smoke or canister (spread). The fitting of larger guns did not, of course, go unchallenged by soldiers and vehicle designers, several of whom would have been only too pleased to make the fighting machines smaller in the interest of mobility, ease of concealment and with reduced costs. There were many attempts to produce smaller weapons with the same penetrative and destructive powers as the existing ones, but, almost inevitably,

Continued on page 96

The Centurion tank arrived just too late to take part in any major operation in World War II, but there can be few tank marques that can boast that it is still in service 50 years after its introduction. It saw combat in Korea in 1950 and in the Suez crisis in 1956 and still serves, in Israel and other nations, to this day.

THE TANK AT WAR IN KOREA: 1950-1953

On 25 June 1950 the North Korean Army, supported by Russia and China, crossed the 38th parallel in a lightning, surprise, pre-dawn attack. It was the Russian T-34s which spearheaded the invasion, initially sweeping all before them. It remained axiomatic that an Army, such as that of South Korea, which was deficient in adequate tank and anti-tank forces would be swept aside by an Army whose armoured forces did not much exceed 240 tanks, those being T34/76s and T34/85s. It was equally true, too, that, even in this kind of limited war, ultimate success depended upon the maintenance of that small superiority in tank numbers along with its momentum. But thereafter, as the opposition increased, and the length their lines of communication extended, the North Koreans began to wilt, until, with the goal of Pusan almost in sight, they were brought to a final halt and then thrown back by the combined forces of the United Nations, the first time that the United Nations had gone to war.

The United Nations steps in

As it was, the North Koreans had it all their own way only until they began to meet the US, British and Australian tank forces. The US contingent had M24 Chaffee light tanks, armed with a 75mm gun, the M4 Sherman and M26 Pershings of the US 1st Cavalry and US 6th Medium Tank Battalion and anti-tank weapons, followed soon afterwards by the Centurions of 8th, The King's Royal Irish Hussars and C Squadron, 7th Royal Tank Regiment of the UK, (armed also with the antiquated but fearsome World War II Churchill 'Crocodile' flamethrowers) and Lord Strathcona's Horse (Royal Canadians).

New tanks in Korea

It was in Korea, in 1950, that the first of the post-war American and British tanks entered the battlefield, these replaced the light 18 ton Chaffees and the heavier Shermans and Pershings which until then had held the ring against the Chinese and North Korean T-34/85s. From the USA came the 44ton M47 Patton with a 90mm gun, armour of 110mm and a speed of 30mph, and from Britain came the latest Mark III Centurion of 49tons, with an 83.4mm gun, 152mm armour and a speed of 21mph. Engine power was now considerably in excess of that with which tanks had begun the war in 1939, when anything in excess of 300hp was unusual.

One of the M24 Chaffee light tanks that confronted the T-34s of the North Korean Army in the early part of the Korean War. These were later replaced by the M47 Patton of the US Army and the British Mark III Centurions.

US Marines re-load an M26 General Pershing in the bleak surroundings of the Korean countryside during the Korean War 1950–1953.

Upgraded technology pays off

Now the M47 Patton power plant was 810hp and the Centurion's 650hp. But it was in gunpower that the new machines, particularly the Centurion, excelled. The M47 Patton used an optical range finder and the Centurion incorporated the first really effective stabiliser which enabled the gunner to maintain elevation and azimuth while the tanks were on the move, thus improving accuracy of shooting during cross-country movement. In fact, by the time these tanks put in an appearance, the North Korean tank threat had been destroyed and the Korean war was on the verge of settling into a trench-style stalemate among steep hills and paddy fields along the Kansas Line close to the 38th Parallel. The tanks were lodged in fortified front line bunkers, employed merely as direct-fire weapons in support of the infantry, without moving more than a few yards in and out of their emplacements every day and night. Armistice was signed on 27 July 1953.

A Centurion of 1st Royal Tank Regiment dug in on the 'Hook' defensive position in Korea, in support of the 1st Commonwealth Division and the 2nd Battalion US Marines. It was commanded by the then Lieutenant George Forty who, later, as a Lieutenant Colonel, was responsible for the improvements to the Tank Museum in Bovington, Dorset, England.

Light Tank M24 Chaffee

Cutaway drawing key

1 M6 75mm gun
2 M64 combination gun mount
3 0.30mm M1919 A4 co-axial machine-gun
4 M71K telescope
5 0.30mm M1919 bow machine-gun
6 0.50mm HB Browning MG M2 (anti-aircraft)
7 Commander's cupola
8 Direct vision blocks
9 Commander's periscope
10 Stowage box
11 Pistol port
12 Radio set, SCR 508
13 M3 grenade launcher
14 Co-driver's door
15 Hull ventilator
16 Portable fire extinguisher
17 Controlled differential
18 Driver's hand levers (Steering brake)
19 Range selector/transmission lever
20 Hand lever transfer unit/shift control
21 Driver's seat
22 Turret control box
23 Turret driving mechanism
24 Stabilizer and turret motor
25 Ammunition storage boxes
26 Fixed fire extinguisher
27 Radiator air inlet grille
28 Two Cadillac 90 V-type 8-cylinder Model 44 T 24 engines

29 Fuel tank covers
30 Fuel compartment vents
31 Final drive sprockets
32 Shock absorber
33 Support arm
34 Track wheel
35 Torsion bar
36 Bumper spring arm bracket
37 Track support roller
38 Compensating wheel and track wheel support linkage
39 Track compensating wheel
40 Compensating wheel link
41 Track wheel link

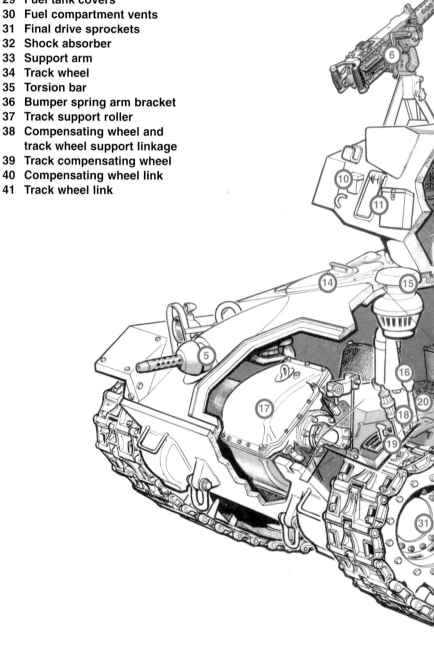

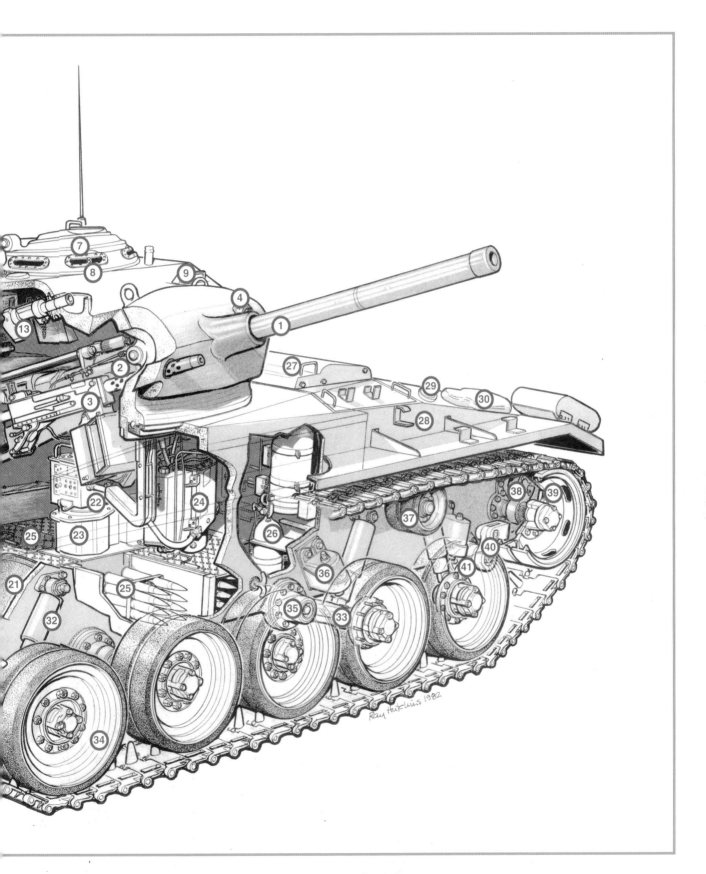

The M48 series covered many variants with the first production models, as shown here, being completed in 1952. Production continued until 1959 with a total of 11,703 units. Further development of this tank resulted in the M60 MBT.

they ended with the high velocity gun still standing top of the choices. However, they were nudged by a newcomer – the rocket propelled anti-tank guided missile (ATGW).

Guided weapons

The ATGW was a product of German inventiveness that had not got beyond the experimental stage in 1945. Their X7 was a rocket steered by signals along a wire, paid out behind, under the guidance of an operator who steered the missile to its target. Developed further by the French, with their SS 10, and closely followed by

the British in the mid-1950s with the infra-red guided Orange William, Malkara and Vigilant. The main attractions of the ATGW were its ability to fly to targets at long range without range-finding and to be fired from the ground or from small vehicles. Armed, as they had to be at their relatively low velocity with CE warheads, they suffered from the inveterate weaknesses of that method of attack. Furthermore they were expensive and demanded a high standard of operator training. The operator's performance was critical since, unlike that of a gunner who could aim, fire and forget his projectile,

The Israeli Sherman M51 'Isherman' was a conversion of the M4A1 stripped back to the hull and fitted with: a Cummins 460hp diesel engine, Easy 8 HVSS suspension, modified steering, transmission, exhaust and wider tracks. A new 105mm D1504 tank gun was fitted which had a 44 calibre and used Israeli manufactured ammunition.

The Soviet T-10 Heavy Tank had the 12.7mm DShKM anti-aircraft machine-gun on the commander's cupola. Its main armament was a 122mm gun with a co-axial KPV series 14.5mm (0.57in) machine-gun.

the ATGW operator might have to spend more than a minute acquiring his target and guiding the missile to it, a performance which put strong demands upon patience, courage and steadiness whilst under fire. Nevertheless, ATGW posed a potent threat to fighting vehicles and, at the same time, offered a way of reducing vehicle size through elimination of the high velocity gun.

Although tanks lay at the core of most armies, a host of reconnaissance, artillery, engineer and infantry fighting vehicles were to be found in close attendance. Gradually the most modern armies were creating all-armoured armies - the principal initial reason for this being the need to give maximum mobility and protection against atomic effects as the threat of the use of nuclear weapons on the battlefield became reality.

Ironically, none among the Russians, the Americans, the French nor the British were often called upon to use their most powerful fighting vehicles in the kind of large scale wars for which they were designed. When they did use them, it was usually in minor confrontations, or in small numbers. Generally any massive encounters involving fighting vehicles were between smaller nations, equipped with the products from the manufacturing nations.

In 1956 the Egyptian President, Colonel Nasser, seized the Suez Canal. The British and French, concerned that the canal would be closed to them, took military action. The Egyptians deployed Russian tanks and 100mm self-propelled guns, without much effect, against the British and French forces. However, under strong pressure from the UN and the US all military operations in the Canal Zone came to a halt. Photograph left shows Centurions disembarking during the Suez crisis.

T–55 MBTs of the East German Army, formerly the German Democratic Republic, in barracks in Berlin; seen during the 'Cold War' before the fall of Communism.

The T–62 entered service with the Red Army in 1963. It went on to replace the T–54 in most front-line units. It differs from the T–54 in having a longer, wider hull, an up-graded turret and armament, and can easily be distinguished from the T–54 by having more evenly spaced wheels and bore evacuator fitted to its 115 mm U–5TS gun. It was used extensively by Arab forces in the Middle East.

Ammunition Improvements

The increased size of ammunition calibres severely reduced the amount of ammunition carried and observation was often impossible, because the far higher velocity of shot caused it to land at the target whilst still obscured by flash, smoke and the dust of discharge. Improvements to ammunition had been among the subjects seriously tackled during the war. The use of low velocity projectiles with Chemical Energy (CE) warheads was one line of approach, but naturally this made range-finding all the more critical. Most work was done in high velocity shot because its flight path almost coincided at the shorter ranges with line of sight through a gunner's telescope, thus minimising the range finding difficulty, while solid shot was less easily defeated by spaced armour than CE warheads. By the time the war was over the shot itself had been improved in material, density and shape which reduced the chances of it breaking up against armour, while its velocity had been increased from the 2,600fps of 1939 to something in the region of 4,000fps. The British Armour Piercing Discarding Sabot (APDS) round, which enabled a relatively greater charge to be applied to the base of a smaller and lighter shot, thus giving it higher speed, was very successful and remains in service. Simply, the shot was cased in a

POST-WAR INFANTRY GUIDED ANTI-TANK WEAPONS

The Israeli B–300 light anti–armour weapon is a man portable, shoulder–fired, semi–disposable, system and is carried, loaded and fired by one man. It has an effective range of 400 metres. It has a calibre of 82mm. The launcher and three rounds weigh 19 kg.

The AT–3 'Sagger', probably the best–known of the Soviet anti–tank guided weapons (ATGW), gained notoriety during the 1973 Yom Kippur war when the Egyptians fired several thousands against the Israeli armour; but with moderate success when compared to other anti–tank systems. It was known to the Soviets as the PTUR–64 'Malatyuka'.

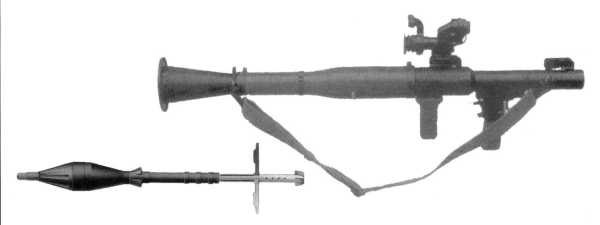

The Soviet RPG-7 anti-tank launcher first appeared in 1962, replacing the RPG-2 which had its origin in the wartime German 'Panzerfaust'. The Soviets improved on the German design by adding a rocket to the actual projectile. This increased the range and also shortened the flight time, so making it easier to hit moving targets. It has been used extensively in Iraq, Afghanistan and other former Warsaw Pact countries.

jacket (or sabot) of some light material, which fell off after the projectile had left the barrel. The Americans, for their part, tried to develop a smooth-barrelled gun firing fin-stabilised ammunition, but this attempt, along with their variable suspension, failed for the time being and left them dependent, for some time, on other nations for the supply of high velocity main armament.

The Levant Wars

It would be for the Israeli and Arab armies to practise tank warfare in the old established mode, while employing the latest fighting vehicles and weapons. The four short principal wars of 1948, 1956, 1967 and 1973, strung together by numerous frontier skirmishes, were mostly fought in wide open terrain, and, although similar in pattern to the campaigns of the

past, would demonstrate the power, defects and limitations of the latest weapon systems. The process was evolutionary, governed by the pace at which more sophisticated equipment was acquired, variations in implementation of tactics and the prowess of commanders at all levels. In 1948, equipment was sparse and pretty basic. The battles were geared to infantry style and pace, under men who treated tanks as ancillary weapons in a way that could be equated with the tank battles of 1918. The campaign of 1956 marked an equivalent turning point to 1940. The Israeli attack on the Egyptians, quite strongly backed by fighting vehicles of most kinds was, nevertheless, mainly conducted the infantry way, with a tendency to shy at any attempt at long-range

strategic tank strikes in the Guderian manner. It was due to the insubordination of tank leaders at the front that the somewhat ponderous initial Israeli attack across the frontier was converted into an all-out lunge which penetrated Egyptian defences, isolated their forward positions and drove full tilt to the banks of the Suez Canal, in a matter of hours, to rout the entire opposing force in the Sinai.

Convinced by now of the tank's dominance of desert warfare, the Israelis concentrated their future rearmament of land forces on the acquisition of main battle tanks, to the detriment of their artillery and infantry. Purchasing US M47s and, above all, British Centurion tanks, armed with the excellent 105mm gun, the Israelis put all their trust in concentrated

In 1963 Israeli Ordnance Corps upgraded the Centurion Mks 3 & 5 by replacing the gun with the 105mm M68/L7 series rifled gun; this fired HEAT, APFSDS–T, HESH and canister rounds and could easily penetrate T–54/55/62 MBT frontal armour at 1800metre range. The first Upgrade Centurions, known by the Israeli name Sho't (Whip) entered service in 1970 and were characterised by their elevated engine deck and external box air filters.

TANK ENGAGEMENTS DURING THE 1967 SIX-DAY WAR

The first major engagement between modern Soviet-built tanks and their US and British rivals began in May 1967 when the Egyptian Army started pouring troops into Sinai. Syria and Jordan were also preparing for hostilities. Egypt had 1,000 tanks including IS-3s, T-54s and T-55s and Centurions while Jordan had about 50 Centurions and 150 lightly-armed Charioteers. Syria's 400 tanks included 150 T-54s. Israeli could field 1,000 tanks, a third Centurions, a third M48s and the remainder a mix of AMX-13s and Shermans. Numbers were in the Arabs' favour but the quality of the Israeli AFVs corrected the disparity.

The Arab build-up was a threat to Israeli survival and so with a surprise pre-emptive strike they eliminated their Arab opponents' air forces on the first day. Then, the Israelis struck hard at the Egyptian defensive positions along the Gaza strip to Kusseima.

The Israeli forces, under the command of General Israel Tal, Major-General Ari Sharon and General Avraham Yoffe intended to stand on the defensive against Jordan and Syria while, on the 5 June, they delivered a knock-out blow against the Egyptians in a three-pronged thrust. On the left, Sharon's division aimed at Kusseima and Abu Ageila; in the centre Yoffe's division made for Kahfan where it could join either Sharon's division on the left or Tal's division on the right as he advanced along the coast road to El Arish. Tal's first objective, the town of Rafah was captured on the first morning after a ferocious tank battle, which also involved infantry and other armoured units. He then struck towards El Arish, bursting through the strongly fortified El Jiradi position by surprise, and bypassed the temporarily demoralised Egyptian 7th Division. However, the Egyptians quickly rallied and reoccupied the concrete emplacements of the Jiradi Pass with infantry, artillery and those IS-3 tanks the Israelis had not destroyed. Thus the road to El Arish was

blocked and the Israeli tanks, already short of fuel and supplies, were under threat. Tal had planned a two-divisional pronged attack to capture El Jiradi but only one, the 7th, was available, but reduced in strength. Tal was ready to move when he was warned that the Egyptians waited in ambush and he was asked to wait until he was able to launch his original two-division attack. However, with knowledge of the desperate situation of the Israeli armour cut off in El Arish, Tal ordered his single battalion of M48s to attack at once, knowing that this meant a virtually unsupported effort except for the sub-units thrown in piecemeal as they arrived from Rafah.

The Egyptians were totally surprised and events moved so fast and disastrously for them that they were unable to use their battle groups to save their frontier forces. On 6 June and the days following they were either caught on the move or attempting a counterattack and were relentlessly harried as they tried to escape. Across the entire battle front the divisions of Tal, Yoffe and Sharon hunted down the Egyptian tanks. At Bir Lahfan Tal's tanks, heavily supported by artillery, made a brilliant assault and picked off the Egyptians guns and tanks with deadly shooting, driving the survivors on to a line of Yoffe's tanks to the south. In the north the Jordanian Army was annihilated and the Syrian infantry bolted, their AFVs were deserted, and so were lost the Golan Heights.

The M551 Sheridan Light Tank entered service with the United States Army in 1966. The Sheridan saw service in Europe, South Korea and Vietnam.

tank attacks. In the Six Day War of 1967, the Israelis aimed their blows at the enemy weak spots while their 105mm tank gunners took a heavy toll of the Russian T-54s and T-55s opposed to them. In every way and in every field, the Israelis were superior, both on land and in the air. High velocity guns, virtually alone, accounted easily for the rather defective and distinctly badly crewed enemy tanks. Indeed, from the Arab side, it was only the Centurion tanks, manned by the Jordanian Arab Legion, which put up a good fight and earned high praise from the victorious Israelis. But the lessons drawn by the triumphant Israelis led to an overwhelming assumption of tank superiority to the exclusion of due concern about the latest, developing, anti-tank weapons coming

into service. They overlooked the peril of short range hand-held weapons of the bazooka kind, such as the Russian RPG 71 and positively decried the dangers inherent in ATGW, having seen just a few fail during the Six Day War.

Between 1963 and the next outbreak of major hostilities in 1973, the Arab nations, chiefly Egypt, Syria and Iraq, not only built up their tank forces, with Russian T-54s, T-55s and the latest 37ton T-62s carrying the 115mm gun, but also acquired a great many RPGs and Sagger ATGW to counter the Israeli tank army. For their part the Israelis bought many Centurions and derivations of the US M47, the M48 and M60, arming the latter and some Easy Eight Shermans with 105mm guns. For their infantry they

The M48A2 – (also known as Product Improved M48) had a redesigned engine compartment to incorporate new fuel-injection petrol engine, and increased fuel load, to reduce the battlefield IR signature. The running gear was changed and the 90mm main gun control-systems, together with the tank's fire-control system, (with its gunner's stereoscopic rangefinder sight), were updated.

The M48A5 conversion programme was initially started to bring the M48 series tanks in the US Army up to an equivalent M60A1 standard. The first vehicles chosen were 360 M48A3s as these were deemed the easiest model to convert. A new 105mm M68 rifled gun was installed and ammunition stowage modified to accept 54 105mm rounds; a new top loading M60 style air cleaner was fitted in the hull together with a solid state regulator; the the suspension and tracks were upgraded and the engine and transmission changed.

acquired some American M113 tracked APCs to supplement the old half-track carriers of World War II vintage. But their artillery had largely to make do with older equipment on the grounds that it would be the tanks which contributed the principal fire power role.

Yom Kippur War mistakes

When the battle was joined in 1973 the old folly of omitting to apply the principles of co-operation between all arms stood blatantly revealed. Israeli tanks which charged emplaced Egyptian infantry with their Saggers and RPG 7s were almost annihilated. It was only the failure of the Egyptians, in their turn, to instantly follow up a badly shaken opponent which gave the Israelis the opportunity to recover.

On the other hand, when tank versus tank fighting, on the grand scale, broke out on the Northern Front, masses of Syrian and Iraqi tanks rolled in against a smaller number of well-emplaced Israeli machines, the advantages of tanks in a well-prepared defence was well demonstrated. The Arab fighting vehicles were shot to pieces by the rapid and accurate fire of 105mm guns in the hands of first class Israeli commanders and gunners, and the survivors were overrun by infantry and destroyed within a few hours. It was the same, too, when the

The XM60 105mm gun tank prototypes were an outgrowth of the M48 series, with the M60 production model being equipped with the old hemispherical M48–style turret and a new design of hull chassis. These were quickly followed by the definitive M60A1 model which used a narrower shaped turret with greater ballistic protection and stowage arrangement changes for internal and external equipment.

Egyptians, belatedly, attempted to exploit their initial success. Their tanks, like those of their allies in the north, found themselves pitched into a charge against a hull-down enemy possessing good fire positions, able to manoeuvre against the Egyptian flank and rear. Once more Egypt's tank forces were destroyed in quantity and her army routed.

The Yom Kippur War of 1973 did most certainly mark a turning point in fighting vehicle warfare, coming as it did when many new weapons were first used in reasonably large quantities. Headline news was made for ATGWs, on the presumption, by misinformed military correspondents, that they had doomed the tank to extinction. Cooler judgement later demonstrated that the ATGWs had forfeited some of their effectiveness when measures with artillery, and close co-operation by armour with infantry, were properly applied.

In the excitement of the ATGW's undeniable initial impact the success of the high velocity gun in accounting for the vast majority of tank losses on both sides was rather overlooked.

Night fighting devices

Less well advertised too was the introduction of night fighting instruments, for the first time on a large scale, into a big tank battle. Infra-red and low-light image intensifiers were employed by both sides and led, in the opening stages, to several night actions. For some time the existence of these instruments, to enable crews to move and shoot in darkness, had offered the possibility of combat round the clock, but, in practice, the ability of the human being to sustain that level of activity indefinitely was not feasible. Exhausted crews simply called off the battle when they could no longer, through intense fatigue, think or see clearly.

Night fighting tactics

Infra-red night fighting instruments had been developed during the Second World

YOM KIPPUR 1973: WAR ON TWO FRONTS

The main difference between the Arab attack on Israel on 6th October 1973 and their previous aggressions lay in the combination of surprise with synchronised effort. The Egyptians and the Syrians struck heavy blows together, preventing the Israelis from concentrating fully against one before the other, whilst the Israelis were caught totally unawares enjoying the holiday of the 'Day of Atonement'. In the north, the Syrians, with 1500 tanks, were intent on recapturing the Golan Heights and, in the south, the Egyptians assaulted the Israeli fortifications lining the Suez Canal. Brilliant Israeli counterattacks finally won the day.

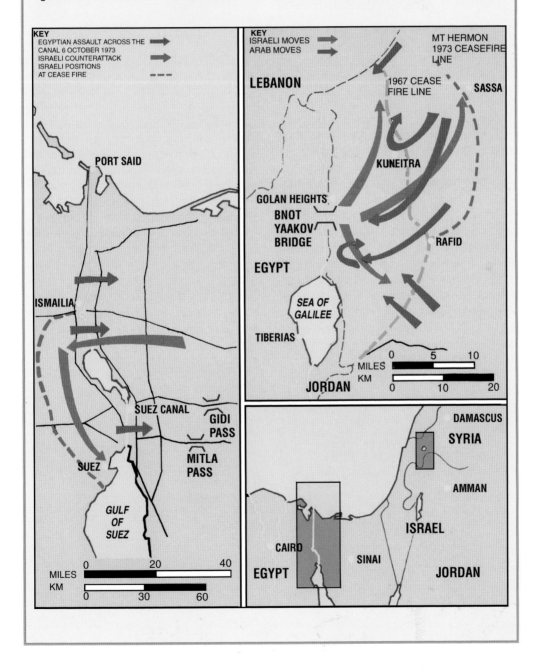

KEY
EGYPTIAN ASSAULT ACROSS THE
CANAL 6 OCTOBER 1973
ISRAELI COUNTERATTACK
ISRAELI POSITIONS
AT CEASE FIRE

PORT SAID

ISMAILIA

SUEZ CANAL

GIDI
PASS

MITLA
PASS

SUEZ

GULF
OF
SUEZ

MILES
KM
0   20   40
0   30   60

KEY
ISRAELI MOVES
ARAB MOVES

MT HERMON
1973 CEASEFIRE
LINE

1967 CEASE
FIRE LINE

SASSA

LEBANON

KUNEITRA

GOLAN HEIGHTS
BNOT
YAAKOV
BRIDGE

RAFID

EGYPT

SEA OF
GALILEE

TIBERIAS

MILES
KM
0   5   10
0   10   20

JORDAN

DAMASCUS

SYRIA

AMMAN

CAIRO

SINAI

ISRAEL

EGYPT

JORDAN

The Vickers Defence Systems' Chieftain MBT was developed from 1958 onwards with the first full production standard vehicles being delivered to the British Army in 1966. The Mk 2 tank shown equipped the 11th Hussars in the British Army of the Rhine (BAOR). Over the years a number of variants have been produced.

War; but it was not until the 1960s that their presence, in large numbers, became noticeable on Soviet tanks. Until then most tanks, with a need to see and shoot in the dark, had depended upon white light searchlights or flares. Tactical night fighting techniques were constantly under consideration as new devices were invented and brought into service. Gradually the 'active' infra-red equipment, which could be detected, were overtaken by the 'passive' low-light image intensification instruments, by the low-light television cameras which could provide a picture of the battlefield to crew commanders, and by 'far IR' heat sensors, none of which could be immediately detected.

The proliferation of instruments and other gadgets on offer to fighting vehicles began to assume alarming proportions. Not only was their cost extremely high, but, unless precautions were taken, a fighting compartment could be cluttered with devices which, individually or collectively, stretched a crew's operating capacity beyond the limit.

A case could always be made out for the advantages of one gadget or another, but in the final analysis a choice had to be

Towards the end of 1989, Egypt signed a technical assistance agreement with Teledyne Continental Motors (TCM) of USA to provide technical support for the design of the RAMSES II MBT. This was the continuation of a contract which had been signed in November 1984 for TCM to upgrade the firepower and mobility of a T-54 MBT.

The Israeli Sherman M51 'Isherman' was a conversion of the M4A1 stripped back to the hull and fitted with: a Cummins 460hp diesel engine, Easy 8 HVSS suspension, modified steering, transmission, exhaust and wider tracks. A new 105mm D1504 tank gun was fitted which had a 44 calibre and used Israeli manufactured ammunition. The M51 saw action in all of the Israeli wars.

made between what was essential and what was only desirable. Range finders were considered essential if the criteria of excellent hit/kill by better guns were to be satisfied. Optical range finders were never entirely satisfactory; the British, most of all, preferred using simple fire and correction techniques as installed on the Centurion and, later, on the new 54ton Chieftain. These used a sub-calibre machine-gun firing tracer ammunition co-axially with its 120mm gun, in order to establish the range.

Laser rangefinders
The adaptation of lasers to range finding in the 1960s offered the chance of much simpler and accurate methods of

The Leopard 1A4 was the final production model of the Leopard 1 series. It is virtually the same as the Leopard 1A3 but with a computerised fire control system coupled to a fully stabilised main armament in place of the gunner's mechanically linked stereoscopic rangefinder sight. A total of 250 were built of which 150 were transferred to Turkey as military aid.

The French AMX-13 Light Tank shown here was fitted with an FL-10 two-man turret armed with a 75mm (2.95 in) gun. Other versions were armed with 90mm (3.54 in) or 105mm (4.13 in) guns. It was a very popular vehicle and saw service throughout the world.

measuring distance to the target, and was soon being incorporated in the sighting systems of most main battle tanks; but, even these can have their drawbacks, sometimes being confused by smoke and dust, and almost invariably introducing an additional complexity for commanders and gunners to cope with.

The arrival of the helicopter

These fighting vehicles did not possess sophisticated anti-aircraft weapons and the armed helicopter had a big role to play in these land battles, but the chances of the helicopter becoming a dominant weapon remained remote at the time.

Furthermore, developments in the field of armoured protection, due to inventions made in the 1960s, now throw doubt upon the viability of the helicopter's main armament the ATGW. The invention in Britain of composite Chobham armour (q.v.) at once reduced the effectiveness of CE warheads with which all ATGW were armed. The resultant increase of this protective factor, commensurate with savings in weight and bulk were, of course, of great assistance to the tank designer, who is always seeking reductions in weight of both guns and missiles. At a stroke, therefore, the family of ATGWs current were made

Production of the GIAT AMX-30 series began in 1966. It is currently the French Army's main MBT and will remain in service until it is fully superseded by the Leclerc. It is in service with many countries throughout the world. AMX-30 is armed with a 105mm gun co-axial with a 20mm cannon.

The Swedish Stridsvagn 103 (S-tank) had problems because it had to rely on its tracks to lay the gun accurately. The driver had also to lay and fire the main armament and the radio operator, seated behind the driver, was responsible for reversing the vehicle if required. The tank was not a success and the Swedish Army is now using upgraded Leopard 2s, designated Stridsvagn 122 MBT.

obsolescent, thus reducing the value of the ATGW helicopters. In addition, fighting vehicle designers were compelled to reconsider fundamentally the shape, size and layout of a new generation of machines to replace those which had been made obsolescent.

Once more the compromises inherent in all design enterprises had to be re-shuffled, but this time the problems led to an examination of radically new shapes – even of new combinations of operational functions – for fighting vehicles.

Long before the last shots had been fired in Vietnam, the first of a new generation of very fast, much more powerful tanks had been built or designed in an effort to improve mobility and speed. The 40ton German Leopard tank of 1961 had a power plant of 830hp and a speed approaching 40mph; the French AMX-30 with a 720hp engine could go as fast, although neither could do this easily across rough ground because of suspension limitations. There

is little use in moving at 40 miles an hour if, at the end of the course the crew lies battered and bleeding from being thrown about the fighting compartment!

The Swedes produced the most radical design of all. This was their turretless S tank of 1961 which remained in service well into the 1990s. Its 105mm gun was fixed within the hull and was aimed at the target by means of elevating and tra-versing the entire vehicle. Suffering from these tactical limitations as it did, its well sloped hull and ingenious suspension offered something for the future.

MBT 70: failed German-US effort

Less well received was an imaginative US/West German effort in the 1960s to produce a fast, well armed and armoured tank for the 1970s, the much publicised MBT 70 (or XM 803). Its suspension was based on that of the failed T95, and its engine was of 1,400hp. It was to carry the 152mm Shillelagh gun/missile launcher which was controlled from the turret. In

The AMX-B2 was announced in June 1979. The French Army ordered 50 of these vehicles with first deliveries made in January 1982 to the 503rd Regiment. This variant is essentially an AMX-30 with an integrated fire-control system based on a laser range-finder and a thermal system. There are many variants to the AMX-30 with this one being armed with the GIAT Industries 105mm smoothbore gun fitted with a magnesium alloy thermal sleeve.

The Leopard 1 MBT was accepted for service with the Federal German Army in 1963 with the first production model being delivered in September 1965. It has an all-welded hull with an all-cast steel turret. It is armed with a 105mm L7A3 rifled gun.

the turret was to be found not only the commander and gunner but also the driver in a contra-rotating sub-turret of his own. Immensely expensive, and held suspect by the Germans, who doubted the effectiveness of the Shillelagh's infra-red link, and preferred a conventional high velocity gun, XM803. The whole project was vetoed on grounds of excessive cost.

Small but efficient

Likewise the US Sheridan light, airborne tank threw up so many mechanical difficulties at first that it lost the confidence of its crews and was often relegated to a minor role, and yet, with the advent of the ATGW, the survival chances of light tanks in combat were enhanced. Small vehicles presented more difficult targets and even the smallest could mount an ATGW to engage, with success, even the biggest opponent at a range out to 4,000 metres if required.

The US Army fielded the M551 Sheridan Light Airborne Tanks as fast armoured reconnaissance with M2 and M3 Bradleys of 1st Armored Division and 1st US Cavalry Division, each vehicle being armed with a 25mm gun and TOW missiles.

Originally fielded in 1967 the T-64 did not reach the Soviet Forces in Eastern Europe in large numbers until 1974. The tank had a number of innovative design features including an autoloader with a 6-8rpm rate of fire. The T-64A shows the fully stabilised 125mm 2A26M2 smoothbore gun that used a rotating carousel magazine at the bottom of the turret basket.

COLD WAR COMBAT ENGINEER VEHICLES

The AMX-30 Combat Engineer Tractor, or Engin Blindé de Génie (EBG), was designed for use in forward areas and is fitted with a front-mounted dozer blade, a hydraulic winch, an auger which can bore 220mm diameter holes to 3m depth and a working arm which is used to lift obstacles out of the way.

The Soviet (IMR) Combat Engineer Vehicle is based on the T-55 chassis with a hydraulically operated crane that has full 360° traverse, a pair of pincer-type grabs which are used to remove obstacles, and, on the hull front, is mounted a hydraulic dozer blade.

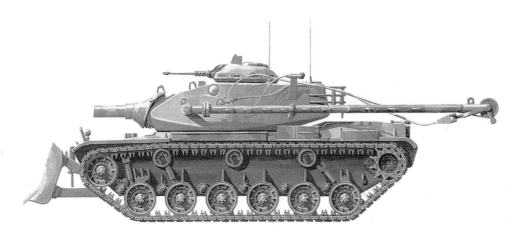

The M728 Combat Engineer Vehicle (CEV) was based on the hull of the M60A1. It was equipped with a bulldozer blade and a large 'A' frame boom. It also mounted a 165mm demolition gun designed to break up concrete obstacles.

CHAPTER SIX

The Fighting Vehicle Comes into its Own

Despite the advancement of main battle tanks during this period there were continuing hot-spots of trouble throughout the world which required lighter vehicles that were more acceptable to the civilian population. Faster and cheaper was the order of the day and many ordinary type motor vehicles were converted to armour to fill the need and light armoured personnel carriers and infantry fighting vehicles were forefront on the drawing boards of the weapons and armoured vehicles designers. The troubles in Northern Ireland began in depth in 1969 and this requirement for lighter vehicles couldn't have been proven better; it was obvious that main battle tanks would have been too intimidating to the local people, too slow, too heavy for local roads, too destructive in their firepower and far, far too expensive to use on a daily basis. To prove the point further, the troubles continue to this day when surveillance, street by street, is still required throughout the province, the excessive cost of heavy tanks for this long period would have been prohibitive. This state of affairs also applies to the Balkans, Afghanistan and many other areas. Only in Israel are main battle tanks to be seen in a security role and television pictures show the results of their use.

Because of this requirement the number and variety of fighting vehicles possessed by the belligerent nations has increased manyfold in response to the demands of nationalism throughout the world and the spread of local insurrections.

Pressure mounted also because of the East/West confrontation known as the Cold War.

Although tanks lay at the core of most armies, a host of reconnaissance, artillery, engineer and infantry fighting vehicles were to be found in close attendance. Gradually the most modern armies were creating all-armoured armies – the principal initial reason for this being the need to give maximum mobility and protection against atomic effects as the threat of the use of nuclear weapons on the battlefield became reality. Though some infantrymen would claim vehemently that underground positions provided the best protection from nuclear attack, they knew too, that the time must come when they would have to move on the surface. For this reason they called for armoured personnel carriers which, ideally, could keep pace with the tanks they supported, and be protected from nuclear attack.

Something better was needed than the half-tracked APCs and the tanks, with their turrets removed, which had sufficed in the Second World War. Overhead armour, some sort of armament and a good cross-

The FV 1609 Humber one-ton armoured personnel carrier, or, 'Pig' as it became known, entered service with the British Army in the early 1950s. It had been withdrawn from service but heightening civil disorder in the province required its return, where it has done sterling work.

country performance were normally called for at first, with the Germans opting to enable their infantrymen to actually fight from the vehicle instead of dismounting. The solutions varied from the inadequate British 6-wheeled 10-ton Saracen, the USA's heavy 19-ton tracked M59, the 15-ton German tracked HS30, armed with a 20mm cannon, to the much more sophisticated, if cramped, 13-ton Soviet tracked BMP of the mid-1960s with its 76mm gun and Sagger ATGW. Although these vehicles were intended to play a subsidiary part in battle, their incorporation of many of the features to be found in a tank could not be ignored.

Their proliferation on the battlefield automatically raised a requirement for some sort of rapid fire anti-armour weapon system, because, it was argued, the expensive ATGW or the big tank gun were inappropriate for use on such relatively insignificant targets. Thus a demand was made for an anti-APC weapon – a gun of between 20mm and 40mm – which could be mounted in armoured cars, as well as on the many different APCs of later design.

Ironically, none among the Russians, the Americans, the French nor the British were often called upon to use their most powerful fighting vehicles in the kind of

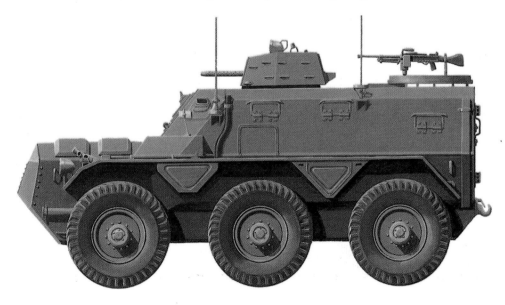

The FV 603 Saracen was first produced in 1952 and was a member of a family of 6x6 vehicles. Its production run lasted for 20 years. It served in Aden, Libya and Malaya. It remained in service with the British Army in Northern Ireland until 1984.

Developed by Daimler Ltd., the Ferret Scout Car (FV 721) was in production for home and export markets until 1971, and was still being used by the British Army until 1983. The version shown is the Mk 2/3 which had a one-man turret armed with a 7.62mm (0.3 in) machine-gun.

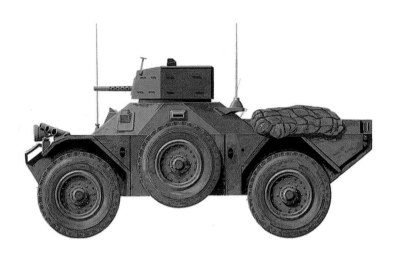

large scale wars for which they were designed. When they did use them, it was usually in minor confrontations, or in small numbers. Generally any massive encounters involving fighting vehicles were between smaller nations, equipped with the products from the manufacturing nations.

Civil actions

The interminable armed insurrections which broke out well before the Second World War ended inevitably involved fighting vehicles, including heavy tanks, since these at that time were regarded as the best way to minimise casualties while

at the same time they could terrorise and quickly suppress poorly armed revolutionaries and lawbreakers. Although the use of minimum force is a keystone of peacekeeping, the use of armoured vehicles, with tanks in particular, the very antithesis of that principal, did not deter the powers employing these in putting down riots and local dissent. For example, the British used tanks in dealing with the civil wars in Greece, India, Palestine, Egypt and to a far lesser extent, due to the difficult terrain, in Malaya. The French used them in Indo-China and in Algeria, and the Russians in East Germany, Hungary and Czechoslovakia and, later, in

The Alvis Saladin (FV 601), shared many common automotive components with the Saracen 6x6 APC. It was armed with a 76mm (3in) gun and served with the British Army in Malaya and Cyprus. Alvis of Coventry built a total of 1177 vehicles for the home and export markets.

The Hornet Malkara tank destroyer shown in the travelling configuration, with the launcher and its two missiles in retracted position at the hull rear. It was replaced by by the Ferret Mk 5 fitted with the Swingfire missile system.

Afghanistan. In immediate impact, the shock effect of tanks was often valuable, but, as time went on, it became noticeable that crowds became accustomed to the weaknesses of these clumsy vehicles in built-up areas. Even during World War II the Russians used 'Molotov Cocktails': home-made incendiary bombs, bottles filled with gasoline or kerosene, lit from a rag fuse, and thrown into the cupolas of unsuspecting German tanks. Moreover, the arrival of tanks, far from suppressing violence, actually acted as a provocation, the appearance of these emotive machines frequently stirring up resentment, which, when transmitted by the news media and used as propaganda, were counter-productive in quelling insurrection.

At first the British, and gradually most other Western nations, drew back from the use of tanks. They decided that, if armoured vehicles were in demand to deal with a particularly dangerous situation, tracked vehicles should be excluded, even tracked APCs, because the Press tended to refer to them as tanks. Wheeled armoured cars were found to be more acceptable, with wheeled scout cars and APCs preferable. By the mid-1970s, in Northern Ireland for example, all tracked armoured vehicles had been withdrawn by the British who preferred to use Saracens, Humber 4-wheelers, Ferret scout cars and, above all, lightly armoured Land Rovers. It appeared that the less sensitive Russians had not learned this lesson.

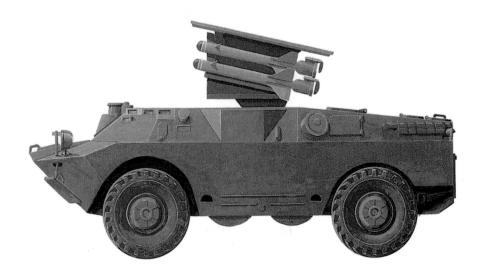

The Soviet BRDM–2 Amphibious Scout Car carried six AT–3 'Sagger' ATGWs which could be launched from, or away from, the vehicle. It was used successfully by the Egyptian Army in the Middle East campaign of 1973.

The M113 formed the base for many variations for military functions such as mortar carriers, field aid stations etc. Model shown is the Armoured Personnel Carrier M113A2 version and was used by the U.S. Army 1st Infantry Division in Vietnam during the mid-1960s.

The Vietnam War

No war in history had been the testing ground for so many new weapon systems as that of Vietnam. When the French were doing their best to defeat the Vietcong in what was then known as Indo China, and approaching their final defeat of 1954 at Dien Bien Phu, armoured vehicles of Second World War vintage were in use and making only a limited contribution to what was, essentially, an infantryman's war. When the Americans entered the Vietnam War they used all types of weaponry to hand – and invented some during the conflict – to make the infantryman's task easier and less costly. Fighting vehicles such as M48A3s and M41A3 Walker Bulldogs were used, but the 15-ton Sheridan airborne tank, with a fairly good cross-country performance

and amphibious capability, gave protection and fire-power, in paddy and jungle throughout the monsoon season, where mobility was at a premium in conditions once deemed impossible for armour. To the fore in practically every operation, however, were infantry M113 APCs, many of them provided with supplementary armament mounted in sub-turrets, several with heavy weapons such as the 106mm recoilless rifle. These also had good cross country performance and could go to places that the tanks could not. Various self-propelled guns and howitzers were used, the M109 SPH was crewed by the U.S. Army 11th Armored Cavalry, The M110 SPH was employed by the U.S. Army 8th Artillery and the U.S. Marine Corps used the M55 SPG and the extraordinary looking M50A1 Ontos anti-tank vehicle.

Similar to the American M113 the FV432 armoured personnel carrier was accepted by the British Army in 1962. It was fitted with a Peak Engineering Ltd., one-man turret armed with a 7.62mm (0.3in) machine-gun and four electrically operated smoke dischargers on either side.

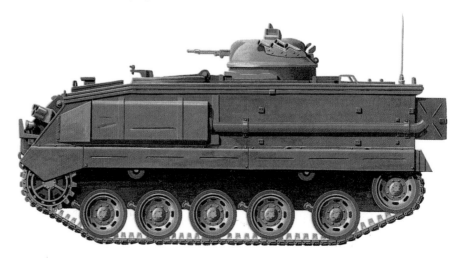

Used only by the Soviet Air Assault Divisions the BMD airborne combat vehicle operated extensively in Afghanistan. It was fitted with an NBC system and was fully amphibious. The BMD could be carried slung under a heavy-lift helicopter or dropped from transport aircraft by parachute.

But for armour to go to many places in Vietnam extensive engineer assistance was needed to clear routes, cross water obstacles and open up country, which, previously, had hardly seen any sort of vehicle, let alone a fighting one. Tanks fitted with rollers for the mine sweeping of roads, and engineer vehicles of all sorts were developed like the M728 Combat Engineer Vehicle (CEV) crewed by troops of the U.S. Army 11th Armored Cavalry Regiment and others (often based on the M113) to help push through undergrowth and thick jungle in the approach to an objective. All these vehicles and many others were used with varying degrees of success, and each at various times was equipped with the latest sensing and viewing devices to make the detection of the enemy easier.

Likewise the US Sheridan light, airborne tank threw up so many mechanical difficulties that it lost the confidence of its crews and was often relegated to a minor role, and yet, with the advent of the ATGW, the survival chances of light tanks in combat were enhanced. Small vehicles presented more difficult targets and even the smallest could mount an ATGW to engage, with success, even the biggest opponent at a range out to 4,000 metres if required. It was with this in mind that the British produced a new family of light reconnaissance AFVs in the 1960s, capable of being air-lifted in the C-130 Hercules aircraft, and could be armed with: a 76mm gun, a 30mm HV automatic cannon, or a Swingfire ATGW. Though this Armoured Vehicle Reconnaissance family was lightly armoured, its progeny were fast, at 50mph, and with a power to

The German Marder 1 Infantry Fighting Vehicle is a formidable vehicle almost resembling a tank but armed with an externally mounted 20mm cannon, and a coaxial 7.62mm MG over a two-man turret; the hull superstructure armour is well sloped to add protection. The Marder 1 IFV is based on a special tracked chassis originally developed in the early 1960s to create a common platform for a whole host of armoured vehicles of which an IFV was only one component.

Based on the chassis of the Mercedes-Benz Unimog 4x4 truck, the Thyssen Maschinenbau UR-416 APC is used in many roles such as airport patrol and riot control. It has exceptional cross-country mobility and is easy to operate.

weight ratio of 25hp/ton and a track-to-ground pressure of 5.2lb/in, they could cross almost the softest bog or paddy.

Scorpion variants

In January 1972 this new range of light armoured vehicles came in to service with the British Army. This was the Alvis Scorpion CVR(T) and its variants which included: Scorpion (FV101), armed with a 76mm L23 gun; Scorpion 90 mounting a Cockerill MkIII 90mm gun; Striker ATGWV (FV102); Spartan APC (FV103); Samaritan Armoured Ambulance (FV104); Sultan Armoured Command Vehicle (FV105); Samson ARV (FV106), Samson ARV (FV106) and Scimitar Reconnais-

sance Vehicle (FV107). The Scorpion was also delivered to the Belgian army early in 1973 and in 1979 the Royal Air Force Regiment ordered 150 members of the Scorpion family (including Spartan, Scorpion, Sultan and Samson) for the defence of Royal Air Force airfields in Germany.

The hull of the Scorpion was made of all-welded aluminium armour and provided the crew with protection from frontal attack by 14.5mm projectiles. The remainder of the hull was protected against 7.62mm armour-piercing rounds. The aluminium armour was particularly effective against shell splinters.

During the Falklands campaign in

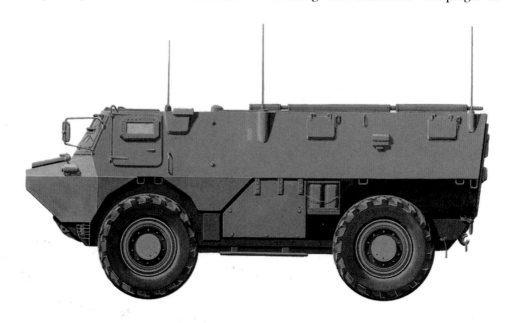

The Renault VAB (Véhicle de l'Avant Blindé) APC was exported to several African and Middle East countries; amongst these over 400 were sold to Morocco where they were in action, in the Sahara, against the Polisario guerrillas. The model shown is not fitted with water jets under the rear of the hull, nor with a roof-mounted weapon station.

British troops rest during the Falklands War when Argentina invaded the islands in 1982. The vehicle shown is one of the two Scorpions which saw action in the Battle for Goose Green in the eastern Falklands supporting the 2nd Battalion, of the British Parachute Regiment.

1982 the British Army deployed two Scorpions, a Samson armoured recovery vehicle and four Scimitars. The ground forces were heavily dependent on helicopters and tracked vehicles for mobility. The tracked reconnaissance vehicles, Scorpion and Scimitar, performed well in boggy conditions, covering an average of 350 miles each. One vehicle withstood a shell which landed 1.5 metres away; another ran over a mine which severely damaged the vehicle but left the crew unharmed.'

Scorpions were also used by the forces of Ireland, New Zealand, Honduras, Oman,

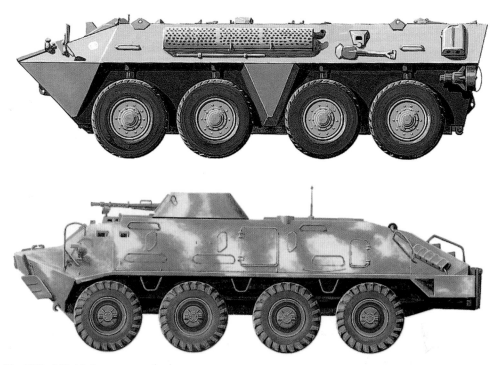

The Saudi Arabian Al Fahd AF-40-8-1 (8x8) Armoured Personnel Carrier is shown here without armament; other versions carry 106mm recoilless rifles and TOW missile launchers. A wide range of variants has been produced.

The BTR-60P APC was widely used when the former Soviet Union invaded Afghanistan in 1979. Afghan Mujahadeen guerrillas would ambush Soviet APCs and other vehicles from above in the mountainous passes, so the enclosed personnel compartment seemed an advantage; however, the occupants were often knocked out by machine-gun fire or RPG-7 ATGWs. BTR-60s were encountered, and quickly destroyed, by United States forces in Grenada in 1983.

VARIANTS OF THE SCORPION AND SCIMITAR SERIES

Combat Vehicle Reconnaissance (Tracked) Scorpion (FV101) was first delivered to the British Army in early 1972. British Army Scorpions had an NBC System at the rear of the hull with optional kit which included NBC detector kit, vehicle navigation system and a Normalair-Garrett air-conditioning system. The latter were fitted as standard in vehicles supplied to the United Arab Emirates. If the NBC System was not fitted there was room for a further five rounds of 76mm ammunition.

Scorpion 90 was fitted with a 90mm Cockerill Mk III gun. This vehicle carried 35 rounds of ammunition which could deal with all types of target and inflict severe damage to MBTs.

Sultan Armoured Command Vehicle (FV 105) were first delivered to the British Army in 1977 as a replacement for the Saracen command vehicle. It had a crew of five or six: commander/radio operator, radio operator, driver plus two or three additional crew members.

Samson Armoured Recovery Vehicle (FV 106) entered service with the British Army in 1978. A heavy-duty winch was fitted inside the hull and was driven from the main engine. It had a maximum pull of 12,000kg.

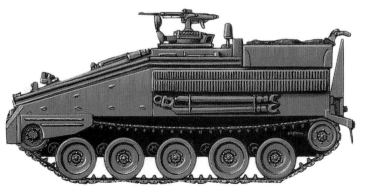

Striker Missile Launch Vehicle (FV 102) carried 10 Swingfire anti-tank missiles. It entered service with the British Army in 1978 and by 1986 was allocated at least one per troop of each reconnaissance regiment allotted to 1 (BR) Corps in Germany.

Spartan Armoured Personnel Carrier (FV 103) entered service with the British Army in Germany in 1978 and was used for a variety of roles such as missile resupply to Striker, carrying Royal Engineer assault teams and Royal Artillery Blowpipe SAM teams.

Samaritan Armoured Ambulance (FV 104) had the same hull as the Sultan command vehicle. It was unarmed and carried four stretcher cases or five sitting cases, large doors at the rear of the hull gave easy access. Medical supplies could be carried on the top of the hull and at the rear of the vehicle.

Scimitar Reconnaissance Vehicle (FV 107) had the same hull as the Scorpion but was armed with a 30mm Rarden cannon instead of the 76mm gun. First deliveries to the British Army were in 1974 and later each mechanised infantry battalion in BAOR (Germany) had been issued with eight Scimitars for close reconnaissance work.

The Hungarian PSZH-IV Armoured Personnel Carrier is also referred to as the FUG-2. Its main armament is a 14.5mm KPVT MG with a coaxial 7.62mm PKT MG. This vehicle is fully amphibious and propelled through the water by two water-jets at the rear of the hull.

The BMP-1 was first shown publicly in 1967 and created quite a stir in the West by its apparent combination of mobility and gun/missile firepower. Time was to demonstrate that, despite its many innovations, the BMP-1 was not the wonder vehicle it first appeared to be for its low silhouette had to be paid for by a cramped interior for the occupants and the main armament was not as powerful as was at first thought.

Spain and the United Arab Emirates.

Early APCs such as half-tracks carried a variety of weapons, usually machine guns, these measures were primarily defensive. In general the early APCs had to depend on supporting arms such as tanks and artillery to cover their movements. Fire support by APCs for other APCs was very limited. What weapons were carried were usually served by crew or infantry squad members having to expose themselves to incoming fire and artillery bursts through an open hatch or cupola to operate whatever weapon was involved. But once that weapon was protected within a turret the potential of what was to become the IFV was realised.

Protection for the occupants and crew expanded to incorporate collective chemical and nuclear warfare protection systems while more consideration was given to protecting vehicle occupants against land mine detonations. The relatively low cost APC had become the far more costly IFV.

It was not long before the APC became the father to the IFV. By the 1960s a series of projects in which APCs assumed combat turrets with cannon type weapons appeared. The old APC thus became less of a personnel carrier and more of a combat vehicle capable of producing its own fire support on the move and of operating in unison with other similarly armed vehicles to attack or defend objectives. The number of combat roles for the old infantry carriers began to expand. From being a simple 'battlefield taxi' the personnel carrier began to assume patrolling, surveillance and

COLD WAR SELF-PROPELLED HOWITZERS

The M110 self-propelled howitzer is armed with a 203mm (8inch) M2A2 howitzer in an M158 mount. It was introduced in 1962 and was used by the US Marine Corps in Vietnam. It was also in service with the British Army of the Rhine during the early nineteen-eighties. It is operated by a team of 13, five of whom (commander, driver, and three gunners) are carried on the gun, with the rest in the M548 tracked cargo carrier which also carries the ammunition.

The Swedish Bofors Bandkanon 1A 155mm Self-propelled Gun was the first fully automatic self-propelled gun to enter service with any army. However it was also the slowest and heaviest, difficult to conceal and had limited mobility.

The M56 90mm airborne self-propelled anti-tank gun, often called the Scorpion, was developed specifically for the US 82nd and 101st Airborne Divisions. It was completely unprotected for the crew and, when fired, the recoil sent the vehicle back several feet and the dust obscured the target!

The French Mk F3 155mm Self-propelled Gun was a 155mm gun based on the Modéle 50 towed weapon mounted on to the rear end of a shortened AMX-13 chassis. It was replaced in French service in the late 1960s by the 155mm GCT.

reconnaissance roles plus, as it carried a viable weapon, the ability to engage similar enemy vehicles and remove them and their precious cargoes from the battlefield. Protection for the occupants and crew expanded to incorporate collective NBC systems while more consideration was given to protection against land mine detonations.

Proliferation of BMP series

If there was one vehicle that marked the complete transition from APC to IFV it was the Soviet BMP-1. When the BMP-1 appeared, in 1967, other IFVs such as the British MCV-80 (now the Warrior), the German Marder 1 and the American M2/M3 Bradley IFVs, were already in the pipeline but the appearance of the well-armed, well-protected and agile BMP-1 accelerated their development processes.

Combat experience in Afghanistan was to demonstrate that the BMP-1 design had its limitations, especially in the 73mm low velocity gun armament, so it was gradually supplemented by the BMP-2 with its more versatile 30mm cannon. Eventually the

formidable BMP-3 appeared, but today the latest Bradleys, Warriors, and many other Western IFVs are on a technical and firepower parity with the ex-Soviet APC/IFV fleets that once seemed such a formidable challenge.

BMP-1s were exported to many nations and remain in service in large numbers, having seen combat in Afghanistan, the Middle East (including the Iran-Iraq War), Chad and Angola.

IFV tactics

One of the current tactical problems for IFV borne infantry is how to make the best use of all this potential firepower. Operations no longer involve a headlong rush at an objective and the subsequent dismounted foot attacks of the APC era. Instead infantry tactics are now very much a matter of fire fights, mutual inter-IFV fire and manoeuvre support, and inter-vehicle engagements at long ranges. While such tactics are familiar to tank crews, all this is quite novel to the infantry for whom the only solution is a course of thorough retraining and subsequent

Although meant to replace the French Mk F3 SPG the GCT 155 Self-propelled Gun (Grande Cadence de Tir) was first deployed in Saudi Arabia. It was also used by Iraq in the Gulf War.

COLD WAR SELF-PROPELLED GUNS

The first M109 howitzer was issued to the US Army in 1963 . It was used as the basis for several other vehicles, like the longer barrelled improvement M109A1, which entered service in 1973. The short-barrelled version, shown here, mounted the M126 howitzer barrel.

Employed by the Royal Artillery in regiments of the British Army of the Rhine the Abbot 105mm self-propelled gun saw service in West Germany during the Cold War. The 105mm gun was manufactured by the Royal Ordnance Factory in Nottingham, England.

The M1973 152mm self-propelled gun/howitzer was known as the SO-152 Akatsiya (Acacia) by the Soviet Army. This vehicle formed the basis for other chassis designs including the SA-4 'Ganef' launcher and the GMZ minelayer.

experimentation to discover how best to go about their tasks in the future.

Campaigns such as that in the Persian Gulf in 1991, during which IFVs were deployed by the West for the first time on any significant scale, could provide only an inkling of how to proceed. The future for the infantry seemed to indicate more time in gunnery and mission simulators as new skills were assimilated and less time spent in pounding around training areas.

There is no firm line of thought as to which path the next generations of APCs and IFVs might take. There seems to be a general reluctance to follow the usual tank path of 'larger and heavier' for the design limits of AFVs appear to have been reached. Some IFVs, such as the German Marder, already resemble light tanks and certainly weigh as much. To emphasise this point there are already some IFVs being considered as platforms for low recoil 105mm guns originally intended for mounting on tanks. While such upgrades

will remove such heavily-armed vehicles from the IFV category the fact that such an option is available demonstrates how the IFV/APC has grown from a mobile armoured box to a powerful armoured combat vehicle.

No firm preference for tracks over wheels has emerged. Both have established their place on the battlefield. Tracks may provide more mobility but wheels are less complex and expensive and, in general terms, more suited to long range operations.

There seems to be a general acceptance that protection levels will have to increase to counter ever-growing threats that ATGWs and close-in infantry anti-armour weapons can produce but a point will be reached where the weights imposed by thick armoured carapaces will seriously impede performance. However, relatively lightweight non-metallic armours are already in service and further developments in this area are to be expected.

LATE COLD WAR SURFACE-TO-AIR MISSILE SYSTEMS

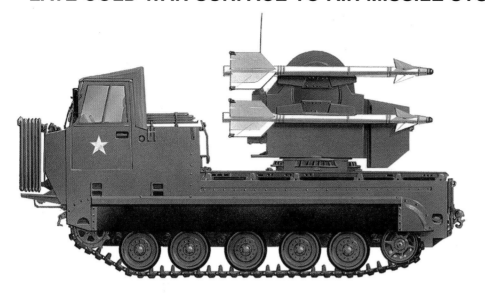

The M48 Chaparral low-level self-propelled SAM system was developed in the early 1960s. It consists of a modified M548 tracked carrier with a missile launch system, originally the MIM-72A, but later replaced by the much improved MIM-72C which was slightly heavier but with a more powerful HE blast fragmentation warhead.

The Rapier surface-to-air missile system was developed by the British Aircraft Corporation (now BAE Systems) to replace the 40mm Bofors guns with a reliable SAM system. First production units were completed in 1971. The tracked Rapier consists of a modified M548 tracked cargo chassis fitted with an eight-missile launcher in ready-to-launch position.

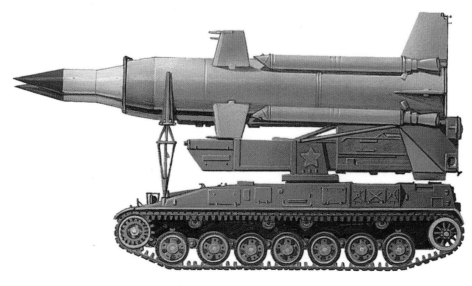

The SA-4 'Ganef' medium to high altitude SAM system was known as 'Krug' by the Soviet Army. This surface-to-air missile system was developed in the late 1950s and was first seen in public during the 1964 parade in Red Square, Moscow. It served with Czechoslovakia, East Germany and Poland during the Cold War.

CHAPTER SEVEN

Modern Russian Tanks and their Derivatives

From the first prototypes of the T-54 in 1945, many of which are still in service (so is the T34-85!) the Soviet/Warsaw Pact countries, now known as The Russian Federation and Associated States, have used successive T-series tanks up to the present advanced T-80 and T-90 series. Since the end of the Russian occupation of Afghanistan few of these vehicles have seen action but defence requirements demand that development must continue. There are so many variants that description becomes complicated, however, the following may describe the most well-known of them but, of course, there are other variants apart from main battle tanks such as: armoured vehicle-launched bridge systems (AVLB); armoured recovery and repair vehicles (ARRV); combat engineer vehicles (CEV) and armoured demining vehicles (ADV). These have not been shown because of lack of space.

Russian T series MBTs
T-80 series and T-90 MBT. These all saw service in many conflicts until the collapse of communism and several continue their fighting role with various armies throughout the world.

Developed in the late sixties the T-72 was the standard tank successor to the T-55 and T-64 series MBTs and by 1981 had largely replaced them on the Soviet tank factory production lines. It offered comparable protection and firepower capabilities to the T-64/80 models but was slower and less agile.

The T-72A/T-72M1 were the result of a mid-seventies redesign of the basic T-72 model. This redesign was based around the availability of a new form of special armour that used ceramic elements in a laminated structure. The former Warsaw Pact allies, Czechoslovakia (now separated as the Czech Republic and the Slovakian Republic) and Poland have produced their own versions of the T-72A.

The T-72B and its variants were the main tank models used in the Soviet Central Group of Forces. The T-72B was essentially a further development of the T-72A model with a number of modifications that include a more powerful engine, improved armour protection and an upgraded fire-control system to fire the AT-11 Sniper semi-laser guided ATGW. Radiation liners are fitted to the turret top, sides and rear.

The T-72S and its variants are the export versions of the T-72B series. The tank is armed with a 125mm 2A46 M smoothbore gun that fires HEAT, APFSDS, HE-Frag ammunition and the AT-11 Sniper ATGW. The gun is fitted with a carousel type automatic loader carrying 22 rounds. The rest of the 45-round total ammunition load is carried in the hull and turret.

In 1984 the T-80 began to appear in the Groups of Soviet Forces in Eastern Europe and by 1990 had almost totally supplanted the various T-64 variants in the

The T–72A/T–72M1 series tanks were the result of a mid–seventies redesign of the basic T–72. This was based around the availability of a new armour that used ceramic elements in a laminated structure. The T–72G shown was the Russian export version of the T–72A built by Poland and then Czechoslovakia. This was the best tank fielded by the Iraqi Army during the 1990–1991 Gulf War, it carried a 125mm smoothbore gun firing a fin-stabilised armour–piercing shot similar to that of the Abrams M1A1.

Western and Northern Groups. The fire-control system includes a laser rangefinder, advanced ballistic computer, thermal sleeve on the gun barrel and a gun barrel warp sensor. The ammunition fired is the standard 125mm family types: APFSDS-T, HE-FRAG(FS) and HEAT-FS – with the additional capacity for the AT-8 Songster radio command guided ATGW. The complete fire system allows targets out to 2500 metres to be effectively engaged by APFSDS-T ammunition and targets out to 4000 metres by the AT-8. The tank also has a limited shoot-on-the-move capability at low speeds. The gun uses a carousel-type autoloader with a 28-round capacity. Beneath the glacis plate is a toothed dozer/plough with which the

tank can dig its own fighting position within 15-20 minutes. It can also be fitted with KMT-5/6 mine roller/ploughs.

The T-80B was an improved production model of T-80, with, initially, an SG-1000 gas turbine developing 1000hp and later the 1100hp GTD-1000F gas turbine.

The T-80BK was a command version of T-80B with additional radio, second antenna on turret roof, land navigation system but with no ATGW capability.

The variant T-80BV was the T-80B with bolts/brackets added all over the hull glacis and turret top, sides and front to take ERA boxes.

The T-80U and its variants are the latest derivatives of the T-80 series. T-80U was

The M–84 is an upgraded version of the Soviet T–72 MBT built under licence in the former Yugoslavia. In latter years assembly of the M–84 was undertaken in Croatia at the Duro Dakovic Workshops, SlavanskiBrod.

The Type T-72 CZ is the Czech-oslovak version of the Soviet T-72 built under licence. There are two variants: T-72 CZ M3 and T-72 CZ M4. The upgrade work was carried out, in the main, by VOZ, the government-owned military repair company.

first seen in 1985. It is fitted with improved armour protection over the T-80B series with an updated main gun and a computerised fire-control system. The tank is armed with a 125mm 2A46M1 smoothbore gun that fires HEAT, APFSDS, HE-Frag ammunition and the AT-11 Sniper ATGW. The gun is fitted with a carousel type automatic-loader carrying 28 rounds. The remaining 17 rounds are carried in the hull and turret.

First seen in 1993 the T-90 and its variants are derivations of the T-72S series MBT family. Armament is the same as for the T-80U series of MBTs. The T-90 is armed with a 125mm 2A46M1 smoothbore gun that fires HEAT, APFSDS, HE-Frag ammunition and the AT-11 'Sniper' ATGW. The major difference from the T-72S is the fitting of the TshU1-7 Shtora optronic jamming system to confuse enemy ATGW systems. The

The Slovakian ZTS T-72 M2 series MBT is an upgrade of the Russian-designed T-72M1MBT which has a new fire-control system with a ballistic computer and a modernised 125mm smoothbore gun.

The T-72M was an upgraded T-72 with laser rangefinder assembly replacing coincidence rangefinder and increased main gun ammunition supply.

Further development of the T-80B resulted in the T-80BV shown here. Externally it is recognised by the addition of first-generation explosive reactive armour (ERA) to the hull and turret whose design and function are identical with the T-64BV MBT.

The installation of ERA gave the T-80BV a high degree of battlefield survivability against HEAT warheads fired from NATO anti-tank weapons.

The T-72S and its variants are the export versions of the T-72B MBT series. The tank is armed with a 125mm 2A46M smoothbore gun that fires HEAT, APFSDS, HE-Frag ammunition and the AT-11 'Sniper' ATGW. The T-72S Shilden shown was first seen in 1987 and is the export version of the T-72B. It is fitted with an ERA boxed armour package.

As the T-72 series increased in size the Soviets stopped T-64 production and switched their factories to production of the T-80 model. Whilst derived from the T-64 and retaining that vehicle's fully stabilised 125mm main gun and fire-control system the T-80 (T-80U shown) also featured either a gas turbine or diesel engine, different suspension system, road wheels and tracks and a smoother transmission.

Shtora has two optronic infra-red illuminators that produce spurious IR coded pulse signals to jam IR guidance of enemy ATGW.

T-90S, first seen around 1994, is the export version of the T-90. Fitted with the same boxed ERA package as the T-90 it is identical in almost all physical respects to the T-90.

The T-80UM is a refined descendant of the T-80U main battle tank. The 'U' designation is the Russian equivalent for the English word 'improved'. Among the improvements to be found on the T-80UM

is the introduction of the GTD-1250-G 1250hp gas turbine power unit. The T-80UM1, which is designated 'Snow Leopard', features the Arena defensive aid suite. A radar system detects incoming missiles and an on-board computer performs a threat appraisal and initiates the launch of fragmentation charges that cause premature detonation of incoming missiles. The T-80UM2, which is designated 'Black Eagle', is largely a T-80U fitted with a Drozd 2 defensive aids suite. The Drozd system appears less sophisticated than its Arena counterpart,

Developed in the late sixties the T-72 was the standard tank successor to the T-55 MBT and by 1981 had largely replaced it on the Soviet production lines. It offered comparable protection and firepower capabilities to the T-64/80 models but was slower and less agile. The T-72M shown was an upgraded T-72 with laser rangefinder assembly replacing coincidence rangefinder.

Another view of the T-80UM1 which clearly shows the explosive reactive armour. There are several variants of the T-80. These include a Command Staff Vehicle which uses the T-80U chassis and is designed to provide control and communication functions for motorised rifle and tank divisions at brigade, regiment and battalion level; and an Armoured Transport Loading Vehicle designed to resupply tanks with 125mm ammunition.

The T-80UM1 Bars (Snow Leopard) is fitted with the Arena Defensive Aid Suite (DAS). The Arena DAS has a mast mounted radar system which senses incoming missiles. The main armament is the 125mm 2A46M-4 smoothbore gun/ missile launcher with a 7.62mm PKT coaxial machine-gun. It is also fitted with a pintle-mounted 12.7mm NSVT machine-gun and eight 81mm smoke grenade dischargers. T-80s are fitted with the KAKTUS explosive reactive armour system. They have been sold to Pakistan, Ukraine, South Korea and Cyprus.

The T-90 is a further development of the T-72M MBT and incorporates some of the advanced features of the late production T-80 MBT. It has the same armament as the later T-80 marques. It is fitted with the latest generation Kontact-5 explosive reactive armour which gives protection against chemical energy and kinetic energy attack. It is now in service with the Russian Army.

but it does have a 360° arc of protection.

Many experts believe that the T-80UM2 is purely a technology platform, others maintain that it will be the next front line tank if it can fight off the challenge from the new Uralvagonzavod tank which carries a 152mm main gun.

Al-Khalid (also referred to as MBT 2000 or P-90) was brought into service in the Pakistani Army in November 2000. It is a hybrid construction based on the Type 59 (10%) Type 69-11 (15%) and Type 85 (20%). The remaining 55% is of new design jointly undertaken between the Chinese and Pakistan's Heavy Industries Taxila. The turret and hull are of all

The Type 90-11 has many similarities with the NORINCO Type 85-11M but is intended primarily for the export market. Featuring an uprated power unit and improved armour the 90-11 was scheduled for production in the early part of the new millennium. At the time of writing, prototypes were undergoing evaluation in trials.

Inheriting a good design standard from its predecessor, the Chinese Type 85–IIM MBT offers a range of improvements in terms of power pack, armament and armour to make it a worthy competitor in current–day battlefield scenarios. These and the Type 90–II are incremental advances on the basic Type 59 which in turn was an upgrade from the Russian T–54 supplied to China in the early 1950s.

welded steel armour construction with additional composite armour on the frontal arc. The armour is modular, facilitating ease of replacement. During trials armour protection of the hull and turret defeated live firings of all types of 120 and 125mm tank projectiles and other selected anti-tank ammunition. The sophisticated fire control system includes a two-axis stabilised dual magnification sight for the gunner and a similar sight for the commander which also features, hunter killer capability and a range of sensors which allows the Al-Khalid to engage moving targets during night or day. The MBT 2000 Al-Khalid is armed with a 125mm smoothbore gun coaxial with a 7.62mm machine-gun, a 12.7mm anti-aircraft machine-gun and, mounted either side of the turret, a bank of four electrically operated smoke grenade dischargers.

The Pakistani MBT 2000 Al-Khalid is equipped with a 125mm smoothbore gun fitted with a thermal sleeve and a fume extractor, a combination of which has been shown to improve first round kill rate. This gun can fire HEAT and HE-FRAG rounds and a laser guided projectile fitted with a HEAT warhead. The Al-Khalid is manufactured in Pakistan by Heavy Industries Taxila, the photograph shows one on display fitted with explosive reactive armour.

CHAPTER EIGHT

International Tank Design

Although many believe that the days of the heavy main battle tank are almost over, because of the significant advances in anti-tank weapons of all types in recent years, most countries still plan to use them at least for the next decade. In fact, countries are still procuring or producing them on a significant scale. While Israel, Japan, Italy, India and Korea, amongst others, continue to manufacture their own tanks, others, such as Greece and Turkey, tend to purchase upgraded versions of existing models. France supplies the GIAT Industries Leclerc to the United Arab Emirates and Germany furnishes the needs of Spain, Sweden, the Netherlands and others with Leopard 2 MBTs. Vickers Defence Systems of the UK provide several MBT types to various countries and the USA continues to supply the world with the many variants of the M60 and M48 series and several Middle Eastern countries with the Abrams series of MBTs.

The Israelis produced many upgraded allied tanks during the several wars with the Arab nations. These include the Sho't, which was an upgraded Centurion MBT fitted with Blazer explosive reactive armour and armed with a 105mm gun.

The Mag'ach series was produced from upgraded M48s and M60s. The first of these, the M48 Modified Patton variant, was the original 200 ex-West German M48A2C procured in 1962-4 and modified during 1966-8 with 105mm L7 rifled main gun. Approximately 40 of these served in the 1967 Six Day War, the remainder used by the Israelis were the 90mm gun version.

Some 600 plus Modified Patton M48, M48A1, M48A2 and M48A3 model vehicles were upgraded in 1968-75 and were called, by the Israelis Mag'ach, (and unofficially called M48A4 by the Americans) to an equivalent M60 standard. The M48 Mag'ach was a 1979-80 conversion of the Improved M48 Mag'ach, these, together with over 150 M48A5s procured during 1977-79, were fitted with Blazer reactive armour and also heavier anti-aircraft/personnel armament.

They were used extensively in 1982 Lebanon War.

The M60/M60A1 Mag'achs were standard models procured during 1970-77 and modified with Israeli equipment such as radios, stowage facilities etc. The M60A1 version was used successfully by the Israelis in the 1973 Yom Kippur war. The M1980 had further modifications to the M60/M60A1 Mag'ach which resulted in the original M60 series Mag'ach tanks being further upgraded with Blazer reactive armour, a new Israeli fire control system, CL-3030 IS-10 smoke discharger system, and heavier anti-aircraft/personnel armament. These models also saw action in the 1982 Lebanon War.

Mag'ach 7 was a standard M60A3 model procured from 1979 onwards and rebuilt 1988 onwards with new passive armour package for turret, hull and side skirts, new diesel engine, transmission and tracks and a new state-of-the art FCS equivalent to that fitted to the Merkava Mk 3.

The 17 M88 and 30 M88A1 ARVs used by the Israeli Army are based on M48 automotive components which have also

been upgraded with the Blazer reactive armour and heavier anti-aircraft/personnel weapon package.

The Israelis also operate over 50 M48/M60 AVLBs and 15 M728 Combat Engineer Vehicles all with local modifications.

Israeli upgrades

The Israeli Sabra is based on the American Patton M60A3. However, the extent of its radical upgrade and modernisation, by Israel Military Industries, makes this 1960 tank a worthy opponent for all MBTs well into the 21st century. Its main armament is a 120mm smoothbore gun capable of firing NATO standard smoothbore ammunition including the APFSDS rounds. Additionally, externally mounted machine guns of 7.62mm calibre or 5.56mm are available and a 60mm mortar system supplied by Soltam provides

further protection. Although the Sabra is currently fitted with modular passive armour protection the Sabra Mk II will be fitted with explosive reactive armour. Also planned is a fire-control system which will provide a stable gun platform when the tank is on the move.

Enter the Merkava

In 1974 came the first prototype of the Merkava Mk 1 MBT, followed, in 1982, by the Mk 2, which built on the success of the Mk 1. It is powered by a Mk 1-TCM AVDS-1790-6A-12 air-cooled turbo-charged diesel developing 908hp.

These tanks took part in the 1982 Peace for Galilee War destroying a large number of Soviet supplied T-55 and T-62 medium tanks as well as several T-72 vehicles. The Merkava Mk 2s were armed with a 105mm gun mounted in a beautiful

Externally the Merkava Mk 3 appears very similar to the two earlier Merkava marques apart from the main gun, which is a 120mm Israeli designed and built smoothbore cannon with a distinctive Vishay Israel thermal sleeve. The main gun fires both Israeli and NATO type 120 mm smoothbore ammunition families and the two 7.62mm FN MAG anti-aircraft machine-guns are specially modified versions developed for the Merkava family with variable height capability mounts.

In mid 1991 Israel started to develop the Merkava Mk 4, a new generation of MBTs built entirely by the Israeli Ordnance Corps. Few details have been given but it is thought that this tank will mount a new 140mm smoothbore gun firing a new 140mm APFSDS-T round. Production has started and the Merkava 4 is now beginning to replace earlier Merkavas in service with the Israel Defence Force.

shaped turret that presented a frontal area of only one square metre. Also they had a rear compartment which seated escorting infantry; nevertheless, they had much room for improvement.

This came with the Mk 3 62000kg version of this machine which has the well-sloped, cast armour of the Mks 1 and 2, but its similarly frontally installed engine is the TCM AVDS-1790-9AR air-cooled turbo-charged diesel developing 1200hp. The Merkava 3 is armed with a 120mm gun, which is an Israeli designed smoothbore cannon carrying a distinctive Vishay Israel thermal sleeve. The armour package is of an advanced special passive type that is integrated into the basic tank design and contains approximately 50% of its make-up as replaceable modules, this allows for easier levels of repair and replacement by more modern armour developments as they become available. The basic cast steel turret has attachments for special armour modules at the front

The Japanese Type 74 has a cross-linked hydro-pneumatic suspension system with a very unusual aspect – the capability to raise or lower itself completely, to tilt itself either forwards or backwards and to incline itself to either side – so as to match its ground clearance to the terrain it is moving over or to enable it to engage targets either higher or lower than the main gun's normal elevation/ depression limits can accommodate.

and sides, as have the sponsons and nose positions. Full length special armour side skirts are also provided – it could match the best in existence and have certain in-built tactical advantages to spare.

Merkava 4

The Merkava Mk 4 retains the hull design of its predecessors but there the similarities fade away. This latest Mark is equipped with a new 120mm smooth bore gun designed to produce high muzzle velocities essential for the kinetic energy ammunition carried. Additionally, the LAHAT, laser homing anti-tank missiles can be launched from the Mk 4. Like the earlier Merkavas, the Mk 4 can carry a small infantry squad under armour protection, allowing them to disembark, unseen by the enemy, through a rear door.

Japenese designs

A project began in 1962 to produce a tank to succeed the Japanese Type 61, the first tank to be designed post World War II, and which is now being phased out of service with the Japanese Ground Self-Defence Force (JGSDF).

Two prototypes were constructed at the Maruko works of Mitsubishi Heavy Industries (MHI) with the first, called the STB-1, completed in 1969. This was followed in 1971 by STB-3 and on through to the final model the STB-6 in 1973. MHI completed the first Type 74 in 1975 for the JGSDF and at the end of production had completed a total of 873 of this marque. The gun fitted in the Type 74 is a locally-built Royal Ordnance 105mm L7 series rifled tank gun firing APFSDS-T, HESH-T, APDS-T and smoke type ammunition.

Variants of the Type 74 include the Type 78 Armoured Recovery Vehicle, which is very similar in appearance to the AMX-30D and Leopard 1 ARVs. This vehicle has a hydraulically operated dozer blade at the front and a hydraulic crane on the right side of the hull. The Type 87 Twin 35mm Self-Propelled Anti-Aircraft Gun system variant is armed with twin Oerlikon Contraves 35mm KDA cannon fitted in a two-man power-operated turret.

Type 90 MBT

The Technical Research Headquarters of the Japanese Self-Defence Agency began research and development of a new Japanese MBT in 1976. This was designa-ted the TK-X and was also manufactured primarily by MHI with the later designation Type 90. Trials of early models, fitted with a

The Mitsubishi Type 90 MBT has a hull and turret feature of special composite armour in its construction with the latter having the characteristic slab-sided appearance of modern Western MBTs. The number of crew has been reduced to three by the adoption of an automatic loading system for the license-built 120mm-Rheinmetall smoothbore tank gun which fires APFSDS-T and HEAT-MP-T rounds.

Japanese 120mm gun, took place through to 1986. Between 1986 and 1988 a second series of prototypes were built which incorporated changes resulting from these trials and armed with the Rheinmetall 120mm smoothbore gun as fitted to the US Abrams M1A1/M1A2 and German Leopard 2 MBTs. No details have been given at the time of writing but it is likely that extensive use of composite armour has been used in the hull, turret and frontal area of this tank.

Variants of the Type 90 are the Type 90 Mineclearing MBT fitted with the Type 92 mineclearing roller system; the Type 90 Armoured Recovery Vehicle, fitted simi-

larly to the Type 74 ARV but with an additional hydraulically operated winch, and the Type 90 AVLB fitted with a scissors type bridge which can span a gap of up to 20 metres.

Italian designs

The Italian Otobreda OF-40 MBT was designed by Otobreda and FIAT from 1977 specifically for the export market. The OF-40 (O for Otobreda, F for FIAT and 40 for its approximate weight in tons) uses components of the Leopard 1 MBT and resembles it in appearance. The only customer to date is the United Arab Emirates (Dubai) and it is no longer being

The OF-40 is of conventional MBT design of all welded steel construction. Main armament comprises a 105mm rifled gun designed by Otobreda which can fire standard NATO ammunition including APFSDS.

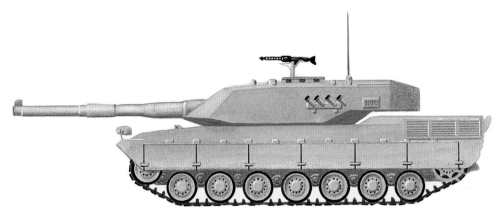

The fire control system of the C1–Ariete is the latest generation computerised full solution modular Officine Galileo TURMS model which, together with gunner's and commander's optical day/thermal vision night sight assemblies and laser rangefinder module, allows high single shot kill probability engagements against both moving and stationary targets whilst the Ariete itself is either moving or stationary. If the primary fire control system fails completely then the gunner can use a manual back-up periscopic sight with a set of aiming graticules.

marketed. Remaining OF-40 Mk 1s are being upgraded to Mk 2s. There is an OF-40 ARV variant and the hull can be used to mount other weapon systems.

Ariete MBT

In 1984 Otobreda and IVECO formed a consortium to handle a new generation of armoured fighting vehicles for the Italian Army. In that year the Italian Army had agreed the specification of the Ariete MBT, with Otobreda having overall responsibility and IVECO being responsible for the power pack and suspension. The first Ariete was delivered in 1995 with final deliveries in 2001.

Apparently studies have begun for a Mk 2 version of the Ariete but as yet there are no firm plans for the Ariete Mk 2 to go into production.

Indian developments

Among other nations capable of design, development and manufacture of fighting vehicles is India. The Arjun is India's first indigenous MBT design and has been developed by the Indian Army's Combat Vehicle Research and Development Establishment (CVRDE) over a protracted period from 1974. A total of 17 prototypes and 20 pre-production vehicles have been used in an extensive test and

The Indian Arjun MBT has new composite armour developed by the Indian Defence Metallurgical Laboratory called Kanchan armour. Arjun is armed with a locally designed stabilised 120mm rifled gun fitted with a fume extractor and thermal sleeve, and a coaxial 7.62mm machine gun.

The Indian Arjun MBT has new composite armour developed by the Indian Defence Metallurgical Laboratory called Kanchan armour. Arjun is armed with a locally designed stabilised 120mm rifled gun, firing similarly developed APFSDS, HEAT, HESH, HE and smoke round types, is fitted with a fume extractor and thermal sleeve, and a coaxial 7.62mm machine gun. The associated fire control system is a full-solution integrated follow-on to the computerised Bharat Electronics Tank Fire Control System Mk 1B used on Vijayanta MBTs and is fitted with a combined day/night thermal imaging gunner's sight assembly with built-in laser rangefinder.

evaluation programme of all the various tank sub-systems with the first pre-production series vehicle delivered in 1988. The type entered service with the Indian Army in 1996.

Republic of Korea developments
The K1 MBT also known as the Type 88 or Republic of Korea Indigenous Tank (ROKIT) was developed from 1979-84 by the US General Dynamics, Land Systems Division under contract to the South Korean government. This was to meet a requirement for a locally built MBT suitable for use by the small stature South Korean personnel. Limited production

The next generation K1 MBT is the K1A1, this is armed with a 120mm smoothbore gun, firing the same types of ammunition as the M1A1/M1A2 Abrams family and is fitted with full night vision equipment and a latest standard fire control system. It is believed that the K1A1 is being developed as a response to a new North Korean MBT design armed with a 125mm gun system based on imported Russian/Chinese technology.

began in 1985 and full series manufacture in 1988.

The low profile K1 MBT uses a hybrid torsion/hydro-pneumatic suspension system and is armed with a 105mm M68A1 rifled gun that is fitted with fume extractor, thermal sleeve and Muzzle Reference System (MRS). The ammunition carried includes HEAT, APFSDS-T, HESH and smoke types. Armour protection is provided by both conventional steel armour plate and special armour configurations. An individual crew protection NBC system is installed.

Khalid programme

The Khalid MBT programme resulted from the defunct Shah of Iran's order for the British made Vickers Defence Systems' FV4030/2 Shir 1 and FV4030/3 Shir 2 MBTs that was cancelled in 1979 by the Islamic Iranian government.

Jordan then ordered 274 Khalid tanks that are essentially similar to the Shir 1

model but with minor changes in equipment to suit Jordanian Army requirements. The FV4030/2 was based on the Chieftain Mk 5 design but with evolutionary changes to overcome problems encountered in service. These included a new 1200hp engine, a new automatic transmission and the fitting of an improved bogie type suspension.

The main armament comprises a Royal Ordnance 120mm L11A5 rifled gun with fume extractor, thermal sleeve and Muzzle Reference System. Ammunition types used include smoke, HESH, APDS and/or APFSDS. These are loaded into the breech with either a separate bag or rigid combustible case charge. The turret mounted 7.62mm MG can be fired from inside the commander's station. The fire control system is the Computer Sighting System derivative of the British Army's Chieftain IFCS and is used with the gunner's Pilkington Optronics Tank Laser Sight unit.

The Jordanian Khalid is essentially similar to the cancelled Iranian Shir 1, that was itself an evolution of the Chieftain Mk 5. The Khalid remains in service with the Royal Jordanian Army in 2004.

CHAPTER NINE

The Gulf Wars

The forces of Saddam Hussein's Iraq invaded Kuwait on 2 August 1990. Earlier in that year Iraq had succeeded in ending a bitter eight year struggle with its neighbour Iran, where its armoured vehicle resources were mostly used from static positions.

Saddam Hussein believed that the West, particularly the United States of America, with his other neighbour, Saudi Arabia, would do nothing if his intentions turned to the oil-rich Kuwait. A shock was felt in Kuwait with the invasion, but a greater shock was awaiting Iraq in the ferocity of the response from the international community. The United States, the United Kingdom, France and their NATO allies stood firmly against Iraq and forced Hussein's forces back across the border. After this war Saddam Hussein refused to abide by international law and so on 21 March 2003 the United States and the UK, this time without France, but with Australian and Polish forces, invaded Iraq in a severe but short war which was won by the coalition forces but which appears to have not quite won the peace, for it has left disquiet in Iraq to the day of writing.

As a result of the 1980s war with Iran the Iraqi Army requested its Ministry of Defence to develop a local armoured vehicle manufacturing/modernisation industrial capability.

Three of the programmes which resulted from this approach involved what could be done with the many thousands of Soviet T-54/55 and Chinese Type 59/69 series MBTs that were in use with the Iraqi Army. The multilayer armour T-55/ Type 69 involved the fitting of add-on multi-layer special composite armour packages and modern night vision equipment. Only a few tanks were seen with this modification and all seemed to be associated with the Iraqi 5th Mechanised Division used in the battles around Khafji. The tanks, mostly modified T-55s, were apparently assigned to tank company commanders. It is believed that Iraq had modernised a small number of its old T-54 MBTs using elements of the Rumanian T-55 upgrade kit. What was probably the most capable of the armoured vehicle modernisation programmes was the rebuilt T-55s. Small numbers of T-55/Type 59/Type 69 MBTs had been totally rebuilt with a raised turret accommodating a locally built Soviet 125mm 2A46 D81T smoothbore gun complete with its auto-loader system, new armoured side skirts, rearranged turret stowage facilities, four-round electrically-fired smoke discharge assemblies and new passive night vision equipment for the crew. The fire control system had also been upgraded to a computerised system standard using component elements for the fire control system model used in the Soviet T-72 MBT.

It is probable that several countries helped Iraq with this particular modification programme including Egypt, Romania and Yugoslavia. Iraq also modified numbers of its T-62 series medium tanks and had a T-series rebuild facility for its Chinese and Russian T-54/55/Type 59/Type 69 family of medium tanks. Licensed production from former

In what was probably the most capable of the armoured vehicle modernisation programmes undertaken by Iraq a small number of T–55/Type 59/Type 69 MBTs have been totally rebuilt with raised turrets accommodating a locally built Soviet 125mm 2A46 D81T smoothbore gun complete with its autoloader system, armoured side skirts, four-round electrically-fired smoke discharge assemblies and new passive night vision equipment for the crew.

eastern bloc countries of the T-72 MBT was also undertaken on a small scale under the name Assad Bablye (Babylon Lion). Many of these tanks were destroyed in the Gulf War of 1991.

British armour in Iraq

Britain fielded Challenger 1 MBTs which, until then, had been untried in desert conditions and in battle. Ironically, the Challenger 1 MBT is an evolutionary derivative of the Shir 2 MBT originally developed for the Shah of Iran's Army but subsequently cancelled by the Islamic Republic of Iran before any production could be undertaken. Compared to the Chieftain MBT it has a more powerful diesel engine, new transmission, improved suspension and extensive use of

Chobham laminated special armour in the construction of the hull and turret. The latter feature gives the vehicle a distinctive slab-sided appearance.

In Operation Desert Storm during this Gulf War, three regiments of Challenger 1 were deployed to Saudi Arabia for use with the First (British) Armoured Division: 14/20th King's Hussars (43 Challenger 1, attached to 4th Armoured Brigade); The Royal Scots Dragoon Guards (57 Challenger 1, attached to 7th Armoured Brigade): and The Queens Royal Irish Hussars (57 Challenger 1, attached to 7th Armoured Brigade). In addition, further Challengers were assigned to the Armoured Brigades and Armoured Division as HQ vehicles and battlefield replacements, the latter including the

Most of the Iraqi modernised T-54 and T-55s were destroyed in the Gulf War of 2003. This model, a T-55A, was armed with a 100mm gun which was practically useless against the armour of Abrams or Challenger tanks and caused little damage to even Bradley and Warrior IFVs.

British and US troops discuss the merits of the Centurion AVRE on the Iraq/Kuwait border during the 1990–1991 Gulf War.

Challenger 1 MBTs seen at rest during the Gulf War of 1990–1991. The MBTs deployed to the region were up armoured prior to the conflict. These tanks were in support of 32 Armoured Engineer Regiment of the British Army which took on the task of clearing up the war debris with their Chieftain AVREs and Chieftain AVLBs.

Divisional assigned Armoured Delivery Group (ADG) with three full squadrons of War Maintenance Reserve Challengers crewed by the Life Guards. Also deployed in Desert Storm were Challenger Armoured Repair and Recovery Vehicles and additional Challenger MBTs as battlefield replacements.

On 18th February 1991, the M110 Self-propelled Howitzers of 74 Heavy Battery (The Battle Axe Company), of 32 Heavy Regiment, Royal Artillery, firing from a position just five miles south of the Iraqi border, in support of 1 (US) Infantry Division, stamped their presence on the Gulf War by being the first British artillery unit to fire against the enemy. This

regiment had established links with their American counterparts, principally the 75th Field Artillery Brigade. This formation was equipped with a mix of M109, M110 and MLRS with close liaison between their respective locating units.

Over 200 Challenger 1s were sent to the Gulf, together with the first 12 production CRARRVs to support the MBTs.

Because of the very nature of the desert battlefield and the Iraqi anti-armour capabilities, a Challenger up-armouring programme was undertaken. This involved the production of special Vickers Defence Systems passive skirt-armour kits for the hull sides and an add-on Royal Ordnance Explosive Reactive

THE GULF WAR 1990-1991: COMBAT MAP FROM 24 FEBRUARY TO 28 FEBRUARY 1991

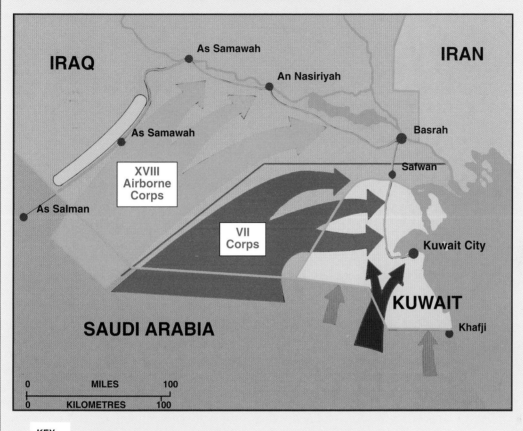

 KEY

 XVIII Airborne Corps comprising US 82nd and 101st Airborne Divisions and US Mechanized Infantry Division

VII Corps comprising British 1st Armoured Division, US 1st and 3rd Armored Divisions, US 1st Infantry Division and US 2nd Armored Cavalry Regiment

French 6th Light Armoured Division (part of XVIII Corps)

 US Marine Corps amphibious landing force comprising 1st and 2nd Marine Divisions (Early attacks 24-26 February)

 Egyptian 4th Armoured Division, Syrian, Saudi Arabian, Kuwaiti and other Arab contingents.

At the beginning of hostilities the Iraqi Army fielded ex-Soviet BMP-2 APCs and 5,500 MBTs which included: T-54/T-55s/T-59/T-69s/T-62s and T-72s, with some Chinese Type 59 and Type 69-2 MBTs, plus a few old Chieftains, M47 and M60 MBTs. Allied armour consisted of 800 M60A3 MBTs of the Egyptian Army and 250 of the Saudi Arabian Army which had the 105mm gun. Saudi Arabia fielded some French-built AMX-30S MBTs as did the Qatar Army whose AMX-30S MBTs were specially modified for desert operations, with sand shields, special filters and lower gear ratio. The Kuwaiti Army had a few British built Chieftain tanks which had managed to escape before the Iraqi invasion. Syria provided a unit of 100 T-62 tanks and the French AMX-30s. The rest of the total of about 4,000 tanks were made up of Challenger 1, Abrams M1A1 MBTs with Bradley and Warrior IFVs.

The full title of this vehicle is: Alvis Vehicles Warrior armoured combat vehicle. The variant shown is armed with a 30mm L21 RARDEN cannon coaxially with a 7.62mm L94A1 Chain gun. All six variants of this vehicle were deployed during Operation Desert Storm, including Artillery Observation and Battery Command Vehicles of the Royal Artillery.

Armour (ERA) package for the bow toe-plate and glacis region. The complete armour upgrading added several thousand kilogrammes to the Challenger's basic combat weight but did not adversely affect its battlefield performance.

Other improvements included: the use of the interim Jericho 2 Depleted Uranium APFSDS round by taking the L26A1 Charm 1 projectile of the CHARM programme and marrying it with an L14 lower pressure charge to increase accuracy and penetration; the enhancing of all the Mk 2 variant Challengers present in the Gulf to the latest Mk 3 standard; the fitting of various equipment to make Challenger fully capable of extended operations in desert conditions; the addition of external fittings to allow the vehicles to carry two 200 litre fuel tanks at the rear; and the addition of a device to a number of Challengers in order to give them the capability of laying down a protective 'tail smokescreen' by pumping atomised diesel fuel into the tank's exhaust system. Most of the improvement

A Challenger 1 at speed during the Iraq War of 1990-1991. The Royal Tank Regiment was the first to be equipped with these vehicles, followed, in 1985, by the Royal Hussars. A modified version, known as the 'Al Hussein' was supplied to Jordan in late 1999.

A Samson armoured recovery vehicle of the 32nd Armoured Engineer Regiment, Royal Engineers, dug in during the 1990–1991 Iraq War. (See entry in Chapter 5)

work and fitting of add-on packages was performed in the Gulf region by the REME and various equipment manufacturers' engineers. All these improvements worked; not one Challenger 1 nor any of its crewmen were lost in combat.

The armament package and fire-control system proved highly successful with the standard L23 tungsten APFSDS-T projectile being highly accurate and lethal out to a range of some 3000 metres. The new L26 APFSDS kinetic energy projectile had only limited use (only 88 being fired in total during combat) whilst the L31 HESH projectile was used in over 50% of the anti-armour engagements. The L31 proved particularly useful, especially against the lighter armour targets, where the tendency was to destroy them in

A Centurion AVRE of 32 Armoured Engineer Regiment moves a destroyed T-55 to clear the road in the suburbs of Abu Khasib during the 1990-1991 Gulf War.

The Warrior MCV is shown here destroying an ikon of Saddam Hussein, the Iraqi President, responsible for the invasion of Kuwait in 1990. Warrior was formerly known as the MCV-80 and is armed with a 30mm RARDEN cannon and a 7.62mm Chain Gun in a two-man turret.

Vickers Defence Systems Challenger 1 is armed with the standard Royal Ordnance 120mm L11A5 rifled tank gun fitted with a thermal sleeve, a fume extractor and a muzzle reference system. Those serving with the 7th Armoured Brigade in Operation Desert Storm were the first to deploy 'Chobham' armour. In early 1991 Royal Ordnance Explosive Reactive Armour (ERA) was installed on the nose and glacis plate.

spectacular fashion. An Iraqi T-55 tank was also destroyed by a first round hit from a Challenger main gun, being used in the direct fire role with HESH, at the extreme range of 5,100 metres.

During Operation Desert Storm six variants of the Alvis Warrior APC, including Artillery Observation and Battery Command vehicles, were deployed in the recapture of Kuwait. Some were converted to use in the MILAN ATGW role. Warrior was also used in the forward observation role for armoured regiments for the first time. Passive armour was fitted in-country in Saudi Arabia and was also fitted to Warrior vehicles in Bosnia.

US armour in Iraq

The 24th US Infantry Division was equipped with the technologically advanced Abrams M1A1 MBT which until Operation Desert Storm had not been tested in battle. Abrams M1A1 is armed with the 120mm smoothbore gun which fires fin-stabilised armour-piercing ammunition which comprises a depleted uranium penetrator carried in a light alloy 'sabot'. Fitting tightly in the barrel this sabot is discarded as soon as the shell leaves the gun muzzle, leaving the long, thin, streamlined penetrator to reach the target. The impact of the penetrator at extremely high velocity punches through the armour and, once inside, the

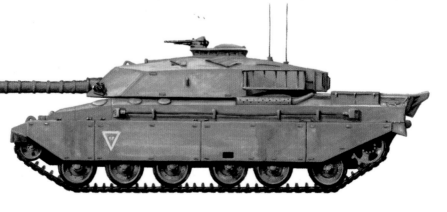

penetrator is destabilised by impact and ricochets around inside the target tank destroying all inside. Depleted uranium is one of the heaviest and most dense metals in existence but has no radio-active properties at all.

In March 1991 the US Department of Defense released provisional information on the performance of US weapons systems in Operation Desert Storm, an extract regarding the performance of the M1A1 MBT reads as follows: *"After 100 hours of offensive operations, the operational readiness rates for both the VII Corps and XVIII Airborne Corps exceeded the Army's 90 per cent standard. Especially noteworthy was a night move by the the 3rd Armored Division covering 200km (120miles). None of the more than 300 tanks in the division broke down.*

"Seven separate M1A1 crews reported being hit by T-72 tank rounds. These M1A1s sustained no damage, attesting to the effectiveness of our heavy armour. Other crews reported that the M1A1 thermal sight allowed them to acquire Iraqi T-72s through the smoke from oil well fires and other obscurants. The T-72

The first M1s were produced in 1978, followed by the M1A1 in 1985 and the first M1A2 in 1986. There have been 3,273 M1 MBTs produced for the United States Army. The model shown here is the M1A1 HA (Heavy Armor) of the 3rd Armored Cavalry Regiment during Desert Storm.

Armed with a 105mm F2 rifled gun the AMX–10RC Reconnaissance Vehicle served with the French Army in Chad during Operation Manta between August 1982 and November 1983. In Operation Desert Storm, two AMX–10RC regiments of the 6th Light Armoured Division of the French Daguet Division carried out the west coverage mission in Iraq for the entire allied forces.

did not have the same advantage. This situation gave the Abrams a significant edge in survivability, engagement range and night manoeuvre. Additionally, tank crews reported that the M829A1 tank round was extremely effective against the T-72. In sum, the combined performance of the Abrams armour, thermal sight and ammunition attest to the systems exceptional lethality and survivability. Of the 1955 M1A1 Abrams tanks in the theatre, four were disabled and four were damaged but are repairable. No M1A1 crew members were killed in many tank engagements. Overall readiness rates exceeded 90 per cent prior to and during combat".

M1A1 successes

During the Gulf War the M1A1 models undertook the brunt of the US Army armour battles destroying large numbers of Iraqi tanks at battle ranges of up to 3500 metres and more. The thermal viewing equipment could see targets at over 5000 metres and positively identify them at 1000-1500 metres. They also allowed enemy positions and vehicles to be seen in the worst of the battlefield conditions, namely the thick oil-fire smoke from the burning Kuwaiti oilfields.

It was found that the 120mm M829A1 APFSDS-T rounds used could be fired through five-foot thick sand berms used to protect Iraqi tanks in hull-down positions and still destroy the target. In another instance an M1A1 hit the turret of a T-72 with an anti-tank round which passed straight through the turret's side armour, the turret interior and the armour on the other side of the turret and then went on to hit and destroy a second T-72. On another occasion an M1A1 destroyed a T-72 by penetrating its frontal armour at a range of 3500 metres.

The M1A1 survivability proved to be on a par with the Israeli Merkava: none was totally destroyed, nine were permanently disabled (mostly by friendly action or in two cases by their own crews when the vehicles had to be abandoned) and nine damaged (mainly by mines) but were considered repairable. Only a few dozen crewmen were injured in combat.

At least seven M1A1s were hit by 125mm fire from T-72s, none had any serious damage caused. One M1A1 suffered two direct hits from anti-tank sabot rounds fired from a T-72 at approximately 500 metres away which simply bounced off its front armour.

The main danger faced by the Abrams was the myriad of Iraqi anti-tank mines obtained from both Eastern and Western sources and these weapons caused the disablement of several M1A1s.

March 2003: Tanks from Charlie Company, 1st Tank Battalion, US Marine Corps, scan the area for enemy personnel and vehicles after coming under mortar fire at the intersection of Highway 1 and 27 while in support of Operation Iraqi Freedom.

April 2003. Charlie Company 1st Tank Battalion M1–A1 Abrams tanks at the Assembly Area at Kerbala en route to Ad Diwaniaya, Iraq during Operation Iraqi Freedom.

Marine Corps tanks in the Gulf

The US Marine Corps also used 60 M1A1(HA) and 18 M1A1 Common Tanks in the Gulf War, but had to borrow the former from the US Army. These equipped the 2nd Marine Tank Battalion and the 4th Marine Tank Battalion assigned to units of the 1st Marine Expeditionary Force.

The US Army also fielded the M551 Sheridan Light Tank as fast armoured reconnaissance with M2 and M3 Bradleys of 1st Armored Division and 1st US Cavalry Division, each vehicle being armed with a 25mm gun and TOW missiles. In March 1991 the US Army issued an initial report on Army Weapons Systems Performance in southwest Asia with the following comment on the Bradley M2/M3: *"Crews reported that the sights were very effective, even during sandstorms. Other crews reported that the 25mm Bush-master cannon was more lethal than expected. There were no reports of transmission failure during offensive operations. Of the 2,200 Bradleys in theatre, three were disabled.*

The M270 Armored Vehicle-mounted Rocket Launcher (AVMRL) entered service with the US Army in 1983, with the first European-built MLRS systems being handed over in 1989. The US Army deployed over 230 MLRS launchers during Operation Desert Storm in the Gulf War of 1990–1991 and 32 Heavy Regiment, Royal Artillery, fielded 16 launchers.

This Bradley is one of the first to have reached Baghdad in the 2003 Iraqi Freedom campaign. It carries the personal belongings of the crew on the outside to gain space inside the vehicle. This photograph was taken during a rest period on the advance up to Baghdad; it appears that a local has taken advantage of the shade.

To date, we have no information on the number damaged. Overall Bradley operational readiness rates remained at 90 per cent or above during combat".

Other armour in the Gulf

Forces from various other states took part in the war, amongst them was a unit of 2,500 men equipped with 100 Soviet T-62 MBTs of the Syrian Army, Egyptian troops with 800 M60A3 MBTs, Kuwaiti forces with British built Chieftains, and Saudi Arabian and Qatari forces with their AMX-30S specially modified for desert warfare. The French used AMX-10RC Reconnaissance vehicles to cover the entire west of the conflict for the whole of the coalition forces.

After Saddam Hussein and his forces had been beaten back into Iraq, President

After successful demonstration trials in the Middle East the MCV–80 was chosen as the future armoured personnel carrier for the British Army, in preference to the American Bradley IFV. In 1984 the MCV–80 was accepted for service and was renamed Warrior by the British Army. A Desert Fighting Vehicle variant known as the Fahris, aimed at the export market, was shown at the British Army Equipment Exhibition in 1990.

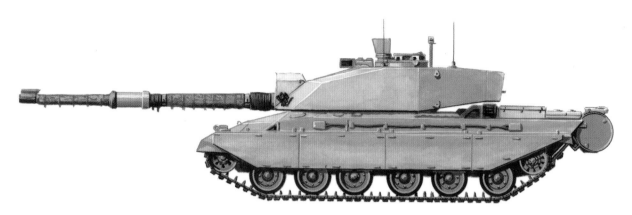

Bush Senior stopped the fighting when Hussein promised to abide by international law. He did not keep his word and, on the strength of intelligence reports of a build up of weapons of mass destruction, the USA, now with President George Bush Junior in command, and with the total support of the British Prime Minister, Tony Blair, a coalition was formed and, with an element of surprise, Iraq was invaded.

Operation Iraqi Freedom

On 21st March 2003 a coalition of US, British, Australian and Polish forces struck again at the regime of Saddam Hussein in Iraq. US troops of 3rd Infantry Division supported by Abrams MBTs and Bradley IFVs advanced towards the town of Umm Qasr while British forces supported by Challenger 2 and Warrior IFVs of the 7th Armoured Brigade made for the Al Faw peninsula en route to Basra. At the same time AS90s of 3rd Royal Horse Artillery, firing from Kuwait, fired the first shots of the war, to emulate their Royal Artillery brothers of 74 Heavy Battery RA, who fired the first shots in the previous Gulf conflict. In consequence of this bombardment, and strikes by US 3rd Infantry Division and the British 7th Armoured Division, Iraq's 51st Infantry Division, one of Iraq's best equipped and trained units, surrendered. Its 8,000 troops, supported by over 200 tanks, stopped fighting.

The Abrams MBTs and Bradleys of the

The Vickers Defence Systems Challenger 2 MBT is armed with a 120mm L30A1 rifled gun with a coaxial 7.62mm L94A1 Chain gun and a 7.62mm L37A2 machine gun, plus 2x5 66 smoke grenade dischargers. It is protected by second generation Chobham armour against both KE and CE attack.

Abrams M1A2 MBTs of US 3rd Infantry on their way to Baghdad during the Iraq War.

An Alvis Stormer of the British Royal Artillery fitted with a Shorts Starstreak High-Velocity Missile installation on Pre-Op training during Exercise Desert Storm.

US 7th Cavalry were ambushed by Iraqi Republican Guard troops on the 25 March but were swept aside by the 25mm cannon fire from the Bradley IFVs. The Cavalry unit, part of the US 3rd Infantry Division, continued its advance to within 50 miles of Baghdad.

On 27 March 2003, a convoy of about 120 T-55s and Type 59 tanks with many APCs was heading southeast out of Basra along roads close to the Iranian border towards the Al Faw peninsula and British lines south of Basra. US Navy and RAF Harrier ground attack jets dropped precision bombs, guided munitions and cluster bombs on the Iraqi armour, which was also successfully shelled by 155mm AS90 SPGs of 3rd RHA and 105mm light field guns of 29 Commando Regiment, Royal Artillery. The whole convoy of T-55s, T-72s with various APCs and IFVs was destroyed.

About 25 M1A2s, supported by Bradley IFVs, moved northwards towards the city centre "to give a poke in the eye" for the Saddam Regime, according to the US Central Command. On 1st April 2003, Colonel David Perkins, of the US 3rd Infantry, who was involved in the tank incursion said: "It was a non-stop gauntlet of both heavy systems as well as light infantry on roofs, shooting down on top of tanks with rocket-propelled grenades and machine guns. It was a full spectrum

The AS90 here is shown with the 155mm/52 calibre ordnance which was fitted to earlier models which were armed with the 155mm/39 calibre barrel. The current 155mm 39 calibre barrel achieves a maximum range, firing assisted ammunition, of 30km, but when fitted with the 155mm 52 calibre barrel this is raised to 40km.

OPERATION IRAQI FREEDOM
MAJOR TANK ENGAGEMENTS OF 14 APRIL 2003
TIKRIT, NORTHERN IRAQ

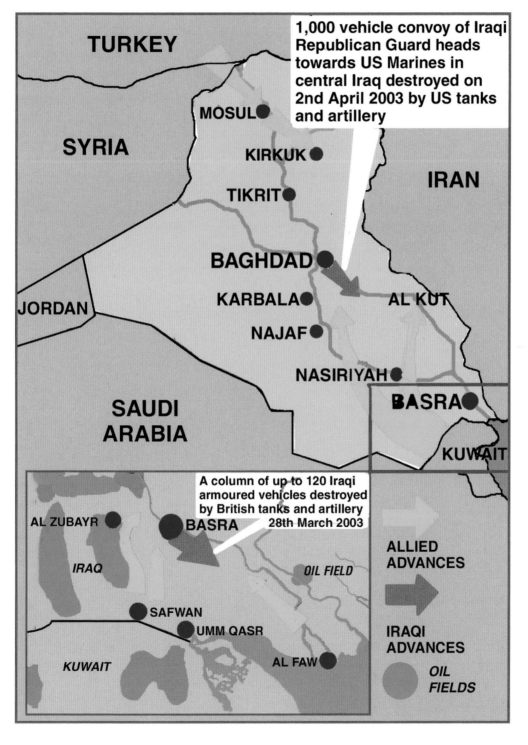

1,000 vehicle convoy of Iraqi Republican Guard heads towards US Marines in central Iraq destroyed on 2nd April 2003 by US tanks and artillery

A column of up to 120 Iraqi armoured vehicles destroyed by British tanks and artillery 28th March 2003

ALLIED ADVANCES

IRAQI ADVANCES

OIL FIELDS

Some of the last battles of Operation Iraqi Freedom were fought around the 14th April 2003 when the Allies launched an assault on Tikrit, the home town of Saddam Hussein. A task force of several thousand marines from the US 1st Marine Expeditionary Force and troops of the British SAS, moved north from Baghdad under the command of Brigadier John Kelly. Its 300 armoured vehicles moved quickly across the plains and destroyed a column of Iraqi armoured vehicles. Iraqi armour stood little chance against superior Abrams and Challenger tanks and Allied self-propelled artillery.

The AS90 Self-propelled gun made its battle debut in Operation Desert Storm. Those of the British 3rd Royal Horse Artillery fired the first shots of 'Operation Iraqi Freedom' as the second Gulf War became to be known.

of very close urban combat." He continued: "We've taken out his defenses, all his prepared organised defenses are destroyed, we have destroyed probably in excess of 1,000 dismounted infantry."

In Najaf, west of Baghdad, US Forces fought a fierce battle for control of a key bridge over the Euphrates River. The infantry was supported in this action by Abrams MBTs and Bradley IFVs. Over 1,000 Iraqi soldiers were killed with about 30 US troops wounded. There were reports of some Abrams MBTs and Bradley IFVs being hit.

By April 6th the US 3rd Infantry Division, with about 25 Abrams MBTs supported by Bradley IFVs had advanced northward into the city of Baghdad and, on reaching the Tigris, swung southwest to the already captured international airport, while, at the same time, at least 30 Abrams MBTs, again supported by Bradley IFVs, moved up the Hilla Road highway into the city from the south in a demonstration of force dubbed 'Operation Thunder Run'. They destroyed countless Iraqi fighting vehicles, mostly

T-55s and T-72s.

US forces rolled into Baghdad during the 13th and 14th of April 2003 and then launched what became the last battle of the war. This took place when an allied assault against Saddam Hussein's home town of Tikrit was launched called 'Taskforce Tripoli'. This force consisted of several thousand US Marines from US 1st Marine Expeditionary Force moving north from Baghdad. The Tikrit Task Force, under the command of Brigadier General John Kelly, included 300 armoured vehicles which moved swiftly across the plains north of Baghdad. These forces destroyed an Iraqi tank column moving outside the town together with an Iraqi force which had attacked the Marines' armoured vehicles.

Meanwhile the British 7th Armoured Brigade had pushed through the outskirts of Basra from the southwest with the 1st Armoured Division launching a second attack, with 3 Commando Brigade, from the southeast seizing control of this important town.

Major John Biggart, leader of C

Squadron, Royal Scots Dragoon Guards, part of the 7th Armoured Division, described how his men drove their Challenger 2 tanks across treacherous marshland to mount a surprise dawn raid on an Iraqi armoured column just outside Basra: "We assaulted them from an unexpected direction. There are only a few routes across the marshland and the men were nervous as we drove across, because the only way over was along a very narrow track. The danger of coming off the track and going into the marshes was considerable and we would have been in a lot of trouble if that had happened. We were coming under fire so that made it even more difficult". The action resulted in the destruction of 14 T-55 MBTs and four MTLV APCs, together with four troop bunkers destroyed, without a single British casualty.

Troubles continue

When the war was declared over the fighting did not stop. Insurgents from the remains of the Iraqi Baath Party, the previous ruling party of Iraq under Saddam Hussein, and terrorists from Al Qaida, an international Muslim terrorist group, began to ambush and bomb coalition forces, especially those of America, around the cities of Baghdad, Tikrit (Hussein's birthplace), Fallujah and other towns and cities in the north of the country. British troops were likewise attacked to a lesser degree around Basra which they had taken quickly during the war.

At the time of writing, this situation continues although, in June 2004, Iraq regained its sovereignty and there is hope that the country will begin to settle down now into relative peace. During this period tanks and other armoured vehicles of the coalition forces continued to help, in a peacekeeping role, but not always with complete success. The insurgents used suicide bombers and other covert systems to attack troops trained in open warfare and not trained to cope with the type of terrorism that was inflicted upon them.

The hull and turret of the M1A2 Abrams MBT is of advanced armor construction similar to the Chobham armour developed in the UK and gives protection against ATGWs and other battlefield weapons. It is composed of steel-encased depleted uranium with two and a half times the density of steel. This depleted uranium is sealed within the tank and has a very low level of natural radio-activity.

CHAPTER TEN

Leclerc, Leopard 2, Challenger and Abrams

G iat Industries of France manufacture the Leclerc MBT. The turret is manufactured at a factory in Tarbes while the hull is manufactured at Roanne. The Leopard 2 is produced by Krauss-Maffei-Wegmann. Krauss-Maffei AG with headquarters in Munich-Allach produced the Leopard 1 and Leopard 2. The firm Wegmann & Co specialised in the development and construction of turret systems for the Leopards 1 and 2 as well as complete artillery systems. In 1999 Krauss-Maffei and Wegmann merged to form Krauss-Maffei-Wegmann (KMW), in Munich and Kassel in Germany. Vickers Defence Systems produce the Challenger series in Newcastle-upon-Tyne in the UK and has been at the forefront of British tank design for many years. In 1971 two companies were awarded contracts to produce a new battle tank for the USA, in 1976 The Defense Division of the Chrysler Corporation won the contract to build the Abrams series. In 1982 Chrysler Defense Incorporated, its tank-building subsidiary, was sold to General Dynamics which is now known as General Dynamics Land Systems.

The Panzer 87 (Pz 87) is the Swiss designation for the Leopard 2 MBT manufactured under licence from Krauss-Maffei in Germany (known as Krauss−Maffei−Wegmann since 1999). The Swiss Army trialled American M1s and Leopard 2s head to head and came to a similar conclusion to the Swedish. The first Pz 87s were delivered by Contraves, the main contractors for the Swiss build, in 1987. The Pz 87s are primarily the same as the German Leopard 2 but they include AN/VCR 12 radio sets, Swiss antennas and machine guns.

160

MODERN TANK TECHNOLOGIES: FIREPOWER

The 1980s witnessed the universal adoption of guns with a calibre of 120mm or more as the most effective weapons for overcoming the latest armour. Thus the whirligig of the gun/armour race spun fighting vehicles in the direction of weightier armament – a trend which militated against men or vehicles whose necessarily lighter anti-tank weapons were automatically outclassed, forcing them to adopt clumsier means of protection for themselves as the only alternative to depending mainly on the tank as the dominant anti-tank weapon system. This situation lasted well into the 1990s.

Gun ammunition technology

The latest guns, introduced from that time are truly formidable, and not simply because of their big calibre and muzzle velocities of about 4,800fps, but for their ability to fire 'conventional' AP Discarding Sabot rounds, such as was fired, firstly, from the British 120mm gun in the Chieftain. To the category of high velocity, Kinetic Energy (KE) ammunition was added the Soviet-developed Armour Piercing Fin Stabilised Discarding Sabot (APSFDS) – an unspun projectile fired from smooth bored guns, such as the 125mm in the T-72 series. It has a velocity in excess of 5000fps. This sort of shot, long sought after, is in the shape of a dart with a high length-to-diameter ratio, stabilised by fins. Penetration is achieved when the long, thin, solid projectile is consumed, as it blasts a way through armour in a molten state, giving a performance in excess of that of the ordinary DS shot. Challengers 1 and 2, and Leopard 2 tanks are armed with 120mm guns firing these projectiles, as were the later versions of the Abrams when it appeared in service with a German 120mm smooth bore gun in about 1986. Before this the Americans used a 105mm gun of British design in the Abrams, firing improved ammunition, including APFSDS.

Those seeking to penetrate armour by more sophisticated means have been compelled to go away from the Chemical Energy (CE) type of ammunition in the direction of KE ammunition. They have done so because the latest arrangements of spaced, composite armour are less vulnerable to CE attack and because KE rounds are the most accurate in flight, giving, in their latest versions and means of aiming, a high chance of a hit and penetration at ranges of 2,000 metres – which is about the optimum range of engagement in all but desert tactical situations.

The Vickers Defence Systems Challenger 2 MBT is shown here firing its 120mm L30 gun on the ranges at Lulworth Cove in southern England. This model is fitted with peacetime training skirts.

MODERN TANK TECHNOLOGIES: POWERPLANTS

Also involved in the adoption of each new item of improved equipment is the matter of reliability. In no field has this been more susceptible to criticism and complaint than that of automotive and cross-country capability and performance. The demand for new power plants that have more than twice the output of those of 1945 has, inevitably, stretched engineering ingenuity to the extreme. The desire to move at higher speeds across country has brought about the development of hydro-pneumatic suspensions. Each new system contributes almost as many fresh problems as it has solved. Nearly always the introduction of more powerful equipment has been matched by difficulty in its accommodation in the limited space available. The doubling of power plant output, for example, called for bulkier cooling systems, all of which had to be fitted-in under armour. Suspension units of greater strength took up extra space which might otherwise have been allocated to the engine or the fighting compartment – and so on.

An important advance in power plants was the adoption of the gas turbine engine. The Textron Lycoming AGT 1500 multi-fuel gas turbine developing 1500hp, as fitted in the Abrams tank, is a fine example of the art of attempting to make something bigger and more powerful fit into a relatively small space and keep going longer than its predecessors; it runs on a wide range of fuels, including petrol, diesel and paraffin, and it has the advantage of a very low cooling requirement and the claimed ability to run for 19,300km without needing an overhaul.

It is in competition with the conventional Perkins Condor CV-12 TCA liquid-cooled diesel engine, installed in the Challenger, which develops 1,200hp and the MTU MB 837ka-501 V-12 multi-fuelled turbocharged diesel, developing 1500hp, in the Leopard 2 tank – an engine which is thought to be capable of uprating to 2000hp for further development of this marque.

The Spanish Leopard 2A5 is known as the 2A5E and in 1999 it was announced that it will be armed with the new Rheinmetall DeTec 120 mm L/55 calibre smoothbore gun. This gun barrel is 1.3 metres longer than the L/44 which it replaces, resulting in a much higher muzzle velocity, thereby increasing armour penetration capability. A Bazan MTU V–12 diesel engine is fitted as standard and the Spanish Indra EWS company has been awarded a contract to supply 219 fire control systems. 200 Leopard 2A5Es will be built at 40 per year and it is intended that 85% of the platform content will be Spanish.

MODERN TANK TECHNOLOGIES: TARGET ACQUISITION

The design of target acquisition and fire control systems lies at the root of accurate shooting. Advances in the type and nature of these have been considerable and on a broad front since the 1950s. The invention of the laser and its adaptation to range finding, in the 1960s, when allied to improved optical devices, sensors and ballistic computers, made possible fire control systems which enable the commander and gunner to obtain and feed in all the essential target, ammunition and ballistic data. All of this can be achieved prior to engaging the target with a high chance of a first round hit, and without ranging by fire and observation. Most improved tanks of the developed nations now have fire-control equipment of this type fitted, to the exclusion of old fashioned range-finders and ranging guns.

Night vision systems

In line with progress with fire control systems has come a proliferation of night vision equipment. Designed to acquire targets in the reconnaissance role, and to enable their engagement, they can be used even on the darkest night. No longer is there a total dependence upon active illuminating star-shells, white or infra-red searchlights, with all their inadequacies. The emphasis is firmly on 'passive' devices, such as electronic image intensifiers, thermal imagers which react to heat radiation from the target and present a photographic image on a screen, and Low Light Television cameras which preclude detection. Low Light Television not only provides the vehicle commander and gunner with a picture of the target at night, but also provides a source of radio or cable transmissions of the target to remote command posts. This information can then be used by senior commanders and staff at the front. A further advantage of the TV display lies in its ease of usage compared with the prohibitive strain imposed on anybody staring into an Image Intensifier device any longer than 30 minutes without rest.

Other considerations

Training and handling times and the expense of fitting these many varied pieces of auxiliary equipment get no less as the years go by. As previously pointed out, careful consideration of the tactical, technical and economic desirability associated with each device, or combination of devices, has to be made prior to adoption. To idealists and designers it is axiomatic that every aid is essential. But, strict limitations are imposed upon the average tank manufacturer purchasing the right instruments to do the best job on the battlefield.

The Leopard 2A6 EX is a Leopard 2A6 with the 120mm/L55 barrel and a number of additional improvements which includes an auxiliary power unit.

A total of 250 Leopard 1A5s was built, of which 150 have been transferred to Turkey as military aid after modification to the new build Leopard 1T1 (1A3) standard already in service with the Turkish Army.

The requirement for the Leopard 2 MBT grew out of the defunct American-German MBT-70 programme which took place in the late sixties. Krauss Maffei were contracted in the early seventies to build a series of prototypes armed with both 105mm and 120mm smoothbore tank guns. In 1977 the version fitted with a 120mm gun and an advanced torsion bar suspension was selected for production as the Leopard 2. Subsequently a series of variants have been built.

At the time of writing the German army is upgrading 225 2A5 tanks to the 2A6 configuration. The Royal Netherlands Army has ordered 180 upgrades and 219 are to be built, under licence, in Spain by General Dynamics, Santa Barbara Sistemas.

A new 120mm L55 smoothbore gun will replace the shorter 120mm L44 gun used on earlier Leopard marques. This results in a greater proportion of the available energy in the barrel being converted to projectile energy which increases the range and target

The Leopard 2A6 is believed by many commanders to be one of the best tanks in the world. Based on the highly successful Leopard 2A5, this tank, developed by Krauss–Maffei–Wegmann of Munich, commenced delivery in March 2001.

The GIAT Industries Leclerc is France's third generation MBT replacement for the current AMX-30/AMX-30 B2 fleet. Apart from having the usual tank design characteristics of firepower, mobility and protection the Leclerc is introducing a fourth dimension to French tank construction - that of a real-time combat capability using a digital multiplex data bus to integrate the on-board electronic systems so as to allow automatic reconfiguration of the various pieces of equipment such as the fire control computer, gun-laying computer etc to overcome complete battlefield failure or damage.

penetration. The L55 gun is compatible with modern 120mm ammunition and advanced high penetration rounds. The Leopard fitted with this gun is known as the 2A6EX. Using the new LKE2 DM53 kinetic energy round, the L55 gun can fire to a range of 5,000m. Additionally, the 2A6 has two 7.62mm machine-guns, one mounted coaxially, the other roof-mounted, and a 4-tube SAM launcher.

Leclerc MBT programme

The French GIAT Industries Leclerc has the latest generation gunner, commander and driver's day/night sights incorporated in its design. The gunner's SAGEM HL-60 and commander SFIM HL-70 sights have integral passive thermal imaging and laser rangefinding capabilities with the former also having a built-in land navigation facility. These sights coupled with the digital data bus and computer fire control allows up to five targets per minute to be engaged compared to the three of current generation automatic computer fire control equipped tanks. First round hit probability of a target at 2000 metres range with the Leclerc firing from the stationary position is over 80% whilst with it moving the same value is achieved at 1500 metres.

The armour used in the hull and turret of the Leclerc is of modular special armour ceramic composite and multi-

Continued on page 170

Krauss-Maffei-Wegmann Leopard 2 MBT

Cutaway key

1   120mm smooth bore gun
2   Muzzle reference system
3   Driver's headlamps
4   Wing mirror folded down
5   Front of turret is of arrowhead design for improved protection
6   Frontal arc of turret and hull front is of advanced armour which provides a very high level of protection against anti-tank projectiles
7   Gunner's stabilised day/ night sighting system
8   Commander's periscope
9   Commander's hatch
10 Commander's stabilised sighting system
11 Radio antenna
12 Ready use 120mm ammunition stowed in turret bustle
13 High performance power pack consisting of 1,500hp diesel coupled to fully automatic transmission
14 Exhaust outlet

15 Driver's reclining seat
16 Co-axial 7.62mm machine gun
17 Reserve ammunition stowed to left of driver
18 Loader's periscope
19 Loader's 7.62mm machine gun
20 Banks of 76mm electrically operated smoke grenade launchers
21 Frontal armoured side skirts
22 Dual rubber tyred road wheels
23 Torsion bar suspension
24 Double pin track
25 Drive sprocket

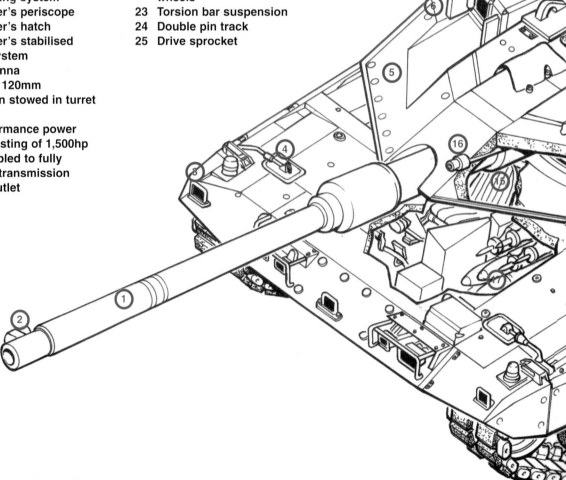

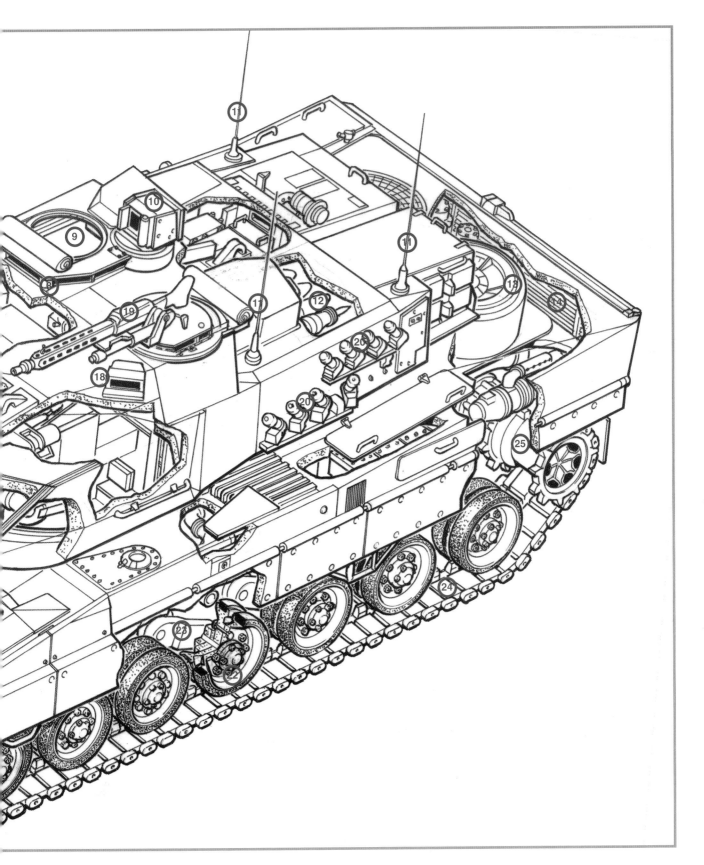

Giat Industries Leclerc MBT

Cutaway key

1   120mm smooth bore gun
2   12.7mm co-axial machine-
    gun
3   Frontal arc of Leclerc
    includes an advanced
    armour package for a high
    level of protection
4   Internal stowage box
5   Rear part of muzzle
    reference system
6   Gunner's day/thermal sight
7   120mm gun mantlet
8   Gunner's day periscopes
9   Gunner's roof hatch
10 Commander's independent
    stabilised sight
11 Blow out panels in turret
    roof
12 Met sensor
13 Bustle mounted automatic
    loader with ready use
    ammunition
14 120mm APFSDS-T
    ammunition
15 Powerpack consists of
    1500hp diesel coupled to
    automatic transmission

23 Driver's periscopes
24 Driver's seat
25 Headlamps and indicators
26 Driver's steering controls
27 Revolver magazine holding
    reserve 120mm ammunition
28 Thermal sleeve with
    integrated fume extractor
29 Muzzle reference system

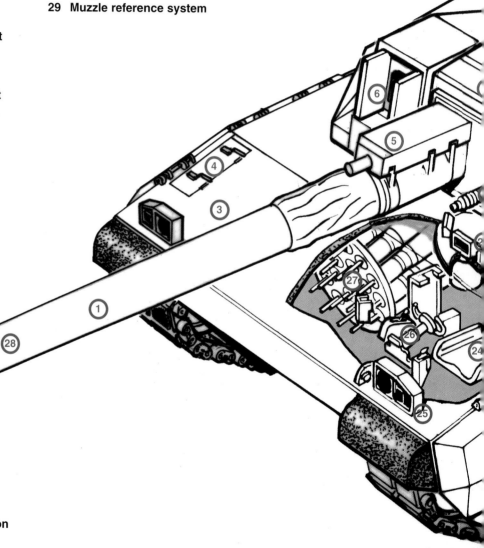

16 Rear drive sprocket
17 Dual rubber tyred road
    wheel
18 Dual rubber pin track
19 Hydropneumatic suspension
20 Track return rollers
21 Front armoured side skirts
22 Commander's seat

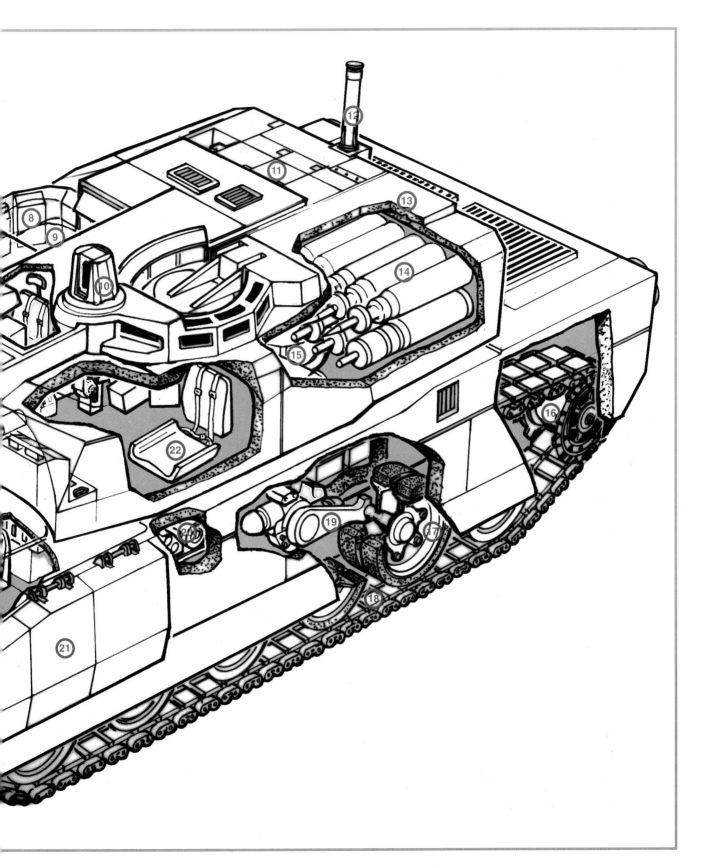

This French Army Leclerc is deployed to Qatar for training. The main armament of the electric power operated turret is the GIAT Industries 120mm smoothbore L52 tank gun with a Muzzle Reference System and a 22-round automatic loader system so as to reduce the turret crew number to two.

layer steel types which provide a significant degree of frontal arc protection against KE as well as the more conventional anti-tank round types. The modularity allows for rapid package upgrading to meet new threats as they develop. Additional roof and belly armour protection is also provided against attack from those directions.

The main armament of the Leclerc's electric power operated turret is the GIAT Industries 120mm smoothbore L52 tank gun with a Muzzle Reference System and a 22-round automatic loader system so as to reduce the turret crew number to two. The maximum effective rate of fire is 12rpm. The ammunition carried is of the APFSDS (with both tungsten and depleted uranium projectiles) and HEAT types with semi-combustible cartridges.

Challenger 2 MBT

Development of the Challenger 2 started as a privately funded venture in 1986. 'Proof of principle' testing for the UK Ministry of Defence (MoD) lasted until September 1990. The initial contract for 127 Challenger 2 MBTs plus 13 Challenger 2 Driver Training tanks was placed in June 1991. In the Spring of 1999

the UK MoD announced that "*Challenger 2 had exceeded the most rigorous reliability targets ever set anywhere, during a demanding series of trials under battlefield conditions*".

Although Challenger 2 is one of the heaviest tanks in the world mobility and crew safety are not sacrificed. It is one of the best protected and together with the superb 120mm L30A1 rifled gun and excellent crew training makes the Challenger 2 a truly formidable fighting force.

The hull and powerpack are similar to that used in Challenger 1 but the hydro-pneumatic suspension, transmission, and running gear are to a higher standard than the Challenger Improvement Programme (CHIP) requirements. The major change is the use of a completely redesigned turret, made with second-generation Chobham laminated special armour and fitted with the high pressure 120mm L30 CHARM 1 rifled gun system firing APFSDS-T (the depleted uranium CHARM 3 Kinetic Energy projectile type for use against both special passive and ERA armour), HESH and smoke rounds. The gun features a chromium lining to provide a harder and smoother surface, which in turn,

Challenger 2 is fitted with a state-of-the-art fire-control system based on the CDC Mission Management Computer System. There is also a joint SAGEM/Vickers Defence Systems SAMS stabilised gunner's sight system. A separate Pilkington Optronics thermal imaging TOGS surveillance sighting system is mounted in a protected box over the main gun. There is built-in capacity for future fitting of the Battlefield Information Control System (BICS).

provides increased round velocity, accuracy and target penetration. It comes complete with a thermal sleeve, fume extractor and muzzle reference system which all boost the first round kill probability. The 120mm L30A1 rifled gun is supported by a Boeing 7.62mm chain gun, located to the left of the main turret, which is now manufactured under licence by Royal Ordnance (BAE Systems). There is also a 7.62mm L37A2 General Purpose Machine Gun mounted on the cupola.

Advanced fire control
Challenger 2 is fitted with a state-of-the-art fire-control system based on the Computing Devices Company (CDC) Mission Management Computer System. At the time of installation this digital system was an improved version of the computer fitted to the M1A1 Abrams MBT. There is also a stabilised gunner's sight system. This features an integral carbon dioxide laser rangefinder and a commander gyro-stabilised day-sight assembly with integral laser rangefinder. A separate Pilkington Optronics thermal imaging (TOGS) surveillance sighting system is mounted in a protected box over the main gun for displays, on individual monitors distinct from their sights, to the gunner and commander positions. There is capacity for future fitting of the

Vickers Defence Systems Challenger 2 MBT

Cutaway key

1 Muzzle reference system
2 120mm L30A1 rifled tank gun
3 Thermal sleeve for L30 rifled tank gun
4 Fume extractor
5 Smoke grenade launchers
6 Thermal Observation and Gunnery Sight
7 7.62mm co-axial machine gun
8 Gunner's stabilised day/thermal sight with laser rangefinder
9 Hull and turret incorporate latest Dorchester advanced armour system
10 Commander's stabilised panoramic sight

16 Long range fuel tanks
17 Stowage box
18 Headlamps
19 Driver's day periscope
20 Gunner's seat
21 Loader's periscope
22 Commander's seat
23 Loader's hatch
24 Exhaust outlet for 1,200hp Perkins diesel engine
25 Driver's reclining seat
26 Driver's steering tillers
27 All 120mm charges are stowed below turret ring
28 Diesel fuel tanks in side of hull
29 Stowed towing cables

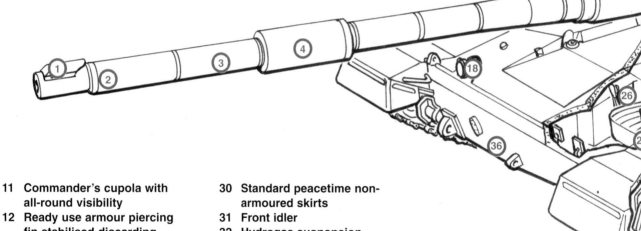

11 Commander's cupola with all-round visibility
12 Ready use armour piercing fin stabilised discarding sabot projectiles in turret bustle
13 NBC and environmental control system in turret bustle
14 Radio antennas
15 Powerpack consisting of Perkins 1,200hp diesel coupled to David Brown TN54 transmission

30 Standard peacetime non-armoured skirts
31 Front idler
32 Hydrogas suspension system
33 Rubber-tyred road wheels
34 Double-pin track with rubber pads
35 Drive sprocket
36 Well sloped glacis plate

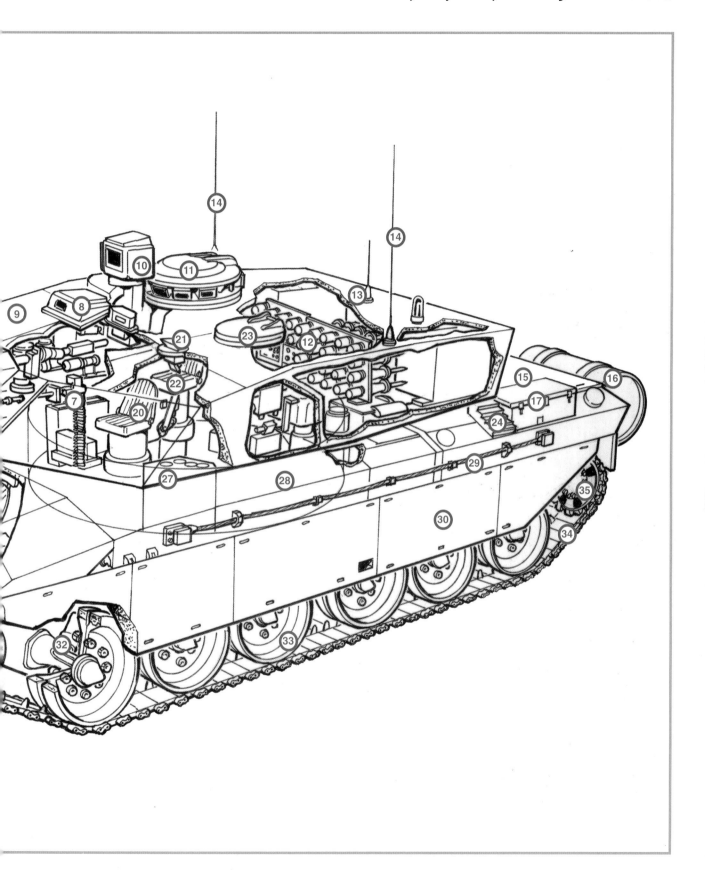

The sole export customer of the Challenger is the Omani Defence Force. Its tanks have a number of modifications to suit Middle East conditions, especially one to maintain full engine power of 1,200hp in temperatures of up to +52ºC. Other changes include replacing the loader's 7.62mm machine gun with a pintle mounted 12.7mm M2 machine gun.

Battlefield Information Control System (BICS). The roof-mounted SIFM stabilised sight gives the commander a full 360º vision capability with magnification and includes a range finder.

Crew safety is one of the key design parameters of Challenger 2 with the second generation Chobham armour giving significantly increased protection against KE and CE attack. A filtered over-pressure system provides NBC protection with all the electronic systems protected against electromagnetic pulses likely to be generated in a nuclear detonation.

Challenger 2 is powered by a Perkins 26.1 litre V-12 diesel engine which develops 1,200hp at 2,300rpm giving a power to weight ratio of 19.2hp/tonne. This drives a David Brown TN54 epicyclic transmission unit with hydrostatically transmitted power which provides infinitely variable output.

British deployment
The British Army has equipped two regiments with the Challenger 2. The first was fielded in 1995 and comprises a Regimental HQ (with two MBTs) and three squadrons (each of four three-vehicle troops). The Regimental total of 38 Challenger 2s is a significant reduction when compared to current regimental totals of 43 or 57 MBTs.

Part of the first Challenger 2 order was

for the only support tank variant to date, a Driver Training tank model. In 1994, a second contract for 259 Challenger 2 MBTs and nine Driver Training tanks was placed. The aim is to equip all British Army tank regiments with Challenger 2. The remaining Challenger 1s will be converted to other uses.

Challenger 2E upgrade

Challenger 2E is a derivative developed for the export market and is known as Desert Challenger. Modifications include the Perkins power unit being replaced by the German MTU EuroPowerPack, comprising the MTU 883V-12 diesel engine, developing 1,500hp, which drives a transversely mounted Renk HSWL 295 TM automatic transmission unit. This power unit is currently installed in the French Leclerc and some US M1A2 Abrams platforms. To complete the unit a new cooling and air filtration system is fitted. This unit gives Challenger 2E a maximum road speed of 65km/h and a road range of 550 kilometres.

Other improvements include an enhanced commander's interface which comprises a roof-mounted stabilised panoramic sight with day and second generation thermal imaging channels, a control and display channel with high level command and control facilities. Design changes in the driver's area include a compact steering wheel to replace the tillers and the fitting of a third-generation image intensifying viewer as a control and display panel. An optional 12.7mm machine gun can be fitted to provide an under-armour firing capability.

Export order

In early 1993 Oman placed an order for Challenger 2s to replace its existing Chieftain fleet. The initial order is for 18 Challenger 2s, two Driver Training tanks and four support Challenger 1 ARRVs. The Omani Challenger 2 is a modification which enables it to retain its operating efficiency in Middle Eastern climates and conditions. The main upgrade is to the cooling system. New, larger, radiators and fans have been installed and new air intake louvres have been introduced to generally cool the vehicle and reduce its thermal signature. With these modifications full engine power can be retained in temperatures in excess of

Unloading the Challenger 2E which has been developed by Vickers Defence Systems for the export market. It was originally called Desert Challenger and has been demonstrated in the Middle East. It uses the same engine, the German MTU EuroPowerPack, as that installed in the French Leclerc MBT.

The basic M1 Abrams was developed in the seventies by General Dynamics, Land Systems Division, as the follow-on to the M60 MBT series, with considerably improved protection, firepower, mobility and maintenance aspects. The major new feature, however, was the fitting of a multi-fuel gas turbine engine.

50°C. Other modifications include the replacement of the loader's 7.62mm machine gun with a pintle-mounted 12.7mm M2 machine gun and the tracks replaced by the single pin type. An improved communications fit, higher specification air conditioning system and provision for a Magellan GPS, complete the internal modifications.

US Abrams series MBTs

The General Dynamics, Land Systems Division, M1A1 Abrams is the successor to the M1/Improved M1 MBT models. Although it uses the same basic design of the Improved M1 it has a 120mm M256 Rheinmetall smoothbore gun; collective NBC system; improved digital computer fire-control system with a state-of-the-art stabilised gunner's day/night sight assembly; integral laser rangefinding and thermal imaging capabilities, together with improved transmission and suspension systems. The gun fires APFSDS-T (depleted uranium type) and HEAT-MP-T ammunition.

In late 1989 the US Army adopted the M1A1 Heavy Armour (M1A1(HA)) version for deployment in Europe. This has additional steel encased depleted uranium armour mesh added to the M1 standard advanced Chobham type armour configuration. In late 1990 the M1A1 (Common Tank) version entered production with 67 engineering changes that made the vehicle suitable for use by

The first production model of the General Dynamics Land Systems M1A1 Abrams MBT was completed in August 1985. When production of this model ended in 1993 a total of of 4,796 vehicles had been built at the Lima, Ohio and Detroit, Michigan, Tank Plants in the USA.

An M1A1 Main Battle Tank manœuvres on the battlefield in Umm Qasr, Iraq on March 23, 2003 in support of Operation Iraqi Freedom.

the US Marine Corps. A total of 221 were built for the US Marine Corps between 1990-92.

The follow-on M1A2 (or M1 Block II) entered US Army field trial testing in mid-1992. This has further special passive armour hull and turret improvements to defeat kinetic and chemical energy rounds; added roof protection to reduce the threat from fielded top-attack ATGW and anti-tank bomblets, it has also a complete digital Intervehicular Information System (IVIS) to replace the current wiring; independent Commander and Driver thermal viewing systems (the CITV and DTV systems). There is a POS/NAV land navigation system; an updated digital fire-control system with new ballistic computer and the capability to carry and fire a new generation of advanced 120mm 'smart' ammunition types that are currently being developed to deal with various battlefield targets.

In 1988 Egypt ordered 524 M1A1 with the majority being built under licence from kit form. In addition Saudi Arabia ordered 315 M1A2 with deliveries completed in 1994. Kuwait also chose the

22 March 2003: M1A2s of US Marine Corps, 1st Tank Battalion sit in an assembly area near Az Zubayr, Iraq in support of Operation Iraqi Freedom.

General Dynamics Land Systems Abrams M1A2 MBT

Cutaway key

1 M256 120mm smooth bore gun
2 Muzzle reference system
3 Thermal sleeve of gun
4 Fume extractor
5 Frontal arc of hull and turret includes advanced armour for a high level of protection
6 Gun mantlet
7 Gunner's day/thermal sighting system
8 Commander's remote controlled 12.7mm machine gun
9 Commander's cupola with day periscope
10 Commander's hatch
11 Loader's hatch with integral periscope
12 Met sensor

20 Dual rubber tyred road wheels
21 Torsion bar suspension
22 120mm ammunition stowed below turret
23 Loader's seat
24 Double pin track with rubber pads
25 Rear drive sprockets
26 Access doors
27 Retainer ring

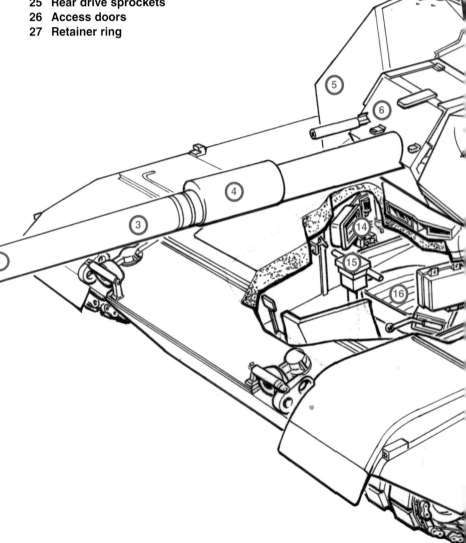

13 Ready use 120mm ammunition stowed in turret bustle with blow out panels in roof
14 Driver's instrument panel
15 Driver's steering yoke
16 Driver's reclining seat
17 Breech of 120mm gun
18 Powerpack consisting of 1,500hp gas turbine coupled to automatic transmission
19 Armoured side skirts

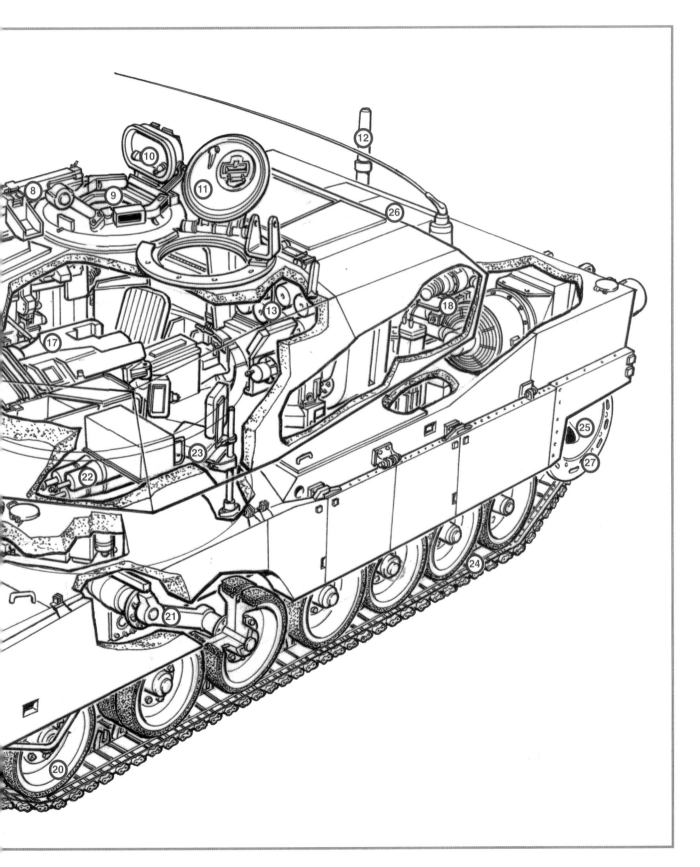

M1A2 as its next MBT, ordering 218 in October 1992 with deliveries made between 1994 and 1996.

In 1994 General Dynamics was awarded a design study of the M1A2 System Enhancement Package (SEP); this is aimed at being introduced into the current US Army M1A2 upgrade programme and as a retro-fit kit for those M1A2s already introduced. The result will be an M1A2 suitable for the digital battlefield. The essence of the M1A2 System Enhancement Program (SEP) is to enhance the tank's digital command and control facilities to push its evasive and destructive powers to the limit through the efficient use of digital technology. Key to the SEP upgrade is the introduction of an open operating system that will facilitate more modular growth to keep the M1A2 at the forefront of tactical technology.

Second generation forward looking infrared (FLIR) sighting systems will replace the current thermal imaging system and commander independent thermal viewer. The introduction of this advanced FLIR will provide the gunner and commander with radically improved target acquisition and engagement capability in both day and night-time scenarios. Target acquisition is improved by around 70% and firing accuracy improvement in the order of 45%. Furthermore, an increased range of 30% is envisaged. This will provide a range advantage over most targets which will boost the M1A2's lethality yet provide a safety margin for its crew.

The digital command and control system places identifying markers on coloured flat screens which enables crews to see where they are on the battlefield, the position of the enemy and the rest of the squadron. The use of common graphics and digitally encoded e-mail facilities allow tactical information to be disseminated throughout the squadron to enable the battalion commander to effect a swift efficient kill.

Key to the success of the M1A1 and

M1A2 MBTs has been the AGT 1500 power unit. A two-phase engine development programme is underway to provide this 'queen of the digital battlefield' with an engine befitting its status. An additional project is assessing the feasibility of developing an under-armour auxiliary power unit. This unit will allow mounted surveillance to take place without the main engine running and without flattening the tank's batteries.

The object of the SEP initiative is to improve lethality, survivability, mobility, sustainability and provide increased situational awareness and command and control enhancements necessary to provide information superiority on the battlefield.

In September 1994 the US awarded a contract to General Dynamics Land Systems worth US$5 million to conduct preliminary design of the M1A2 System Enhancement Package (SEP). The requirements for this programme were established at the System Requirements Review/Functional Design Review in February 1995 and include 15 modifications into the M1 to M1A1 upgrade production and to all previously produced M1A2 MBTs to a single M1A2 configuration.

The essence of the M1A2 System Enhancement Program (SEP) is to enhance the tank's digital command and control facilities to push its evasive and destructive powers to the limit through the efficient use of digital technology. Key to the SEP upgrade is the introduction of an open operating system that will facilitate more modular growth to keep the M1A2 at the forefront of tactical technology.

181

CHAPTER ELEVEN

Modern Fighting Vehicles

So what will be the future for the Main Battle Tank and other fighting vehicles? Following the end of East-West confrontation in the early 1990s it was hoped that the world would become a safer place and that funds could be directed away from armaments to areas of government such as health, education and the environment.

Unfortunately this has not been the case and, if anything, thanks to troubles in Iraq, Africa, the Middle East and other trouble spots, the world is far more unstable and requires an increasing number of peacekeeping operations.

Large numbers of troops and their equipment are tied up with these peacekeeping operations for long periods causing disruption to the various national armies involved. This often leads to the operations ending up being funded from the budgets of the various armies, leading to cutbacks in training and acquisition of new equipment.

Full-scale warfare and peacekeeping operations require different skills and equipment, that suited to mechanised warfare may not be suitable for extended peacekeeping operations, this applies especially to troop carriers. For instance, tracked vehicles are more suitable for mechanised warfare but suffer from a number of disadvantages in extended peacekeeping operations in that they are heavy and expensive to operate and to maintain; but, perhaps, more importantly they appear in the eyes of a civilian population to be offensive and threatening. Wheeled vehicles are less damaging to road surfaces, are easy to operate and maintain, can travel long distances in a short time and are less offensive to a civilian population.

This is the amphibious version of the Steyr–Daimler–Puch Pandur (6x6) Armoured Personnel Carrier, it is armed with a 12.7mm M2 HB machine gun. There are several variants and all have the amphibious function available. The Pandur APC is in service with the armies of Austria, Belgium, Kuwait, Slovenia and the USA.

Alvis Hägglunds Vehicle AB CV 9030 Infantry Fighting Vehicle has a 30mm The Boeing Company Chain Gun fitted as main armament coaxial with a 7.62 mm machine gun. It is now in service with the Norwegian Army and orders are expected from the Swiss Army.

However, development of tracked armoured personnel carriers continues with the Swiss Army selecting the CV 9030CH Infantry Fighting Vehicle (IFV) to meet its future requirements.

Israel is developing very heavy and well protected IFVs which can operate in conjunction with the new Merkava MBTs and Russia has developed IFVs based on T-55 and T-72 chassis.

Another vehicle from the Swedish manufacturer is the Bv 206S articulated armoured all-terrain personnel carrier which is now in service with France, Germany, Italy and Sweden. The larger Bvs 10 articulated all-terrain vehicle is now

in service with the UK's Royal Marines and replaces the older, unarmed, Bv 206 which has been in service for some years.

Experiments were made with an Advanced Composite Armoured Vehicle Platform (ACAVP) which was a joint development programme between the now defunct Defence Evaluation and Research Agency (DERA), Vickers Defence Systems (now Alvis Vickers) and Vosper Thornycroft. It consisted of a composite hull structure fitted with the running gear and power pack of the Warrior IFV. The turret of a Fox armoured car was fitted to simulate the weight of the turret. The experiment was to see if its composite hull

Prototypes of the Alvis Hägglunds BvS 10 APC are undergoing trials to meet requirements for the UK Royal Marines. According to the manufacturer the BvS 10 is a new generation all-terrain armoured vehicle. It is similar to the earlier Bv 206 S but with its two units having increased payload and a level of armour protection up to 7.62mm armour piercing.

The FMC M2 Bradley Infantry Fighting Vehicle is made of all-welded aluminium spaced laminate armour. It is said that the armour of the Bradley M2 can defeat 95 per cent of all types of ballistic attack encountered on the battlefield. Main armament consists of a McDonnell Douglas Helicopter Company M242 25mm Chain gun 'the Bushmaster'.

The standard version of the Dardo Infantry Fighting Vehicle, subsequently evaluated by the Italian Army under the designation VCC-80, had a two-person turret armed with a 25mm cannon and 7.62mm coaxial machine gun. There were also four specialised versions: anti-tank, 120mm mortar, command post and ambulance.

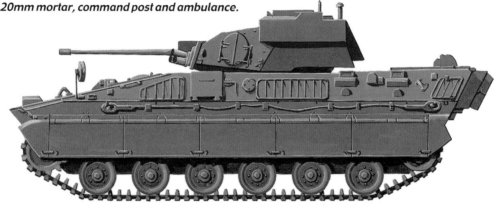

The Mitsubishi Type 89 Mechanised Infantry Combat Vehicle is produced for the Japanese Ground Self-Defence Force. The initial requirement was for 300 vehicles; but, by 1997, only 52 had been built. There are no known variants of this model although a modified version of its chassis may be used for a 155mm self-propelled artillery system.

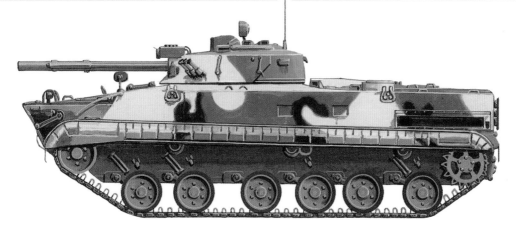

The Soviet BMP-3 Infantry Combat Vehicle made its first public appearance in 1990. The BMP-3 weapon system is known as the 2K23 and consists of a 100mm 2A70 gun, a 30mm 2A72 coaxial cannon and a 7.62mm PKT coaxial machine gun with an additional 2 x 381 smoke grenade dischargers.

The French AMX-10P mechanised infantry combat vehicle has a Giat Industries Dragar one-man turret armed with a Giat Industries 25mm Model 811 dual-feed cannon with coaxial 7.62mm machine gun. Production is complete and it is in service with the armies of France, Greece, Qatar, Saudi Arabia and the UAE, it was also in service with Iraq.

The Amphibious Assault Vehicle AAV7A1, was once called the LVTP7A1 by the US Marine Corps and other users. It is a bulky amphibious tracked vehicle intended to land troops on open beaches so it has to be seaworthy and is thus scaled accordingly. It was used by the US Marine Corps during Operation Desert Storm.

The Armoured Infantry Fighting Vehicle was developed by the FMC Corporation of America specifically for the export market, filling the gap between the basic M113 and the more expensive M2 Bradley. The Netherlands Army was the first to adopt the vehicle followed by the Armies of the Philippines and Belgium.

The M-60P Armoured Personnel Carrier was first seen during a parade held in Yugoslavia in 1965. The version shown is armed with a 12.7mm M2 HB machine-gun but the anti-tank variant, the M-60PB mounts two 82mm recoilless rifles.

First marketed in 1999 the Cadillac Gage LAV-300 Mk II Armoured Vehicle shown here is fitted with a Textron Marine & Land Systems two-person turret armed with a 90mm Cockerill Mk III gun and 7.62mm coaxial machine gun. It is now in service with the forces of Kuwait, Panama and the Philippines.

The Soviet MT–LB multi–purpose tracked vehicle was use for a wide range of roles such as artillery prime mover, command post, cargo carrier and armoured personnel carrier. It was fully amphibious and equipped with an NBC system.

The Alvis Stormer vehicle fitted with the Short Starstreak High–Velocity Missile System. The Stormer uses the technology of the Alvis Scorpion CVR(T) family, but the hull is wider and the original petrol engine has been replaced by a Cummins or Perkins turbocharged diesel engine.

The MaK Wiesel 2 Multi–Purpose Carrier is a further development of the Wiesel 1 Armoured Weapon Carrier, which is armed with a Raytheon Systems Company TOW ATGW system or a KUKA turret armed with a 20 mm Rheinmetall Mk 20 Rh 202 cannon.

The MOWAG Piranha (8x8) APC is manufactured in Switzerland by MOWAG Motorwagenfabrik AG and also, under licence, in the UK and Chile. It is the platform for many variants and is in service world wide. The model shown is the Piranha III APC which has been successfully trialed in Denmark.

was suited to armoured fighting vehicle design and was used for automotive trials only.

Development of wheeled armoured personnel carriers goes on at a pace with the Austrian Steyr-Daimler-Puch Pandur (6x6) vehicle being adopted by Austria itself, Belgium, Kuwait, Slovenia and, recently, because the manufacturer AV Technology is now owned by the US General Dynamics Land Systems, has been ordered by the United States.

Steyr-Daimler-Puch are also developing a new family of Pandur vehicles with an 8x8 configuration which will have a maximum weight of 19 tonnes and be fully air portable

in a C-130 Hercules transport aircraft. These vehicles are designed to be fitted with a wide range of weapons up to 105mm in calibre.

The Diesel Division, General Motors of Canada, having taken over MOWAG of Switzerland, continue to develop the 6x6 and 8x8 Piranha family of vehicles and is currently building the Piranha Generation III (8x8) for the Canadian Army.

The Multi-Role Armoured Vehicle (MRAV) (8x8), now called 'Boxer' is developed by Germany, the UK and the Netherlands but the UK have not, so far, placed a production order and the two other countries are considering their options.

Originally developed in the early 1980s the first firing trials were carried out in the late 1990s. The ASCOD 105 Light Tank is fitted with a General Dynamics Land Systems Low-Profile Turret armed with an externally mounted 105mm M68A1 rifled tank gun.

The 105mm Low Profile Target (LPT) Assault Gun is being developed by the Diesel Division, General Motors of Canada as a private venture to meet the possible operational requirements of the armies of Australia, Canada and the US. It consists of a standard LAV III chassis fitted with a General Dynamics Land Systems Low-Profile Turret (LPT). The vehicle will be air portable.

There is still some concern that the MRAV is too heavy and too large for some of the roles it is intended to undertake and for this reason MOWAG developed, as a private venture, the Piranha IV (8x8) with first examples completed in 2001.

Research is currently majoring on weight, stealth, armour, propulsion, integrated battle management systems and threat awareness but, although defensive mechanisms are constantly improving, these improvements are overshadowed by the development of offensive mechanisms such as Laser homing Anti-tank projectiles, and dual axis stabilised sights which improve first round kill rates.

To counter this, the British are working on a revolutionary idea where a force field is activated as the tank enters combat. This field has the power to vaporise anti-tank grenades and shells on impact. The potential is astounding. In field trials an APC protected by this system survived repeated attacks by RPGs, many from point blank range and was able to move away under its own power.

Prototype of the General Dynamics Land Systems Amphibious Assault Vehicle (AAAV) which is the replacement for the current United Defense LP AAV7A1 which has been in service with the US Marines since 1971. It is now under development and production is expected to commence in 2005.

Many believe that the days of the heavy MBT are now almost over due to advances in anti-armour weaponry, but MBTs have proved their worth in operations in the Balkans and Iraq and most countries plan to operate MBTs for the next decade at least. Some of the MBTs that have only recently been introduced into service have already additional enhancements being studied, especially in target acquisition and battlefield management.

The approach of the Israeli Defence Force is to fit the new Merkava Mk 4 with any one of a range of modular armours which rely heavily on the possession of ELINT (electronic intelligence) to be aware of the type of threat likely to be encountered. They will be rapidly deployed, as the missile approaches, to detonate it before it gets too close.

Krauss-Maffei-Wegmann of Germany are producing a wide range of fighting vehicles apart from their main battle tanks. The PzH 2000 Self-Propelled Howitzer is claimed as the World's Most Advanced Artillery System. It features a 60-round combat load and the newly developed 155mm L 52 main armament has a proven 30km effective range using standard NATO ammunition and 41km range with assisted

shells. A fully automatic shell loader permits a firing rate of 10 rounds per minute. By the end of 2002, 185 PzH 2000 artillery systems had been delivered to the German Army, with deliveries to Greece in May 2003, and contracts existing with the Netherlands and Italy giving rise to the KMW claim that this system is the new "Euro-Howitzer".

This company is also developing the FENNEK Reconnaissance Vehicle in collaboration with a Dutch partner for the German and Netherlands armies. It is a 4x4 vehicle which is armoured to defeat 7.62mm KE rounds as well as AT and AP mines. The FENNEK has a surveillance and reconnaissance unit fitted with a thermal imager, daylight camera and laser range finder which are integrated into a sensor head elevatable to 3.3m above the ground for observation. It can be armed with various automatic weapons from 7.62 calibre to .50 calibre machine gun and 40mm automatic grenade launcher.

Variants of the FENNEK include an artillery forward observer vehicle, a medium range anti-tank vehicle, a combat engineer vehicle and a general purpose vehicle.

The General Dynamics Land Systems M1A1/M1A2 Abrams is the last tank to be

The PzH 2000 Self-Propelled Howitzer is claimed as the world's most advanced artillery system. It is said to feature the performance characteristics required for the future as a result of its progressive technology.

procured by the United States Army. This will remain in front line service for at least 20 years but within ten years is expected to start to be replaced by elements of the very ambitious Future Combat Systems (FCS).

Lead systems integrator for the FCS is The Boeing Company and Science Applications International Corporation (SAIC) with General Dynamics Land Systems and United Defense being responsible for the chassis.

FCS will be a "system of systems" and include not only a family of ground combat vehicles, which could be tracked or wheeled, but also unmanned aerial vehicles and unmanned ground vehicles. All of these will be linked together and be able to share information in real time.

All of the ground elements of FCS must be air portable in a Lockheed Martin C-130 Hercules transport aircraft. The M1A1/M1A2 will be replaced by a direct fire platform while the M2 Bradley infantry fighting vehicle will be replaced by a new infantry vehicle.

In the UK, the Alvis Vickers Challenger 2 MBT will remain in service until at least 2025 when it will be replaced by a new system.

The UK is now working on the Future Rapid Effects (FRES) programme which

The FENNEK is a highly mobile reconnaissance vehicle weighing approximately 10 tons and capable of negotiating 60% grades and 35% side slopes. It has a three man crew consisting of the commander, observer and driver. It features a manually operated gun mount which is operated under armour.

aims to field a complete family of armoured vehicles and other weapons systems within ten years. All of these elements are also required to be fully air portable in a C-130 Hercules aircraft.

Main Battle Tanks have again proved their worth on the battlefields of Iraq and the Balkans, but the lighter Bradleys and Warriors showed their value too. So, what will the future be – MBTs or IFVs? Probably both, for a long time yet.

Currently under development by Krauss–Maffei–Wegmann the Puma is the future Infantry Fighting Vehicle for the German Army. It will be armed with a 30mm dual feed cannon with Air Bursting Munition (ABM) fitted in a remote controlled turret with fully digital fire control system. It will have mine protection against 10kg blast and EFP mines.

WORLD WAR I ARMOURED CARS

Austin-Putilov

Crew:	5
Weight:	5.30 tons
Powerplant:	one 50hp (37.32kW) Austin petrol engine
Dimensions:	length 4.88m; width 1.95m; height 2.40m
Performance:	max. speed 50km/h; range 200km

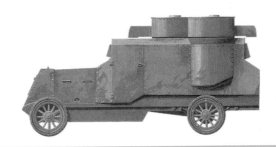

Rolls-Royce

Crew:	3 or 4
Weight:	3.50 tons
Powerplant:	one 40/50hp (30/37.3kW) Rolls-Royce petrol engine
Dimensions:	length 5.03m; width 1.91m; height 2.55m
Performance:	max. speed 95km/h; range 240km

Lanchester (Admiralty Turretted Pattern)

Crew:	3 or 4
Weight:	3.50 tons
Powerplant:	one 40/50hp (30/37.3kW) Rolls-Royce petrol engine
Dimensions:	length 5.03m; width 1.91m; height 2.55m
Performance:	max. speed 95km/h; range 240km

Autoblindo Mitragliatrice Lancia Ansaldo IZ

Crew:	6
Weight:	3.8 tons
Powerplant:	one 35/40hp (26/30kW) petrol engine
Dimensions:	length 5.40m; width 1.82m; height with single turret 2.40m
Performance:	max. speed 60km/h; range 300km

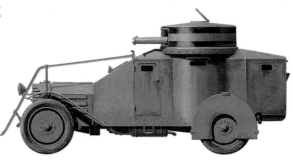

Peugeot Armoured Cars

Crew:	4 or 5
Weight:	5.0 tons
Powerplant:	one 40hp (30-kW) Peugeot petrol engine
Dimensions:	length 4.80m; width 1.80m; height 2.80m
Performance:	max. speed 40km/h; range 14 km

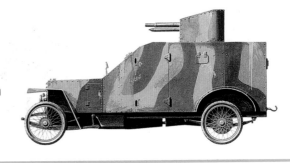

WORLD WAR I BRITISH AND GERMAN TANKS

Medium A or Whippet

Crew:	3 or 4
Weight:	14 tons
Powerplant:	two 45hp (33.6kW) four-cylinder petrol engines
Dimensions:	length 6.10m; width 2.62m; height 2.74m
Performance:	max. speed 13 km/h; range 257km

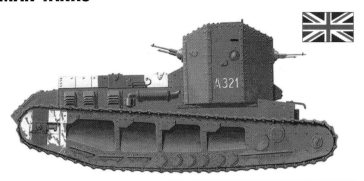

Tank Mk IV

Crew:	8
Weight:	28 tons
Powerplant:	one 105hp or 125hp (78.3 or 93.2kW) Daimler petrol engine
Dimensions:	length 8.05m; width over sponson 3.91m; height 2.49m
Performance:	max. speed 6 km/h; range 56 km

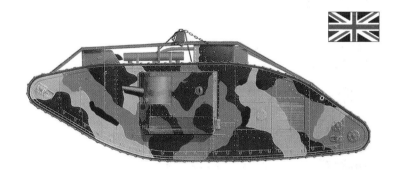

Tank Mk V (Male)

Crew:	8
Weight:	29 tons
Powerplant:	one 150hp (112kW) Ricardo petrol engine
Dimensions:	length 8.05m; width (over sponsons) 4.11m; height 2.64m
Performance:	max. speed 7 km/h; range 72 km

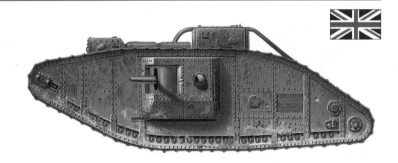

A7V Sturmpanzerwagen

Crew:	18
Weight:	33 tons
Powerplant:	two 100hp (74.6kW) Daimler petrol engines
Dimensions:	length 8.0m; width (over sponsons) 3.06m; height 3.30m
Performance:	max. speed 13 km/h; range 40km

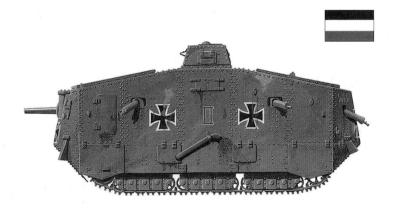

WORLD WAR I FRENCH TANKS

Schneider Char d'Assaut

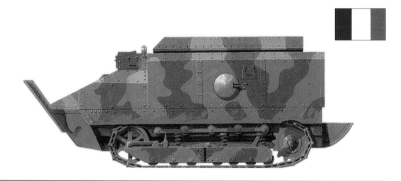

Crew: 7
Weight: 14.6 tons
Powerplant: one 55hp (41kW) Schneider four-cylinder petrol engine
Dimensions: length 6.00m; width 2.00m; height 2.39m
Performance: max. speed 6km/h; range 48km

St. Chamond Char d'Assaut

Crew: 2
Weight: 6.49 tons
Powerplant: one 35hp (26kW) Renault four-cylinder petrol engine
Dimensions: length with tail 5.00m; width 1.71m; height 2.34 m
Performance: max. speed 7.7 km/h; range 35 km

Renault FT-17

Crew: 2
Weight: 6,485 tonnes
Powerplant: one 35hp (26kW) Renault four-cylinder petrol engine
Dimensions: length with tail 5.00m; width 1.71m; height 2.133m
Performance: max. speed 7.7km/h; range 35.4km

M 280 sur Chenilles

Calibre: 280 mm
Length of barrel: 3.35m
Weight: 16000kg (in action, mortar only)
Elevation: + 10° to + 60°
Traverse: 20°
Muzzle velocity: 418m per second
Maximum range: 10,950m
Shell weight: 205kg

WORLD WAR II FRENCH TANKS

Char B-I-bis Heavy Tank

Crew: 4
Weight: 31.5 tonnes
Powerplant: one Renault 6-cylinder petrol engine developing 307hp (229kW)
Dimensions: length 6.37m; width 2.50m; height 2.79m
Performance: max. road speed 28km/h; range 180km

Renault R-35

Crew: 2
Weight: 10 tonnes
Powerplant: one Renault 4-cylinder petrol engine developing 82bhp (61kW)
Dimensions: length 4.20m; width 1.85m; height 2.37m
Performance: max. road speed 20km/h; range 140km

SOMUA S-35 Medium Tank

Crew: 3
Weight: 19.5 tons
Powerplant: one Somua V-850 petrol engine developing 190hp (142kW)
Dimensions: length 5.38m; width 2.12m; height 2.62m
Performance: max. road speed 40km/h; range 230km

Hotchkiss H-35 and H-39

Crew: 2
Weight: 12.1 tons
Powerplant: one Hotchkiss 6-cylinder petrol engine developing 120hp (89.5kW)
Dimensions: length 4.22m; width 1.95m; height 2.15m
Performance: max. road speed 36km/h; range 120km

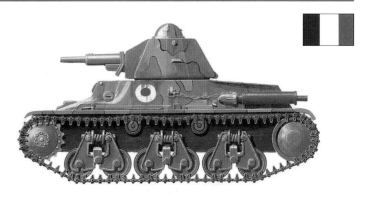

WORLD WAR II US TANKS

Light Tank M3A1 Stuart III and IV

Crew: 4
Weight: in action 12.927 tonnes
Powerplant: one Continental W-970-9A 7-cylinder radial petrol engine developing 250hp (186.5kW)
Dimensions: length 4.54m (14ft 10.75in); width 2.24m (7ft 4in); height 2.3m (7ft 6.5in)
Performance: max. road speed 58km/h (36mph); range 112.6km (70miles)

Medium Tank M3A2

Crew: 6
Weight: 27.24 tons
Powerplant: one Continental R-975-EC2 radial petrol engine developing 340hp (253.5kW)
Dimensions: length 5.64m (18ft 6in); width 2.72m (8ft 11in); height: 3.12m (10ft 3in)
Performance: max. road speed 42km/h (26mph); range 193km (120miles)

Medium Tank M4A3E8

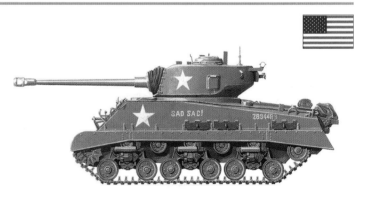

Crew: 5
Weight: 32.284 tonnes
Powerplant: one Ford GAA V-8 petrol engine developing 450 or 500hp (335.6 or 373kW)
Dimensions: length with gun 7.518m (24ft 8in); width 2.667m (8ft 9.5in); height 3.43m (11ft 2.875in)
Performance: max. road speed 48km/h (29mph); range 161km (100miles)

Medium Tank M4A3 SHERMAN

Crew: 5
Weight: in action 32.284 tonnes
Powerplant: one Ford GAA V-8 petrol engine developing 450 or 500hp (335.6 or 373kW)
Dimensions: length with gun 5.905m; width 2.667m; height 2.743m
Performance: max. road speed 42km/h; range 161km (100miles)

WORLD WAR II BRITISH AND SOVIET TANKS

T-28 Medium Tank

Crew: 6
Weight: 28 tonnes
Powerplant: one M-17 V-12 petrol engine developing
                 373kW (500hp)
Dimensions: length 7.44m; width 2.81m;
                 height 2.82m
Performance: max. road speed 37km/h; range 220km

T-37 Amphibious Light Tank

Crew: 2
Weight: 3.5 tons
Powerplant: one 40 bhp petrol engine developing
                 140hp (104kW)
Dimensions: length 3.75m; width 2.00m; height 1.70m
Performance: max. road speed 32km/h; range 180km

Infantry Tank Mks I and II Matilda

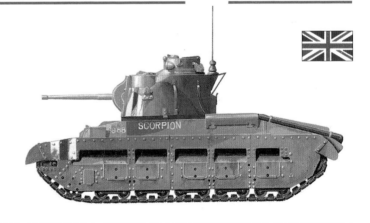

Crew: 5
Weight: 26.9 tonnes
Powerplant: two Leyland 6-cylinder petrol engines,
                 each developing 95bhp (71kW)
Dimensions: length 5.61m; width 2.95m; height 2.51m
Performance: max. road speed 24km/h; range 257km

Vickers Light Tank Mk V

Crew: 2
Weight: 4.88 tonnes
Powerplant: one Meadows ESTL 6-cylinder petrol
                 engine delivering 88bhp (66kW)
Dimensions: length 3.96m; width 2.08m; height 2.24m
Performance: max. speed 52km/h; range 201km

WORLD WAR II BRITISH AND SOVIET TANKS

Light Tank Mk VII, Tetrarch

Crew: 3
Weight: 7620kg (16,800lb)
Powerplant: one Meadows 12-cylinder petrol engine
                 developing 165bhp (123kW)
Dimensions: length 4.305m (14ft 1.5in); width 2.31m
                 (7ft 7in); height 2.121m (6ft 11.5in)
Performance: max. road speed 64km/h (40mph)

Infantry Tank Mk III Valentine

Crew: 3
Weight: 17690kg (39,000lb)
Powerplant: one AEC diesel engine developing
                 131bhp (98kW) in MkIII or GMC diesel
                 developing 138bhp (103kW) in Mk IV
Dimensions: length 5.41m (17ft 9in); width 2.6292m
                 (8ft 7.5in); height: 2.273m (7ft 5.5in)
Performance: max. road speed 24km/h (15mph);
                 range 145km (90miles)

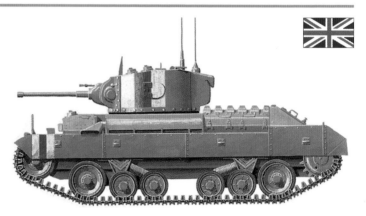

Cruiser Tank Mk VI, Crusader III

Crew: 3
Weight: 20067kg (44,240lb)
Powerplant: one Nuffield Liberty Mk III petrol engine
                 developing 340bhp (254kW)
Dimensions: length 5.994m (19ft 8in); width 2.64m
                 (8ft 8in); height 2.235m (7ft 4in)
Performance: max. speed 43.4km/h (15mph); range
                 with extra fuel tank 204km (127miles)

Mk IV Cromwell Cruiser Tank

Crew: 5
Weight: 27942kg (61,600lb)
Powerplant: one Rolls-Royce Meteor V-12 petrol
                 engine developing 570bhp (425kW)
Dimensions: length 6.42m (21ft 0.75in); width
                 3.048m (10ft); height 2.51m (8ft 3in)
Performance: max. road speed 61 km/h (38 mph);
                 range 278 km (173 miles)

Infantry Tank Mk VII Churchill

Crew: 5
Weight: 40642kg (89,600lb)
Powerplant: one Bedford twin-six petrol engine developing 350hp (261kW)
Dimensions: length 7.42m (24ft 5in); width 2.44m (8ft 0in); height 3.45m (11ft 4in)
Performance: max. road speed 20km/h (12.5mph); range 145km (90miles)

KV-85 Heavy Tank

Crew: 5
Weight: 43 tonnes
Powerplant: one V-2K V-12 diesel engine developing 600hp (448kW)
Dimensions: length 6.68m (21ft 11in); width 3.32m (10ft 10.7in); height 2.71m (10ft 7in)
Performance: max. road speed 35 km/h (21.75 mph); range 150 km (93.2 miles)

T-34/76A Medium Tank

Crew: 4
Weight: 26 tonnes
Powerplant: one V-2-34 V-12 diesel engine developing 500hp (373kW)
Dimensions: length 5.92m (19ft 5.1in); width 3m (9ft 10in); height 2.44m (8ft)
Performance: max. road speed 55km/h (34mph); range 186km (115miles)

IS-2 Heavy Tank

Crew: 4
Weight: 46 tonnes
Powerplant: one V-2-IS (V-2K) V-12 diesel engine developing 600hp (447kW)

Dimensions: length 9.9m (32ft 5.8in); width 3.09m (10ft 1.6in); height 2.73m (8ft 11.5in)
Performance: max. road speed 37km/h (23mph); range 240km (149miles)

WORLD WAR II ALLIED SELF-PROPELLED GUNS/ HOWITZERS & TANK DESTROYERS

Bishop Self-Propelled Gun-Howitzer

Crew:	4
Weight:	7,911kg
Powerplant:	one AEC 6-cylinder diesel engine developing 98kW (131hp)
Dimensions:	length 5.64m; width 2.77m; height 3.05m
Performance:	max. road speed 24km/h; range 177km

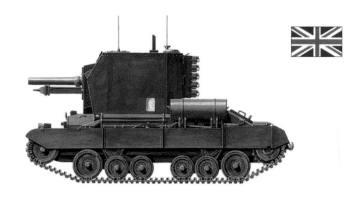

Archer Self-Propelled Anti-Tank Gun

Crew:	4
Weight:	16,257kg
Powerplant:	one General Motors 6-71 6-cylinder diesel developing 143kW (192hp)
Dimensions:	length 6.68m; width 2.76m; height 2.25m
Performance:	max. road speed 32km/h; range 225km
Armament:	one 17-pdr (3in/76.2mm) anti-tank gun

M7 Priest Self-Propelled Howitzer

Crew:	5
Weight:	22,967kg
Powerplant:	one Continental 9-cylinder radial piston engine developing 279.6kW (375hp)
Dimensions:	length 6.02m; width 2.88m; height 2.54m
Performance:	max. road speed 42km/h; range 201km
Armament:	one 105mm howitzer and one 12.7mm machine-gun

M40 155mm Gun Motor Carriage

Crew:	8
Weight:	37,195kg
Powerplant:	one Continental 9-cylinder radial piston engine developing 294.6kW (395hp)
Dimensions:	length 9.04m; width 3.15m; height 2.84m
Performance:	max. road speed 39km/h; range 161km
Armament:	one 155mm gun

3-in Gun Motor Carriage M10

Crew: 5
Weight: 29,937kg
Powerplant: two General Motors 6-cylinder diesel engines, each developing 276.6kW (375hp)
Dimensions: length 6.83m; width 3.05m; height 2.57m
Performance: max. road speed 51km/h; range 322km

Sexton Self-Propelled Gun/Howitzer

Crew: 6
Weight: 25,855kg
Powerplant: one Continental 9-cylinder radial piston engine developing 298kW (400hp)
Dimensions: length 6.12m; width 2.72m; height 2.44m
Performance: max. road speed 40km/h; range 290km

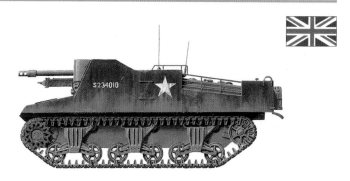

SU-76 Self-Propelled Gun

Crew: 4
Weight: 10,800kg
Powerplant: two GAZ 6-cylinder petrol engines, each developing 52kW (70hp)
Dimensions: length 4.88m; width 2.74m; height 2.17m
Performance: max. road speed 45km/h; range 450km

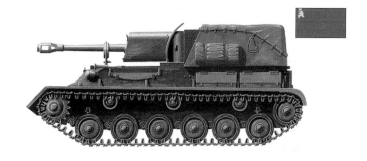

ISU-122 Self-Propelled Assault Gun

Crew: 5
Weight: 46,430kg
Powerplant: one V-12 diesel engine developing 388kW (520hp)

Dimensions: length (overall) 9.80m; length (hull) 6.81m; width 3.56m; height 2.52m
Performance: max. road speed 37km/h; range 180km

WORLD WAR II ALLIED TANK DESTROYERS

3-in Gun Motor Carriage M18

Crew: 5
Weight: 17,036kg
Powerplant: one Continental R-975 C1 radial
             petrol engine developing 254kW
             (340hp)
Dimensions: length 6.65m; width 2.87m;
             height 2.58m
Performance: max. road speed 89km/h;
             range 169km

WORLD WAR II AXIS TANK DESTROYERS

Semovente M.41M da 90/53

Crew: (on gun) 2
Weight: 17,000kg
Powerplant: one SPA 15-TM 18-cylinder petrol
             engine developing 108kW (145hp)
Dimensions: length 5.21m; width 2.20m;
             height 2.81m
Performance: max. road speed 36km/h;
             range 200km

Type 4 HO-RO Self-Propelled Howitzer

Crew: 4 or 5
Weight: about 13,600kg
Powerplant: one V-12 diesel engine developing
             127kW (170hp)
Dimensions: length 5.54m; width 2.29m;
             height 1.55m
Performance: max. road speed 38km/h

WORLD WAR II ALLIED HALF TRACKS

M3 Half-Track

Crew: 13
Weight: 9,299kg
Powerplant: one White 160AX 6-cylinder petrol
             engine developing 109.6kW (147hp)
Dimensions: length 6.18m; width 2.22m;
             height 2.26m
Performance: max. road speed 64.4km/h;
             range 282 km

WORLD WAR II GERMAN TANKS

PzKpfw II Light Tank

Crew:	3
Weight:	10,000kg
Powerplant:	one Maybach NL 38 TR six-cylinder petrol engine developing 140hp (104kW)
Dimensions:	length 4.64m; width 2.30m; height 2.02m
Performance:	max. road speed 55km/h; range 200km

PzKpfw III Ausf M

Crew:	5
Weight:	22,300kg
Powerplant:	one Maybach HL 120 TRM 12-cylinder petrol engine developing 300hp (224kW)
Dimensions:	length 6.41m; width 2.95m; height 2.50m
Performance:	max. road speed 408km/h; range 175km

kleiner Panzerbefehlswagen

Crew:	3
Weight:	5.8 tons
Powerplant:	one Maybach NL 38 TR six-cylinder petrol engine developing 100hp (75kW)
Dimensions:	length 4.45m; width 2.08m; height 1.72m
Performance:	max. road speed 40km/h; range 290km

TNH P-S Light Tank (PzKpfw 38(t))

Crew:	4
Weight:	9,700kg
Powerplant:	one Praga EPA six-cylinder water-cooled inline petrol engine developing 150hp (112kW)
Dimensions:	length 4.55m; width 2.13m; height 2.31m
Performance:	max. road speed 42km/h; range 200km

WORLD WAR II GERMAN TANKS

PzKpfw VI Tiger Ausf E Heavy Tank

Crew:	5
Weight:	55 tonnes
Powerplant:	one Maybach HL 230 P 45 12-cylinder petrol engine developing 700hp (522kW)
Dimensions:	length including gun 8.24m; width 3.43m; height 3.10m
Performance:	max. road speed 46km/h; range 177km

PzKpfw V Panther Ausf A Heavy Tank

Crew:	4
Weight:	45,500kg
Powerplant:	one Maybach HL 230 P 30 12-cylinder diesel engine developing 700hp (522kW)
Dimensions:	length including gun 8.86m; width 3.43m; height 3.10m
Performance:	max. road speed 46km/h; range 177km

PzKpfw IV Ausf H Medium Tank

Crew:	5
Weight:	25000kg
Powerplant:	one Maybach HL 120 TRM 12-cylinder petrol engine developing 300hp (224kW) developing 140hp (104kW)
Dimensions:	length (including armament) 7.02m (23ft 0in); width 3.29m (10ft 9.5in); height 2.68m (8ft 9.5in)
Performance:	max. road speed 38km/h (24mph); range 200km (125miles)

PzKpfw VI Tiger II Ausf B Heavy Tank

Crew:	5
Weight:	69700kg
Powerplant:	one Maybach HL 230 P 30

	12-cylinder diesel engine developing 700hp (522kW)
Dimensions:	length (including gun) 10.26m (33ft 8in); width 3.75m (12ft 3.5in); height 3.09m (10ft 1.5in)
Performance:	max. road speed 38km/h (24mph); range 110km (62miles)

WORLD WAR II TANK DESTROYERS AND HALF-TRACKS

Panzerjäger Tiger (P) Elefant

Crew:	6
Weight:	65 tonnes
Powerplant:	two Maybach HL 120 TRM V-12 water-cooled petrol engines, each developing 395kW (530hp)
Dimensions:	length 8.13m; width 3.38m; height 2.99m
Performance:	max. road speed 20km/h; range 153km

StuG III Ausf E Assault Gun

Crew:	4
Weight:	23.9 tonnes
Powerplant:	one Maybach V-12 petrol engine developing 198kW (265hp)
Dimensions:	length 6.77m; width 2.95m; height 2.16m
Performance:	max. road speed 40km/h; range 165km
Armament:	one 75mm howitzer and two 7.92mm machine-guns

Jagdpanzer IV SdKfz 162 Tank Destroyer

Crew:	4
Weight:	25800 kg
Powerplant:	one Maybach HL 120 petrol engine developing 197.6kW (265hp)
Dimensions:	length 8.58m (28ft 1.8in); width 2.93m (9ft 7.4in); height 1.96m (6ft 5.2in)
Performance:	max. road speed 35km/h (22mph); range 214km (133miles)

SdKfz 9 Schwerer Zugkraftwagen 18t

Crew:	9
Weight:	18000 kg
Powerplant:	one Maybach HL V-12 petrol engine developing 186.4kW (250hp)
Performance:	length 8.25m (27ft 0.8in); width 1.60m (8ft 6in); height 2.76m (9ft 7in)
Performance:	max. road speed: 50km/h (31mph)

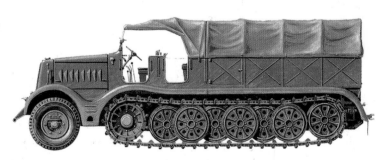

WORLD WAR II AXIS SELF-PROPELLED GUNS/ HOWITZERS & TANK DESTROYERS

Hummel Self-Propelled Howitzer

Crew:	5
Weight:	24,000 kg
Powerplant:	one Maybach V-12 petrol engine developing 198kW (265hp)
Dimensions:	length 7.17m; width 2.87m; height 2.81m
Performance:	max. road speed 42km/h; range 215km

Nashorn SdKfz 164 Tank Destroyer

Crew:	5
Weight:	24,400 kg
Powerplant:	one Maybach HL 120 petrol engine developing 198kW (265hp)
Dimensions:	length 8.44m; width 2.86m; height 2.65m
Performance:	max. road speed 40km/h; range 210km

Marder II Tank Destroyer

Crew:	3 or 4
Weight:	11,000 kg
Powerplant:	one Maybach HL 62 petrol engine developing 104kW (140hp)
Dimensions:	length 6.36m; width 2.28m; height 2.20m
Performance:	max. road speed 40km/h; range 190km

Hetzer Jagdpanzer 38(T) für 7.5 cm Pak 39 Tank Destroyer

Crew:	4
Weight:	14,500 kg
Powerplant:	one Praga AC/2800 petrol engine developing 112 - 119kW (150-160hp)
Dimensions:	length 6.20m; width 2.50m; height 2.10m
Performance:	max. road speed 39km/h; range 25km

SdKfz 138/1 sIG 33 auf Geschützwagen

Crew: 4
Weight: 11500kg
Powerplant: one Praga six-cylinder petrol engine
developing 111.9kW (150hp)
Dimensions: length 4.835m (15ft 10.4in);
width 2.15m (7ft 6in); height 2.40m (7ft 5in)
Performance: max. road speed 35km/h (22mph);
range 185km (115miles)

8.8 cm Pak 43

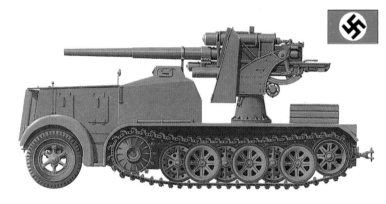

Calibre: 88 mm (3.45in)
Length of piece: 6.61m (21ft 8in)
Length of rifling: 5.125m (16ft 9.8in)
Weight: travelling 4750kg
(10,472lb)
Traverse: 360°
Elevation: -8° to +40°
Maximum range: HE 15150m
(16,570yards)
Armour penetration: 184mm (7.244in) at
2000m (2,190yards)

Type 95 Light Tank

Crew: 4
Weight: 7400 kg
Powerplant: one Mitsubishi NVD 6120 six-cylinder
air-cooled diesel engine developing
120hp (89kW)
Dimensions: length 4.38m (14ft 4in); width 2.057m
(6ft 9in); height 2.184m (7ft 2in)
Performance: max. road speed 45km/h (28mph);
range 250km (156miles)

Semovente L.40 da 47/32

Crew: 2
Weight: 17000 kg
Powerplant: one SPA 15-TM-41, 8-cylinder petrol
engine developing 108.1kW (145hp)
Dimensions: length 5.205m (17ft 0.9in); width 2.20m
(7ft 2.6in); height 2.15m (7ft 0.6in)
Performance: max. road speed 35.5km/h (22mph);
range 200km (124miles)

POST-WAR UNITED STATES MAIN BATTLE TANKS

M24 Light Tank, Chaffee

Crew: 5
Weight: in action 18.37 tonnes
Powerplant: two Cadillac Model 44T24 V-8 petrol engines developing 82kW (110hp) each
Dimensions: length with gun 5.49m (18ft 0in); width 2.95m (9ft 8in); height 2.48m (8ft 1.5in)
Performance: max. road speed 56km/h (35mph); range 161km (100miles)

M26 Pershing Heavy Tank

Crew: 5
Weight: in action 41.73 tonnes
Powerplant: one Ford GAF V-8 petrol engine developing 373kW (500hp)
Dimensions: length with gun 8.79m (28ft 10in); width 3.505m (11ft 6in); height 2.77m (9ft 1in)
Performance: max. road speed 48km/h (30mph); range 148km (92miles)

M41 Light Tank

Crew: 4
Weight: 23,495kg
Powerplant: Continental AOS-895-3 6-cylinder supercharged petrol engine developing 750bhp (560kW)
Dimensions: length with gun 8.213m; width 3.198m; height 2.726m
Performance: max. road speed 72km/h; range 161km

M47 Medium Tank

Crew: 5 (4)
Weight: 42,130kg
Powerplant: Continental AV-1790-5B 4-cylinder air-cooled petrol engine developing 810bhp at 2800rpm
Dimensions: length with gun 8.21m; width 3.51m; height 2.95m
Performance: max. road speed 48km/h; range 130km

M48 Main Battle Tank

Crew: 4
Weight: 44,906kg
Powerplant: Continental AV-1790-5B/7/7B/7C
12-cylinder air-cooled petrol developing
810/2800hp/rpm
Dimensions: length with gun 8.69m (28ft 6in); width
3.361m (11ft 11in); height 3.124m (10ft 3in)
Performance: max. road speed 48km/h (30mph);
range 463km (288miles)

M60/M60A1 Patton Main Battle Tank

Crew: 4
Weight: (M60) 49,710kg (M60A1) 52,610kg
Powerplant: AVDS-1790-2A V-12 air cooled diesel
engine developing 750hp
Dimensions: length (gun forwards) (M 60) 9.31m,
(M60A1) 9.44m; width 3.63m; height
(overall) (M60) 3.31m (M60A1) 3.27m
Performance: max. road speed 48km/h; range 500km

M551 Sheridan Light Tank

Crew: 4
Weight: 15.83 tonnes
Powerplant: one Detroit Diesel 6V-53T 6-cylinder
diesel engine developing 300hp (224kW)
Dimensions: length 6.30m (20ft 8in); width 2.82m
(9ft 3in); height (overall) 2.95m (9ft 8in)
Performance: max. road speed 70km/h (43mph);
range 600km

M103 Heavy Tank

Crew: 5
Weight: 56.7 tonnes
Powerplant: one Continental AV-1790-5B
V-12-cylinder petrol engine
developing 810bhp (604kW)
Dimensions: length with gun 11.32m
(37ft 1.5in); width 3.76m
(12ft 4in); height 2.88m (9ft 5in)
Performance: max. road speed: 34km/h (21mph);
range 130km (80miles)

COLD WAR US AND BRITISH MAIN BATTLE TANKS

M48A1/A2/A3 Series Patton Main Battle Tank

Crew: 4
Weight: M48A1/A3 47,273kg M48A2 47,727kg
Powerplant: M48A1 AV1790-7C V-12 air-cooled petrol engine developing 810hp
Dimensions: length gun forwards M48A1 7.3m M48A2/3 8.69m; width M48A1/A2/A3 3.63m; height M48A1 3.13m M48A2 3.09m M48A3 3.12m
Performance: max. road speed M48A1 42km/h M48A2/A3 48km/h; range M48A1 216km M48A2 400km M48A3 496km

M48A5 Patton Main Battle Tank

Crew: 4
Weight: 49,090kg
Powerplant: as M48A1 but with an AVDS-1790 2A RISE model diesel engine developing 750hp
Dimensions: length gun forwards 9.47m; width 3.63m; height with cupola 3.29m
Performance: max. road speed 48km/h; range 500km

Chieftain Mk3 Main Battle Tank

Crew: 4
Weight: 54,100kg
Powerplant: Leyland L60, No.4 Mk 6a, 2-stroke, compression ignition 6-cylinder (12 opposed pistons) multi-fuel engine developing 730bhp at 2100rpm
Dimensions: length gun forwards 10.79m; width 3.504m; height 2.895m
Performance: max. road speed 48km/h; range 500km

Centurion Mk 5 Main Battle Tank

Crew: 4
Weight: 50,728kg
Powerplant: Rolls-Royce Mk IVB 12-cylinder liquid-cooled engine developing 650bhp at 2,550rpm
Dimensions: length gun forwards 9.829m; width 3.39m; height 2.94m
Performance: max. road speed 34.6km/h; range 102km

COLD WAR FRENCH, GERMAN AND SWEDISH MAIN BATTLE TANKS

AMX-13 Light Tank

Crew: 3
Weight: 15 tonnes
Powerplant: one SOFAM 8Gxb 8-cylinder petrol engine developing 250hp (186kW)
Dimensions: length (gun forward) 6.36m (20ft 10.3in); width 2.5m (8ft 2.5in); height 2.30m (7ft 6.5in)
Performance: max. road speed 60km/h; range 350-400km

AMX-30 Main Battle Tank

Crew: 4
Weight: 34,000kg
Powerplant: one Hispano-Suiza HS 110 12-cylinder, water-cooled supercharged multi-fuel engine developing 720hp at 2,000rpm
Dimensions: length (gun forward) 9.48m; width 3.10m; height 2.29m
Performance: max. road speed 65km/h; range 500-600km

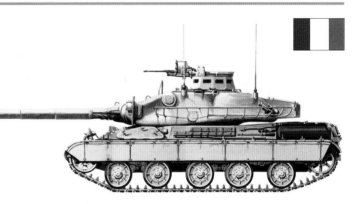

Leopard 1 Series Main Battle Tank

Crew: 4
Weight: 40,400kg
Powerplant: MTU MB 838 Ca M-500, 10 cylinder multi-fuel engine developing 830hp at 2,200rpm
Dimensions: length (gun forward) 9.54m; width 3.41m; height 2.764m
Performance: max. road speed 65km/h; range 600km

Bofors Stridsvagn 103 Main Battle Tank

Crew: 3
Weight: 39,700kg
Powerplant: Rolls-Royce K60 multi-fuel engine developing 240bhp at 3750rpm and, Boeing 553 gas turbine developing 490shp at 38,000rpm
Dimensions: length gun forwards 8.99m; width 3.63m; height 2.14m
Performance: max. road speed 50km/h; range 390km

COLD-WAR SOVIET TANKS

T-10 Heavy Tank

Crew: 4
Weight: 36 tonnes

Powerplant: V-12 diesel engine developing 520hp (388kW)
Dimensions: length (gun forward) 9.00m; width 3.27m; height 2.40m
Performance: max. road speed 48km/h; range 400km

COLD WAR UNITED STATES LIGHT ARMOURED VEHICLES

M56 90-mm Airborne Self-propelled Anti-tank Gun

Crew: 4
Weight: 7.03t onnes
Powerplant: one Continental 6-cylinder petrol engine developing 200bhp (149kW)
Dimensions: length with gun 5.841m (19ft 2in); width 2.577m (8ft 5.5in); height 2.067m (6ft 9.33in)
Performance: max. road speed 45km/h (28mph); range 225km (140miles)

M113 Armoured Personnel Carrier Family

Crew: 2+11
Weight: 10,258kg
Powerplant: Chrysler 75M V-8 petrol engine developing 209bhp at 4000rpm
Dimensions: length 4.863m; width 2.686m; height 2.50m
Performance: max. road speed 64km/h; range 321km

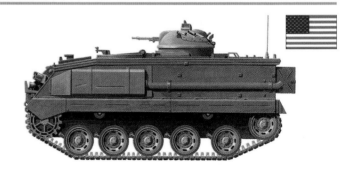

HORNET MALKARA

Crew: 2+11
Weight: 10,258kg
Powerplant: Chrysler 75M V-8 petrol engine developing 209bhp at 4000rpm
Dimensions: length 4.863m; width 2.686m; height 2.50m
Performance: max. road speed 64km/h; range 321km

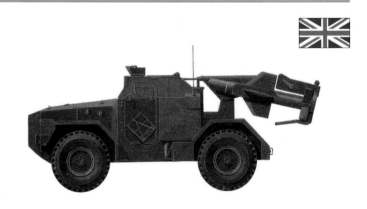

COLD-WAR BRITISH LIGHT ARMOURED VEHICLES

FV432 Armoured Personnel Carrier

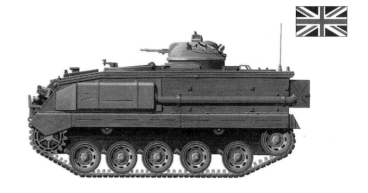

Crew: 2+10
Weight: 15280kg
Powerplant: one Rolls-Royce K60 6-cylinder multi-fuel engine developing 240bhp (170kW).
Dimensions: length 5.251m (17ft 7in); width 2.80m (9ft 2in); height 2.286m (7ft 16in)
Performance: max. road speed 52km/h (32mph); range 483 km (300miles)

Humber 'Pig' Armoured Personnel Carrier

Crew: 2 + 6 (or 2 + 8)
Weight: 5790kg
Powerplant: one Rolls-Royce B60 Mk5A 6-cylinder petrol engine developing 120bhp (89kW)
Dimensions: length 4.926m; width 2.044m; height 2.12m
Performance: max. road speed 64km/h; range 402km

Alvis Saracen Armoured Personnel Carrier

Crew: 2 + 10
Weight: 8640kg
Powerplant: one Rolls-Royce B80 Mk 6A 8-cylinder petrol engine developing 160hp (119kW).
Dimensions: length 5.233m; width 2.539m; height 2.463m
Performance: max. road speed 72km/h; range 400km

Alvis Saladin Armoured Car

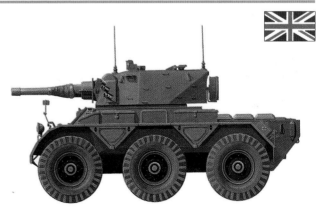

Crew: 3
Weight: 11.59 tonnes
Powerplant: one Rolls-Royce B80 8-cylinder petrol engine developing 170bhp (127kW).
Dimensions: length (including gun) 5.284m; width 2.54m; height 2.93m
Performance: max. road speed 72km/h; range 400km

COLD WAR NATO AND FRENCH LIGHT ARMOURED VEHICLES

Daimler Ferret Scout Car

Crew:	2
Weight:	4,395 tonnes
Powerplant:	one Rolls-Royce 6-cylinder petrol engine developing 129hp (96kW)
Dimensions:	length 3.835m; width 1.905m; height 1.879m
Performance:	max. road speed 93km/h; range 306km

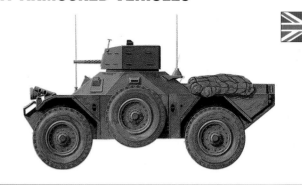

Marder 1 Infantry Combat Vehicle

Crew:	9
Weight:	(combat) 29,207kg
Powerplant:	MTU MB 833 Ea-500 6-cylinder liquid-cooled diesel developing 600hp at 2,200rpm
Dimensions:	length 6.79m; width 3.24m; height (over turret top) 2.985m
Performance:	max. road speed 90km/h; range 520km

UR-416 Armoured Personnel Carrier

Crew:	2+8
Weight:	7600kg
Powerplant:	one Daimler-Benz OM352 6-cylinder diesel engine developing 120bhp (89kW)
Dimensions:	length 5.21m; width 2.30m; height 2.225m
Performance:	max. road speed 85km/h; range 600-700km

Renault VAB Armoured Personnel Carrier

Crew:	2+10
Weight:	13000kg
Powerplant:	one MAN 6-cylinder inline diesel engine developing 235bhp (175kW).
Dimensions:	length 5.98m; width 2.49m; height 2.06m
Performance:	max. road speed 92km/h); range 1000km

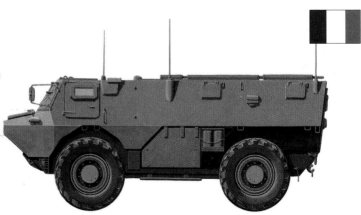

COLD WAR SOVIET ARMOURED VEHICLES

BRDM-2 Amphibious Scout Car
(carries six AT-3 'Sagger' ATGWs)

Crew:	4
Weight:	7 tonnes
Powerplant:	one V-8 petrol engine developing 140hp (104kW)
Dimensions:	length 5.75m (18ft10.33in); width 2.35m (7ft 8.5in); height 2.31m (7ft 7in)
Performance:	max. road speed 100km/h (62mph); range 750km (465miles)

BTR-60 Armoured Personnel Carrier

Crew:	2 + 14
Weight:	10300kg
Powerplant:	two GAZ-49B 6-cylinder petrol engines developing 90hp (67kW)
Dimensions:	length 7.56m (24ft 9.6in); width 2.825m (9ft 3.2in); height 2.31m (7ft 6.9in)
Performance:	max. road speed 80km/h (50mph); range 500km

BMD Airborne Combat Vehicle

Crew:	7
Weight:	6700kg
Powerplant:	Type 5D-20 V-6 liquid-cooled diesel engine developing 240hp
Dimensions:	length 5.40m; width 2.63m (8ft 8in); height 1.97m (6ft 6in)
Performance:	max. road speed 70km/h (43mph); range 320km (200miles)

PSZH-IV Armoured Personnel Carrier

Crew:	3 + 6
Weight:	7,600kg
Powerplant:	Csepel D.414.44 4-cylinder in-line water-cooled diesel engine developing 100hp at 2,300rpm
Dimensions:	length 5.695m; width 2.50m; height 2.308m
Performance:	max. road speed 80km/h; range 500km

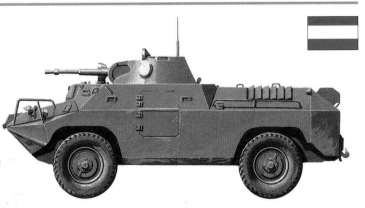

COLD WAR SELF-PROPELLED GUNS / HOWITZERS

M109 155 mm Self-Propelled Howitzer

Crew: 6
Weight: 23,786kg
Powerplant: one Detroit Diesel Model 8V-71T diesel
engine developing 405 hp
Dimensions: length (gun forward) 6.612m;
width 3.295m; height 3.289m
Performance: max. road speed 56km/h; range 390km

M108 105mm Self-Propelled Howitzer

Crew: 5
Weight: (combat) 22,452kg
Powerplant: Detroit Diesel Model 8V-71T,
turbocharged, 2-sdtroke, liquid-cooled
8-cylinder diesel engine developing
405bhp at 2,300rpm
Dimensions: length 6.114m; width 3.295m;
height (with AA gun) 3.155m
Performance: max. road speed 56km/h; range 390km

Abbot 105mm Self-Propelled Gun

Crew: 4
Weight: 16556kg
Powerplant: one Rolls-Royce 6-cylinder diesel engine
developing 240hp
Dimensions: length gun forward 5.84m; width 2.64m;
height without armament 2.49m
Performance: max. road speed 47.5km/h; range 390km

Bandkanon 1A 155mm Self-Propelled Gun

Crew: 5
Weight: 53000kg
Powerplant: one Rolls-Royce diesel engine developing
240hp and
turbine developing
300shp
Dimensions: length gun forward 11.00m; width 3.37m;
height including AA MG Boeing gas
3.85m
Performance: max. road speed 28km/h; range 230km

Mk F3 155mm Self-Propelled Gun

Crew: 2
Weight: 17400kg
Powerplant: one SOFAM 8Gxb 8-cylinder petrol engine developing 250hp
Dimensions: length gun forward 6.22m; width 2.72m; height 2.09m
Performance: max. road speed 28km/h; range 230km

GCT 155mm Self-Propelled Gun

Crew: 4
Weight: 42000kg
Powerplant: one Hispano-Suiza HS 110 12 cylinder water-cooled multi-fuel engine developing 720hp
Dimensions: length gun forward 10.25m; width 3.15m; height 3.25m
Performance: max. road speed 60km/h; range 450km

Palmaria 155mm Self-Propelled Howitzer

Crew: 5
Weight: 46000kg
Powerplant: 8-cylinder diesel engine developing 750hp
Dimensions: length gun forward 11.474m; width 2.35m; height without AA MG 2.874m
Performance: max. road speed 60km/h; range 400km

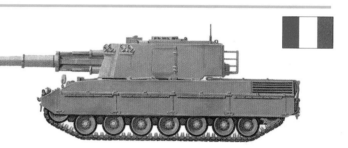

M1973 152mm Self-Propelled Gun/Howitzer

Crew: 6
Weight: 25000kg
Powerplant: one V-12 diesel developing 520shp
Dimensions: length gun forward 8.40m; width 3.20m; height 2.80m
Performance: max. road speed 55km/h; range 300km

M1974 122mm Self-Propelled Howitzer

Crew: 4
Weight: 16000kg
Powerplant: one YaMZ-238V-8 water-cooled diesel engine developing 240hp
Dimensions: length 7.30m; width 2.85m; height 2.40m
Performance: max. road speed 60km/h; range 500km

MODERN MAIN BATTLE TANKS

NORINCO Type 90-II Main Battle Tank (MBT 2000)

Crew:	3
Weight:	(combat) 48,000kg
Powerplant:	Perkins CV12-1200 TCA 12-cylinder, water cooled electronically controlled diesel developing 1,200hp at 2,300rpm
Dimensions:	length: (gun forward) 10.067m width: (with skirts) 3.5m height: (without AA gun) 2.37m
Performance:	max. road speed: 62.3km/h range: 450km

NORINCO Type 85-III Main Battle Tank

Crew:	3
Weight:	(combat) 42,500kg
Powerplant:	V-type diesel developing 1000hp at 2,300rpm
Dimensions:	length: (gun forward) 10.428m width: 3.4m height: (without AA gun) 2.20m
Performance:	max. road speed: 65km/h range: 600km

NORINCO Type 69-II Main Battle Tank

Crew:	4
Weight:	36,700kg
Powerplant:	Type 12150L-7BW V-12 diesel engine developing 580hp at 2,000rpm
Dimensions:	length: gun forwards 8.589m width: 3.307m height: 2.807m
Performance:	max. road speed: 50km/h range: 420-440km

NORINCO Type 59 Main Battle Tank

Crew:	4
Weight:	36,000kg
Powerplant:	Model 12150L V-12 liquid-cooled diesel developing 520hp at 2,000rpm
Dimensions:	length: (gun forward) 9m width: 3.27mm height: 2.59m
Performance:	max. road speed: 40-50km/h range: 420-440-km

Type T-72 CZ M4 Main Battle Tank

Crew: 3
Weight: (combat) 46,000kg
Powerplant: V-46 TC diesel developing 858hp at 2,000rpm
Dimensions: length: (gun forward) 9.55m
width: (withoout skirts) 3.755m
height: (to turret roof) 2.185m
Performance: max. road speed: 60km/h
range: 700km

Ramses II Main Battle Tank

Crew: 4
Weight: (combat) 45,800kg
Powerplant: Teledyne TCM AVDS 1790-5A turbocharged diesel
developing 908hp
Dimensions: length: (gun forward) 9.9m
width: (without skirts) 3.27m
height: (without AA gun) 2.4m
Performance: max. road speed: 50km/h
range: (with external tanks) 600km

Leopard 2A6/2A6EX Main Battle Tank

Crew: 4
Weight: (combat) 59,700kg
Powerplant: MTU MB 873 four stroke 12-cylinder diesel, exhaust turbocharged,
liquid-cooled, developing 1,500hp at 2,600rpm
Dimensions: length: (gun forward) 9.97m
width: (with skirts) 3.74m
height: (over commander's periscope) 3m
Performance: max. road speed: 72km/h
range: 500 km

Leopard 2 to 2A5 series Main Battle Tank

Crew: 4
Weight: (combat) 55,150kg
Powerplant: MTU MB 873 ka 501 V-12 multi-fuel turbocharged diesel
developing 1500hp
Dimensions: length: (gun forward) 9.67m
width: (with skirts) 3.7m
height: (without AA gun) 2.79m
Performance: max. road speed: 72km/h
range: 550km

MODERN MAIN BATTLE TANKS

Leclerc Main Battle Tank

Crew:	3
Weight:	(combat) 54,500kg
Powerplant:	SACEM UD V8X 1500 T9 Hyperbar 8-cylinder diesel developing 1,500hp at 2,500rpm
Dimensions:	length: (gun forward) 9.87m width: (with skirts) 3.71m height: (without AA gun) 2.53m
Performance:	max. road speed: 71km/h range: 450km (with external fuel 550m)

Arjun Main Battle Tank

Crew:	4
Weight:	(combat) 58,500kg
Powerplant:	MTU MB 838 Ka 501 10-cylinder liquid-cooled diesel developing 1,400hp at 2,500rpm
Dimensions:	length: (gun forward) 10.194m width: (with skirts) 3.847m height: (without AA gun) 2.32m
Performance:	max. road speed: 72km/h range: (estimate) 450km

Vijayanta Main Battle Tank

Crew:	4
Weight:	40,400kg
Powerplant:	Leyland multi-fuel L60 developing 535hp at 2,375rpm
Dimensions:	length: (gun forward) 9.788m width: (over skirts) 3.168m height: (without AA gun) 2.711m
Performance:	max. road speed: 48.3km/h range: 354km

T-55 Main Battle Tank variants

Crew:	(Multilayer Armour) T-55/Type 69 - 4, Rebuilt T-55 - 3
Weight:	(combat) T-55 - 36,000kg, Type 69 36,500-37,000kg
Powerplant:	Type 12150L-7BW diesel developing 580hp at 2000rpm
Dimensions:	length: (gun forward) T-55 - 9m, Type 69 8.657m width: T-55 - 3.27m, Type 69 (over skirts) 3.298m height: (overall) T-55 - 2.4m, Type 69 - 2.807m
Performance:	max. road speed: 50km/h range: T-55 - 500km, Type 69 - 420-440km

Merkava Mk2/Mk3 Main Battle Tank

Crew: 4
Weight: (combat) Mk 2-63,000kg, Mk 3-62,000kg
Powerplant: TCM AVDS 1790 6A (9 AR) air cooled turbo-charged diesel developing 908hp (1200hp)
Dimensions: length: (gun forward) Mk 2-8.63m, Mk 3-8.78m
width: (with skirts) 3.7m
height: (without AA gun) Mk 2-2.75m, Mk 3-2.76m
Performance: max. road speed: Mk 2-46km/h, Mk 3-55km/h
range: 500km

M60A1 - MAGACH-7 Main Battle Tank

Crew: 4
Weight: 52,617kg
Powerplant: Continental TCM AVDS-1790-2A 12 cylinder, aircooled diesel developing 750hp at 2,400rpm
Dimensions: length: (gun forward) 9.436m
width: 3.631m
height: 3.27m
Performance: max. road speed: 48.28km/h
range: 500km

C-1 Ariete Main Battle Tank

Crew: 4
Weight: 54,000kg
Powerplant: IVECO V-12 MTCA, turbo-charged, intercooled, 12-cylinder diesel developing 1,300hp at 2,300rpm
Dimensions: length: (gun forward) 9.67m
width: (with skirts) 3.6m
height: (without AA gun) 2.5m
Performance: max. road speed: 66km/h
range: 550-600km

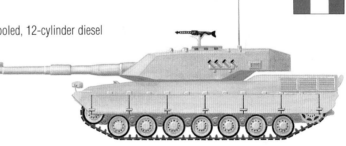

O-F 40 Main Battle Tank

Crew: 4
Weight: (combat) 45,500kg
Powerplant: MTU 90° 10-cylinder, 4-stroke, precombustion chamber, supercharged, multifuel developing 830hp at 2,200rpm
Dimensions: length: (gun forward) 9.222m
width: (with skirts) 3.51m
height: (top of commander's sight) 2.68m
Performance: max. road speed: 60km/h
range: 600km

MODERN MAIN BATTLE TANKS

Mitsubishi Type 90 Main Battle Tank

Crew: 3
Weight: (combat) 50,000kg
Powerplant: Mitsubishi 10ZG V-10 fuel injection diesel developing 1,500hp at 2,400rpm
Dimensions: length: (gun forward) 9.755m
width: (with skirts) 3.43m
height: (overall) 3.045m
Performance: max. road speed: 70km/h
range: 400km

Mitsubishi Type 74 Main Battle Tank

Crew: 4
Weight: (combat) 38,000kg
Powerplant: Mitsubishi 10ZF Type 22 WT 10-cylinder air-cooled diesel developing 720hp at 2,200rpm
Dimensions: length: (gun forward) 9.42m
width: 3.18m
height: (including AA MG) 2.67m
Performance: max. road speed: 60km/h
range: 400km

Hyundai K1 (Type 88 or ROKIT) Main Battle Tank

Crew: 4
Weight: (combat) 51,100kg
Powerplant: MTU MB 871 Ka 501 V-8 liquid-cooled diesel developing 1,200hp at 2,600rpm
Dimensions: length: (gun forward) 9.67m
width: (with skirts) 3.59m
height: (without AA gun) 2.25m
Performance: max. road speed: 65km/h
range: 437km

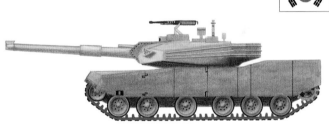

Al-Khalid Main Battle Tank

Crew: 3
Weight: (combat) 45,500kg
Powerplant: Ukrainian 6TD 8-cylinder, 4-stroke, water-cooled, turbocharged diesel developing 1,200hp
Dimensions: length: (gun forward) 6.9m
width: 3.4m
height: (without AA gun) 2.3m
Performance: max. road speed: 60km/h
range: 400km

PT-91 Main Battle Tank

Crew: 3
Weight: (combat) 45,300kg
Powerplant: Multi-fuel S-12U four-stroke, multifuel, supercharged, water-cooled diesel developing 850hp at 2,300rpm
Dimensions: length: (gun forward) 9.67m
width: (with side skirts) 3.59m
height: (turret roof) 2.19m
Performance: max. road speed: 60km/h
range: 650km

T-80U Series Main Battle Tank

Crew: 3
Weight: (combat) 46,000kg
Powerplant: GTD-1250 multi-fuel gas turbine developing 1250hp
Dimensions: length: (gun forward) 9.656m
width: (with side skirts) 3.589m
height: (without AA gun) 2.202m
Performance: max. road speed: 70km/h
range: 440km (with long-range fuel tanks)

T-90 Main Battle Tank

Crew: 3
Weight: (combat) 46,500kg
Powerplant: Model V-84MS 4-stroke 12-cylinder multifuel diesel developing 840hp
Dimensions: length: (gun forward) 9.53m
width: 3.78m
height: (without AA gun) 2.226m
Performance: max. road speed: 60km/h
range: 550km

T-72S Series Main Battle Tank

Crew: 3
Weight: (combat) 46,500kg
Powerplant: V-12 multifuel (V-84) diesel developing 840hp at 2,000rpm
Dimensions: length: (gun forward) 9.533m
width: (with side skirts) 3.59m
height: (without AA gun) 2.228m
Performance: max. road speed: 60km/h
range: (with external tanks) 550km

MODERN MAIN BATTLE TANKS

T-72 B Series Main Battle Tank

Crew: 3
Weight: (combat) 46,000kg
Powerplant: Multi-fuel V-84-1 V-12 diesel developing 840hp
Dimensions: length: (gun forward) 9.53m
width: 3.65m
height: (without AA gun) 2.19m
Performance: max. road speed: 70km/h
range: (with external tanks) 640km

T-72 A, G and M1 Series Main Battle Tank

Crew: 3
Weight: (combat) T-72A-44,000kg, T-72M2-45,500kg
Powerplant: Multi-fuel V-46-1 V-12 diesel developing 780hp
Dimensions: length: (gun forward) 9.53m
width: 3.59m
height: (without AA gun) 2.19m
Performance: max. road speed: 60km/h
range: (with external tanks) 700km

ZTS-T-72 Main Battle Tank

Crew: 3
Weight: (combat) 46,500kg
Powerplant: Model V-84MS 4-stroke, 12-cylinder multifuel diesel
developing 840hp
Dimensions: length: (gun forward) 9.53m
width: (over skirts) 3.78m
height: (without AA gun) 2.226m
Performance: max. road speed: 60km/h
range: 550km

Khalid Main Battle Tank

Crew: 4
Weight: (combat) 45,500kg
Powerplant: 8-cylinder, 4-stroke, water-cooled, turbocharged diesel
developing 1,200hp
Dimensions: length: 6.9m
width: 3.4m
height: 2.3m
Performance: max. road speed: 70km/h
range: 400km

Challenger 1 Main Battle Tank

Crew:	4
Weight:	(combat) 62,000kg
Powerplant:	Perkins Engines (Shrewsbury) Condor 12V 1200 water-based cooled diesel developing 1,200bhp at 2,300rpm
Dimensions:	length: (gun forward) 11.56m width: (with skirts) 3.518m height: (without AA gun) 2.95m
Performance:	max. road speed: 56km/h range: 400km

Challenger 2 Main Battle Tank

Crew:	4
Weight:	(combat) 62,500kg
Powerplant:	Perkins Engines (Shrewsbury) Condor CV12 TCA liquid-cooled diesel developing 1,200bhp at 2,300rpm
Dimensions:	length: (gun forward) 11.55m width: 3.52m height: (without AA gun) 2.49m
Performance:	max. road speed: 57km/h range: 450km

M1A1/M1A1(HA)/M1A2 Abrams Main Battle Tank

Crew:	4
Weight:	(combat) M1A1- 57,155kg, M1A1(HA)- 63,738kg, M1A2/M1A2(SEP)- 61,690kg
Powerplant:	Textron Lycoming AGT 1500 multifuel gas turbine developing 1,500hp at 30,000rpm
Dimensions:	length: (gun forward) 9.828m width: 3.657m height: (without AA gun) 2.438m
Performance:	max. road speed: 66.77km/h range: 465km

M60A3 Patton Main Battle Tank

Crew:	4
Weight:	(combat) 52,617kg
Powerplant:	Continental AVDS-1790-2C RISE V-12 cylinder, air-cooled diesel developing 750bhp at 2,400rpm
Dimensions:	length: (gun forward) 9.436m width: 3.631m height: (with AA gun and cupola) 3.27m
Performance:	max. road speed: 48.28km/h range: 480km

MODERN TRACKED ARMOURED VEHICLES

Giat Industries AMX-10P Infantry Combat Vehicle

Crew:	3 + 8
Weight:	14,500kg
Powerplant:	Hispano-Suiza HS 115 V-8 water-cooled supercharged diesel developing 260hp at 3,000rpm
Dimensions:	length: 5.9m
	width: 2.83m
	height: (overall) 2.83m
Performance:	max. road speed: 65km/h
	range: 500km

MaK Wiesel 2 Multi-Purpose Carrier

Crew:	up to 6
Weight:	(combat) 4100kg
Powerplant:	Audi 4-cylinder TDI diesel developing 109hp
Dimensions:	length: (overall) 4.20m
	width: (overall) 1.852m
	height: 1.7 to 2.11m (depending on version)
Performance:	max. road speed: 70km/h
	range: 550km

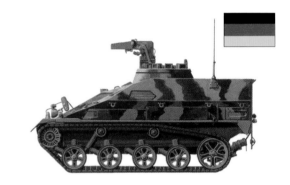

Dardo Infantry Fighting Vehicle

Crew:	2-7
Weight:	(combat) 23,000kg
Powerplant:	IVECO 8260 V-6 4-stroke turbocharged, intercooled diesel developing 520bhp at 2,300rpm
Dimensions:	length: 6.705m
	width: 3.0m
	height: (overall) 2.64m
Performance:	max. road speed: 70km/h
	range: 500km

Mitsubishi Type 89 Mechanised Infantry Combat Vehicle

Crew:	3 + 7
Weight:	27,000kg
Powerplant:	6 SY 31 WA diesel developing 600hp at 2,000rpm
Dimensions:	length: 6.7m
	width: 3.20m
	height: (overall) 2.75m
Performance:	max. road speed: 70km/h
	range: 400km

MT-LB Multi-Purpose Tracked Vehicle

Crew:	2 + 11
Weight:	11,900 kg
Powerplant:	YaMZ 238 V, V-8 cylinder diesel engine developing 240hp at 2,100rpm
Dimensions:	length: 6.454m
	width: 2.86m
	height: (to turret top) 1.865m
Performance:	max. road speed: 61.5km/h
	range: 500km

BMP-3 Infantry Combat Vehicle

Crew:	3 + 7
Weight:	18,700kg
Powerplant:	Type UTD-29M 10-cylinder 4-stroke diesel developing 500hp
Dimensions:	length, (overall) 7.14m
	width: (overall) 3.23m
	height: (over turret roof) 2.30m
Performance:	max. road speed: 70km/h
	range: 600km

Alvis Vehicles Warrior Armoured Combat Veicle

Crew: 3 + 7
Weight: 28,000kg
Powerplant: Perkins Engines Company CV-8 TCA V-8 diesel developing 550hp at 2,000rpm
Dimensions: length: 6.34m
        width: (overall) 3.034m
        height: (turret top) 2.735m
Performance: max. road speed: 75km/h
        range: 660km (at 60km/h)

Alvis Vehicles Stormer Combat Veicle

Crew:	3 + 8
Weight:	12,700kg
Powerplant:	Perkins Engines Company T6.3544V-8 water-cooled 6-cylinder turbocharged, diesel developing 250bhp at 2,600rpm
Dimensions:	length: 5.27m
	width: 2.4m
	height: 2.27m
Performance:	max. road speed: 80km/h
	range: 650km

MODERN TRACKED ARMOURED VEHICLES

Singapore Technologies Automotive Bionix 25 Infantry Fighting Vehicle

Crew:	3 + 7
Weight:	(combat) 23,000kg
Powerplant:	Detroit Diesel Model 6V-92TA diesel developing 475hp at 2,400rpm
Dimensions:	length: 5.92m width: 2.70m height: (overall) 2.57m
Performance:	max. road speed: 70km/h range: 415km

M2 Bradley IFV

Crew:	3 + 7
Weight:	22,666kg
Powerplant:	one Cummins VTA-903T 8-cylinder diesel developing 500hp
Dimensions:	length: 6.453m width: 3.20m height: 2.972m
Performance:	max. road speed: 66km/h range: 483km

Armoured Infantry Fighting Vehicle

Crew:	3 + 7
Weight:	13,687kg
Powerplant:	one Detroit Diesel 6V-53T V-6 diesel developing 264hp
Dimensions:	length: 5.258m width: 2.819m height: 2.794m
Performance:	max. road speed: 61.2km/h range: 490km

M-60P Armoured Personnel Carrier

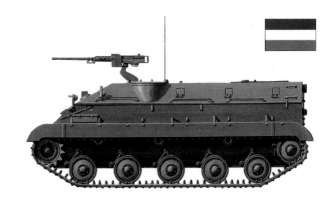

Crew:	3 + 10
Weight:	(combat)11,000kg
Powerplant:	FAMOS 6-cylinder in-line water-cooled diesel developing 140hp
Dimensions:	length: 5.02m width: 2.77m height: (overall) 2.385m
Performance:	max. road speed: 45km/h range: 400km

AS90 155mm Self-Propelled Gun

Crew: 5
Weight: (combat) 45,000kg
Powerplant: Cummins VTA-903T-660 V-8 diesel developing 660bhp at 2,800rpm
Dimensions: length: (gun forward) 9.90m
width: 3.4m
height: 3.0m
Performance: max. road speed: 55km/h
range: 370km (approx)

Hägglunds Pbv 302 Amphibious Armoured Personnel Carrier

Crew: 2 + 10
Weight: (combat) 13,500kg
Powerplant: Volvo-Penta Model THD 100B horizontal 4-stroke turbocharged 6-cylinder in-line diesel developing 280hp at 2,200rpm
Dimensions: length: 5.35m
width: 2.86m
height: 2.5m
Performance: max. road speed: 66km/h
range: 300km

United Defense M4 Command and Control Vehicle

Crew: 9 (depends on role)
Weight: (combat) 25,401-29,937kg (depends on role)
Powerplant: Cummins VTA-903T turbocharged 8-cylinder diesel developing 600hp at 2,600rpm
Dimensions: length: 7.493m
width: 2.97m
height: 2.707m
Performance: max. road speed: 64km/h
range: 483km

M270 Armored Vehicle-Mounted Rocket Launcher (AVMRL)

Crew: 3
Weight: (system loaded) 25,191kg
Powerplant: Cummins VTA-903 turbocharged 8-cylinder diesel developing 500hp at 2,400rpm
Dimensions: length: (travelling) 6.972m
width: (travelling) 2.972m
height: (travelling) 2.617m
Performance: max. road speed: 64km/h
range: 483km

SCORPION SERIES ARMOURED VEHICLES

Alvis Samaritan Armoured Ambulance (FV 104)

Crew:	2
Weight:	8664kg
Powerplant:	Jaguar J60 No 1 Mk 100B 4.2 litre, 6-cylinder petrol engine developing 190hp at 4750rpm
Dimensions:	length 5.07m; width 2.24m; height 2.42m
Performance:	max. road speed 73km/h; range 483km

Alvis Sultan Armoured Command Vehicle (FV105)

Crew:	5-6
Weight:	8664kg
Powerplant:	Jaguar J60 No 1 Mk 100B 4.2 litre, 6-cylinder petrol engine developing 190hp at 4750rpm
Dimensions:	length gun forwards 5.28m; width 2.24m; height 2.42m
Performance:	max. road speed 73km/h; range 483km

Alvis Samson Armoured Recovery Vehicle (FV 106)

Crew:	3
Weight:	8738kg
Powerplant:	Jaguar J60 No 1 Mk 100B 4.2 litre, 6-cylinder petrol engine developing 190hp at 4750rpm
Dimensions:	length 4.79m; width 2.43m; height 2.25m
Performance:	max. road speed 73km/h; range 483km

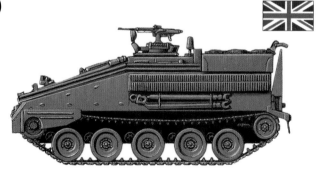

Alvis Scimitar Reconnaissance Vehicle (FV 107)

Crew:	3
Weight:	7756kg
Powerplant:	Jaguar J60 No 1 Mk 100B 4.2 litre, 6-cylinder petrol engine developing 190hp at 4750rpm
Dimensions:	length gun forwards 4.99m; width 2.24m; height 2.10m
Performance:	max. road speed 81km/h; range 644km

Alvis Scorpion Reconnaissance Vehicle (FV 101)

Crew: 3
Weight: 8073kg
Powerplant: Jaguar J60 No 1 Mk 100B 4.2 litre, 6-cylinder petrol engine developing 190hp at 4750rpm
Dimensions: length 4.794m; width 2.235m; height 2.102m
Performance: max. road speed 80.5km/h; range 644km

Alvis Scorpion 90

Crew: 3
Weight: 8573kg
Powerplant: Jaguar J60 No 1 Mk 100B 4.2 litre, 6-cylinder petrol engine developing 190hp at 4750rpm
Dimensions: length gun forwards 5.28m; width 2.24m; height 2.10m
Performance: max. road speed 73km/h; range 644km

Alvis Striker Anti-Tank Guided Weapon Vehicle (FV 102)

Crew: 3
Weight: 8346kg
Powerplant: Jaguar J60 No 1 Mk 100B 4.2 litre, 6-cylinder petrol engine developing 190hp at 4750rpm
Dimensions: length 4.83m; width 2.28m; height 2.28m
Performance: max. road speed 81km/h; range 483km

Alvis Spartan Armoured Personnel Carrier (FV 103)

Crew: 3 + 4
Weight: 8172kg
Powerplant: Jaguar J60 No 1 Mk 100B 4.2 litre, 6-cylinder petrol engine developing 190hp at 4750rpm
Dimensions: length 5.13m; width 2.26m; height 2.28m
Performance: max. road speed 81km/h; range 483km

MODERN WHEELED ARMOURED VEHICLES

Ratel FSV 90 Infantry Fighting Vehicle

Crew:	10
Weight:	(combat) 19,000kg
Powerplant:	Bussing D 3256 BTXF 6-cylinder in-line turbocharged diesel engine developing 282hp at 2,200rpm
Dimensions:	length: 7.212m width: 2.516m height: 2.915m
Performance:	max. road speed: 105km/h range: 860km

Henschel Wehrtechnik Condor Armoured Personnel Carrier

Crew:	2 + 12
Weight:	(combat) 12,400kg
Powerplant:	Mercedes-Benz OM 352A 6-cylinder supercharged water-cooled diesel developing 168hp at 2,800rpm
Dimensions:	length: (including winch) 6.47m width: 2.47m height: (overall) 2.79m
Performance:	max. road speed: 100km/h range: 900km

SIBMUS Armoured Personnel Carrier

Crew:	3 + 11
Weight:	(combat) 14,500-18,500kg (depending on role)
Powerplant:	MAN D 2566 MK 6-cylinder in-line water-cooled turbocharged diesel developing 320hp at 1,900rpm
Dimensions:	length: (hull) 7.32m width: 2.5m height: (to turret top) 2.77m
Performance:	max. road speed: approx 100km/h range: 1,000km max. water speed: (by propellers) up to 11km/h

Steyr-Daimler-Puch Pandur Armoured Personnel Carrier

Crew:	2 + 8
Weight:	(combat) 13,500kg
Powerplant:	Steyr WD 612.95 6-cylinder turbocharged water-cooled diesel developing 260hp at 2,400rpm
Dimensions:	length: 5.697m width: 2.5m height: (to hull top) 1.82m
Performance:	max. road speed: 100km/h range: 700+km

Cadillac Gage LAV-300 Mk 1 Armored Vehicle

Crew: 3 + 9
Weight: 14,969kg
Powerplant: Cummins 6 TCA 8.30-C260 turbocharged, aftercooled 6-cylinder, in-line diesel developing 260hp at 2,200rpm
Dimensions: length: 6.40m
width: 2.54m
height: (MG turret) 2.692m
Performance: max. road speed: 105km/h
range: 925km

Cadillac Gage LAV-150 Armoured Vehicle Range

Crew: 3 + 2
Weight: (combat) 9,888kg
Powerplant: V-504 V-8 diesel developing 202bhp at 3.300rpm
Dimensions: length: 5.689m
width: 2.26m
height: (to turret roof) 2.54m
Performance: max. road speed: 88km/h
range: 643km

AMX-10RC Reconnaissance Vehicle

Crew: 4
Weight: (combat) 15,880kg
Powerplant: Baudouin Model 6F 11 SRX diesel developing 280hp at 3,000rpm
Dimensions: length: (gun forward) 9.15m
width: 2.95m
height: 2.66m
Performance: max. road speed: 85 km/h
range: 1,000km

Panhard ERC Sagaie Armoured Car

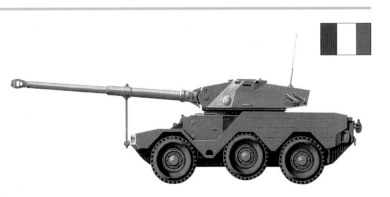

Crew: 3
Weight: (combat) 8,300kg
Powerplant: Peugeot V-6 petrol engine developing 155hp at 5,250rpm
Dimensions: length: (gun forward) 7.693m
width: 2.495m
height: 2.254m
Performance: max. road speed: 95km/h
range: 700 km

Page references in *italics* refer to illustrations.

ABBREVIATIONS

AA	Anti-aircraft	HE-FS	High Explosive-Fin Stabilised
AAAV	Advanced amphibious assault vehicle	HE-T	High Explosive-Tracer
AAV	Anti-aircraft vehicle; amphibious assault vehicle	HEAT	High Explosive, Anti-Tank
ACV	Airborne Combat Vehicle (eg BMD family)	HEAT-FS	High Explosive, Anti-Tank, Fin Stabilised
AEV	Armoured Engineer Vehicle	HEAT-MP-T	High Explosive, Anti-Tank-Multi Purpose-Tracer
AFV	Armoured Fighting Vehicle	HEAT-T	High Explosive, Anti-Tank Tracer
AIFV	Armoured Infantry Fighting Vehicle	HEI	High Explosive, Incendiary
AP	Armour Piercing	HEI-T	High Explosive, Incendiary-Tracer
AP-T	Armour Piercing-Tracer	HEP-T	High Explosive, Plastic Tracer
APC	Armoured Personnel Carrier	HESH	High Explosive, Squash Head
APC-T	Armour Piercing Capped-Tracer	HESH-T	High Explosive, Squash Head-Tracer
APDS	Armour Piercing, Discarding Sabot	HVAP-T	High Velocity Armour Piercing-Tracer
APDS-T	Armour Piercing, Discarding Sabot-Tracer	HVAPDS-T	High Velocity Armour Piercing, Discarding Sabot-Tracer
APER-FRAG	Anti Personnel-Fragmentation		
APERS-T	Anti Personnel-Tracer	IFCS	Improved Fire Control System
APFSDS	Armour Piercing, Fin Stabilised, Discarding Sabot	ICV	Infantry combat vehicle
APFSDS-T	Armour Piercing, Fin Stabilised, Discarding Sabot-Tracer	IFV	Infantry Fighting Vehicle
		IR	Infra Red
APHE	Armour Piercing, High Explosive	IVIS	Intervehicular Information System
AP-T	Armour Piercing-Tracer	KE	Kinetic Energy
API-T	Armour Piercing, Incendiary-Tracer	LAV	Light Armored Vehicle
ARRV	Armoured Recovery and Repair Vehicle	LLLTV	Low Light Level Television
ARV	Armoured Recovery Vehicle	LVTP	Landing Vehicle, Tracked, Personnel
ATGW	Anti-Tank Guided Weapon	MAOV	Mechanised Artillery Observation Vehicle
AVLB	Armoured Vehicle Launched Bridge	MBT	Main Battle Tank
AVRE	Armoured Vehicle Royal Engineers	MCRV	Mechanised Combat Repair Vehicle
BARV	Beach Armoured Recovery Vehicle	MCV	Mechanised combat vehicle
CE	Chemical Energy	MICV	Mechanised Infantry Combat Vehicle
CET	Combat Engineering Tractor	MG	Machine gun
CEV	Combat Engineer Vehicle	MLRS	Multiple Launch Rocket System
CFV	Cavalry Fighting Vehicle	MOLF	Modular Laser Fire Control
CIS	Commonwealth of Independent States	MRS	Multiple Rocket System
CRARRV	Challenger Armoured Repair and Recovery Vehicle	MRV(R)	Mechanised Recovery Vehicle (Repair)
EAOS	Enhanced Artillery Observation System	NATO	North Atlantic Treaty Organisation
ELINT	Electronic intelligence	NBC	Nuclear, Biological and Chemical
ERA	Explosive Reactor Armour	NORINCO	China North Industries Corporation
FCS	Fire Control System	REME	Royal Electrical and Mechanical Engineers
FCV	Forward command vehicle	RFAS	Russian Federation and Associated States
FLIR	Forward Looking Infra-red	SAM	Surface-to-Air Missile
FOV	Forward observation vehicle	SAPHEI	Semi-Armour Piercing, High Explosive, Incendiary
FRAG-HE	Fragmenting high explosive	SAPHEI-T	Semi-Armour Piercing, High Explosive, Incendiary-Tracer
FST	Future Soviet Tank (American intelligence community designation usually suffixed by a number eg FST-1)		
		SFCS	Simplified Fire Control System
		SIRE	Sight Integrated Range Equipment
FV	Fighting Vehicle (British MoD designation usually suffixed by a number and version eg FV4030/4)	TCM	Teledyne Continental Motors
		TOGS	Thermal Observation and Gunnery Sight
		TTS	Tank Thermal Sight
GPS	Gunner's Primary Sight	TWMP	Track Width Mine Plough
GPTTS	Gunner's Primary Tank Thermal Sight	UAE	United Arab Emirates
HE	High Explosive	WarPac	Warsaw Pact
HE-APER-FRAG	High Explosive-Anti Personnel-Fragmentation		
HE-FRAG	High Explosive-Fragmentation		